Caro

The Fatal Passion

Caro

The Fatal Passion

The Life of Lady Caroline Lamb

Henry Blyth

Rupert Hart-Davis   London

Granada Publishing Limited
First published 1972 by Rupert Hart-Davis Ltd
3 Upper James Street London W1R 4BP

Copyright © 1972 by Henry Blyth

ISBN 0 246 10557 7
Printed in Great Britain by
Willmer Brothers Limited, Birkenhead

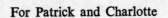

For Patrick and Charlotte

Contents

Contents

List of Illustrations

The jacket illustration of Lady Caroline Lamb by Thomas Hayter is reproduced by courtesy of *The Devonshire Collection, Chatsworth.*

Acknowledgements

First of all, I must acknowledge the great debt which I owe to Lady Salmond for the help which she has given me, and for her kindness in making available to me all her treasured mementoes of Caroline—the sketches, diaries, commonplace books and all the other sad little souvenirs of what was, in so many ways, a wasted life. I feel that Caroline's sketches, which Lady Salmond has allowed me to reproduce in this book, speak for themselves. There is an air of melancholy about them which reflects the tragedy of her fatal passion.

I am also happy to acknowledge the assistance which has been given to me by those who have allowed me to reproduce pictures that are in their possession or to quote from letters which they own; and notably, Mr John Grey Murray, of Byron's publishing firm of John Murray Ltd; the Earl of Lytton; the Earl of Bessborough; Mary, Duchess of Roxburghe; and the Duke of Devonshire.

Finally, as always, I must thank my research expert, Dr Sylvia England, who so painstakingly unravels for me the many threads which lead from the British Museum. But in this case my debt to her is twofold, for it was she who first suggested that I should write a biography of Caroline Lamb. One of her reasons for doing this was that she had already carried out some research into Caroline's story for the late Professor Clarke Olney of the University of Georgia, who died before he could begin his book about her. Before his death, he told Dr England that, if he should fail to write this biography, he hoped that someone else would do so in his place, and that, if they did, he hoped they would deal compassionately with 'poor Caro'.

I believe that I have done so.

Foreword

This book is a biography of Lady Caroline Lamb. Its title, *Caro: The Fatal Passion*, requires some amplification for it may be argued that *The Fatal Passion* savours of melodrama. There may even be those who are churlish enough to suggest that it does not sound original.

The Fatal Passion is melodramatic. And it is not original. It is the title used for Caroline's first novel, *Glenarvon*, when it was reprinted in one volume in 1865, nearly thirty years after her death.

The reader is therefore entitled to ask whether this passion which Caroline developed for Lord Byron was melodramatic and whether it was fatal. It was both.

Equally significant is the word *Caro*. This was the nickname that was given to Caroline in her childhood, and it was the name which she loved. But when she grew up, Caro became Caroline. It was a change that saddened her, for it seemed to separate her from her childhood. Her childhood world had been one of fantasy and unreality and she had no desire to enter the world of maturity, which was materialistic and unromantic.

Byron shared her attitude to reality. Both gloried in melodrama, and a title such as *The Fatal Passion* would have delighted both of them.

It is the tragedy of their two lives that neither was ever destined to discover happiness. Those who inhabit a world of fantasy rarely do so, and the dreams of childhood seldom come true.

Those who inhabit a dream world usually have one thing in common. They find it difficult to tell the truth. It is not so much that they are deliberate liars as that they are incapable of distinguishing between fact and fiction. 'Truth,' said Caroline once, 'is what one believes at the moment.' The historian who sets out to chronicle the events of their lives therefore finds himself at some disadvantage, for their own graphic and detailed descriptions of these events are liable to be wholly inaccurate.

John van Druten, in a book which he wrote some years ago on the art of the playwright, advised authors to develop a theme in their work as well as a plot. This has always seemed to me to be excellent advice, particularly for those who write biographies. In a biography the plot is presented to you ready-made. You cannot change the date or the place of birth of your central character just to suit your own convenience.

In this book there are two central themes which have served me as my guide lines. The first is one that is as applicable today as it was in the early nineteenth century. It is that a permissive society is not necessarily a mature society. Nor is a permissive society necessarily an uninhibited one. A further development of this theme has led me to realize that a permissive society can also be a surprisingly unworldly society, in which the young can still be shocked by behaviour outside the fairly rigid rules of permissiveness which they have laid down.

It is my purpose to show in this book that the central characters behaved in the way that they did because they remained basically very immature. We are really dealing with children, not with adults. They are spoilt children, particularly in Caroline's case; vain children, particularly in Byron's case; simple children, particularly in Augusta's case; and headstrong and very determined children, particularly in the case of Caroline and Annabella. I believe that one of the faults to be found in so many of the biographies that have been written about Byron is that he is treated as a mature adult, which he never was.

I believe that no character assessment should ever be attempted in a biography until the family history of the subject has been studied and also the medical history. The formative years of childhood are of the utmost importance. So are any abnormalities of behaviour which can be traced to mental or physical suffering, or to disease.

I am reluctant to condemn anyone who has a pain in the stomach.

A study of the family history and medical history of Caroline Lamb and of Byron leads to the conclusion that each was born at the wrong time, of the wrong parents, into the wrong social environment and with the wrong attributes. Their upbringing made them unstable. Their outlook made them incapable of coping with reality. They never had a chance. It would have been a miracle had either grown up into a normal and balanced individual.

2

I am not a medical expert, but I have discussed their problems with doctors and psychiatrists. They have confirmed my belief that each was at times both mentally and physically sick, and that each was in urgent need of treatment. But medical knowledge in those days was very limited, and there was not much that the doctors of the early nineteenth century could have done to cure their disabilities. Sometimes the treatment given was well-intentioned but of little value. At other times it was tragically inept and only served to accentuate the suffering rather than to alleviate it. Laudanum, which is a tincture of opium, was freely available without any restrictions.

Of Byron's physical condition in childhood and youth it is only necessary to say that he bit his nails, ground his teeth and either ate voraciously or not at all. He, like Caroline, suffered from tension, frustration and moods of acute depression, accentuated later in life by alcoholism. He ruined a magnificent constitution by gross dissipation.

There may well be readers of this book who consider that I have been unduly tolerant of Byron's sexual extravagances. I certainly feel that he believed himself to be far more wicked than he was. His wife, Annabella, who suffered grievously from a total lack of any sense of humour, was yet blessed with a sturdy common sense. She never thought he was wicked, and gave it as her opinion that he suffered from the effects of a classical education.

But if I seem unduly tolerant of certain aspects of Byron's character, I remain sharply critical of him in other respects. I find his vanity insufferable and his duplicity unforgivable. He was singularly lacking in the attributes of a gentleman.

Several notable scholars have attempted a life of Byron, but scholarship alone is not sufficient when assessing character. Such an assessment must depend to a large extent on the writer's knowledge of human nature, and particularly his knowledge of women.

In the past Caroline has been frequently condemned for her childishness and petulance, which were certainly aggravating and often intolerable. She has also been condemned for her exhibitionism. And it has been assumed that because she threw herself at Byron's head and indulged, as a married woman, in a succession of flamboyant affairs whilst wearing indecent dresses, she was over-sexed, and indeed something of a nymphomaniac. But a study of nymphomania suggests that these are often the symptoms of frustration and frigidity rather than of advanced sensuality.

The curious thing about Caroline and Byron was that each was a

3

puritan at heart. Each was highly emotional, but I doubt if either was highly sexed.

This book is not merely an assessment of Byron or a character study of Caroline Lamb. To me it is also an essay on the problems of growing up.

One

Caro - The Formative Years

There were two Carolines.

Caroline was tiny and exquisite. Her animated face was eager and expressive. Her hazel eyes were large and enquiring, and they gave to her face a look of child-like innocence. Her hair was fawn-flaxen and a mass of curls. Her mouth was a red rosebud, and when she laughed—which was often—she showed her even white teeth. Her hands were slim and exquisite. Her small feet were never still. Her figure was that of a boy, and there was a mercurial quality about her body as there was also about her mind, so that she seemed always to be poised for a new adventure. Her movements were quick and graceful.

Her voice was soft and persuasive, and she spoke with a child-like lisp. Words tumbled from her in a cascade of sudden thoughts and half-finished sentences. She was warm-hearted, generous and affectionate. The words of love which came from the passionate little mouth were deeply romantic. She had small, kittenish ways of showing her affection, with kisses that brushed the cheek and with tiny, intimate caresses.

At times she looked so fragile and forlorn that men felt the urge to comfort her and to protect her. She was so vulnerable, and she could so easily be hurt. She had no knowledge of the harsh realities of life. She inhabited a world of dreams, and like a child she believed that one day her dreams would all come true.

This was the first Caroline. An enchanting girl.

The second Caroline was physically the same. She had the same face, the same figure, the same elfin look, the same vulnerability. But the second Caroline was spoilt, selfish and neurotic. Her small mouth could spit venom as well as lisp endearments. The rose-bud lips could pout and sneer. The hazel eyes could blaze with anger. The tiny feet could stamp in fury, and the fragile body could stiffen with an implacable resolve.

5

Her moods varied from day to day and from hour to hour. Her temper was violent and she had no self-control whatever. When crossed, or denied anything on which she had set her heart, she would scream, bite, kick and scratch. In her tantrums, she would smash china, fling valuable ornaments out of the window and herself onto the floor in a paroxysm of uncontrolled fury.

She would vent her temper on anyone—both on those who could stand up to her and on those, like the servants, who were forced to bow to her will. She could prove herself both spiteful and unforgiving. She was a rebel against discipline and against convention. When forbidden to do something she did it. She was obsessed with the desire to focus the limelight upon herself. She was happy to behave in an outrageous way in order to command attention.

This other Caroline was neither fragile nor helpless. Her stubbornness and determination made those who associated with her, and especially the women, feel an urgent desire to subdue her spirit and to humiliate her pride. She disliked her own sex and her own sex heartily disliked her.

Caroline had no ethics and few principles. She lied brazenly and without compunction.

This was the second Caroline. A detestable girl.

Somewhere in between these two extremes was the real Caroline. And to those who loved her—and there were few enough of them as the years passed by—there remained the image of the girl that she might have been had circumstances been different. She was a tragic little figure, and her own worst enemy. She always remained a child and never grew up.

In her defence it could be said that both she and her lover, Lord Byron, were the victims of circumstance. Character is fashioned by heredity, the influences of childhood, medical history and the pressures of environment.

Both Caroline and Byron were born at the wrong time, and of the wrong parents. Each suffered from serious mental and physical disorders which the doctors of the day were unable to diagnose, let alone to cure. Each grew up in a harmful environment, and the forces which controlled their lives were largely destructive. Fate was against them from the outset, and it would have been remarkable if either had ever revealed any sort of normality. Each craved for affection and understanding.

The Victorian age branded each as being immoral and depraved, but in fact neither was at heart either sinful or depraved, but only childish and vain. It was not that they were evil, but rather that neither ever learnt to distinguish good from bad, or fact from fiction. Like children they lied because this was the easiest way to evade the harsh realities of life. Their selfishness was deplorable and their vanity insufferable, but these were faults which a normal upbringing could have cured. It was their misfortune that nothing about their way of life, either in childhood or in adolescence, bore the slightest resemblance to normality. Each was at heart a frustrated actor with a weakness for melodrama. It is not surprising, therefore, that every major incident in their respective careers was invariably melo-dramatic, usually sensational and often absurd.

Byron, with his strongly-developed sense of humour, was better able to appreciate the absurdities and futilities of life. Caroline suffered the more because whatever her faults may have been she was never cynical. Her fantasies were real to her.

Caroline was destroyed by life. She treasured her fantasies like a child treasures its toys, and when they were taken away from her one by one she lost interest in living.

Caroline Ponsonby—Caro, as she was known in childhood, and Caroline Lamb as she became after marriage—was the only daughter and third child of Frederick Ponsonby, 3rd Earl of Bessborough and his wife, the former Lady Henrietta Frances Spencer.

Caroline was therefore a typical product of the Whig aristocracy that had commanded the fortunes of England during the eighteenth century. Her father was a Whig statesman of negative character. Her mother was a social butterfly, of singularly permissive outlook and of sadly promiscuous habits, but child-like and enchanting none the less.

But although both her parents were ineffectual and weak, neither showed any indication of that wilful eccentricity which characterized their only daughter, and they were at a loss to account for Caro's remarkable wrong-headedness. They were both happy to drift through life, enjoying the pleasures of the senses to the full, whereas Caro seemed constantly on the attack. Hers were failings that they found it hard to comprehend, let alone to eliminate or control.

From whom, they asked themselves sadly, did Caro inherit her temper and her rebellious outlook? Not from either of them, and not from any of her grandparents. And so they had to go a great deal further back in their family tree to discover an ancestor who had in any way resembled Caro.

Caro's grandfather on her mother's side had been John Spencer,

7

1st Earl Spencer. He in his turn had been the grandson of Charles, 3rd Earl of Sunderland, who had married Lady Anne Churchill, the favourite daughter of the great Duke of Marlborough and his remarkable wife, the excitable and unstable Sarah Jennings.

This formidable woman was Caroline's great-great-great-grandmother, and the similarity between the two seemed to develop as Caroline grew older. And yet, in many ways, Caroline seemed also to resemble her great-great grandmother, Anne, Countess of Sunderland, who had been Sarah's favourite child. Anne had been a woman of sweetness and infinite charm, and Caroline—in her moods of tranquillity and warm affection—could resemble her as well as Sarah.

By tradition, Churchill women were beautiful, and this tradition had been maintained throughout the succeeding generations. By tradition, also, the Churchill's had large families, and Anne was the mother of five—three boys and two girls. Her third son, the Hon. John Spencer, inherited not only the Sunderland estate but also a large part of his grandmother's great wealth on her death, for Sarah had always been devoted to him.

He married Georgina Carolina Carteret, the third daughter of John Carteret, Earl Granville, and herself an heiress to a considerable fortune. On his death in 1746 he was survived by his only son, John Spencer, who became the 1st Earl Spencer in 1765. In 1755 he married Georgiana, eldest daughter of the Right Hon. Stephen Poyntz, and by her had three children—a son and heir to the earldom, George John, and two daughters—Georgiana and Henrietta Frances, who was Caroline's mother.

This is where the majority of those who have written about Caroline's story have chosen to begin. Normally, one would consider that a study of a child's parents is sufficient, and that research into ancestry is unnecessary. But in Caroline's case her parentage and childhood explain much, but not everything.

The two Spencer girls—Georgiana and Henrietta—in no way resembled either their father, at one time plain Mr John Spencer, of Althorp, or their mother, a woman of austere outlook and strong personality. Nor did they resemble their brother, George John, who was bookish and had red hair. However they closely resembled each other, being beautiful, feckless and naïve. They were a devoted pair, and their devotion lasted throughout their lives.

Mr Spencer had entered the House of Commons as the Whig member for Warwick shortly before he married Miss Poyntz, who came of an ancient Berkshire family. He received no fewer than four

8

peerages in the course of as many years, but the only public office which he ever appeared to have filled was President of the Lying-In Society.

There was little reason why the negative 1st Earl Spencer and the very positive Miss Poyntz should have brought into the world two daughters whose outstanding qualities were beauty and fecklessness. They were an enchanting pair who were caught together for posterity in Rowlandson's equally enchanting study of the sweetness of life in eighteenth-century London. In *Vauxhall Gardens*, which he exhibited at the Academy in 1784, all Society seems to be represented. The Prince is there, whispering slyly into the ear of Perdita Robinson, whose arm is dutifully linked in that of her dwarfish husband. Major Topham, that leader of Mayfair fashion, is there, quizzing the company through his monocle, and in a supper-box on the left are Dr Johnson, Boswell, and Goldsmith (although then deceased).

And in the very middle of the picture, dainty and delightful, and looking for all the world like two little shepherdesses who have escaped from a sylvan study by Watteau, are Georgiana in white and Henrietta in blue. Both are ringletted and both are wide-eyed and innocent. But whereas Georgiana is eager and animated, her sister seems lost in reverie. It is a picture to look at and to love.

Not long before, when they had set out together on an expedition to canvass help for Charles Fox in the Westminster Election, a wit had said of them that they were the two loveliest portraits that had ever appeared on a *canvas*.

Here were two sweet and adorable girls, who always loved unwisely and always too well. Men were their obsession and their downfall. They could no more resist the call of passion than they could resist the call of the gambling tables. They gambled as freely with their honour as they did with their money. They lost consistently, but never learnt their lesson. Just one more romance—just one more throw of the dice—and then they would reform.

Had they been born men, they would have been looked upon as rakes; but they did not indulge in sexual experience out of daredevilry, or as a means of self-assertion, as is the case with many raking young men. They were not vain, and although they delighted in their good looks, they never preened themselves. Nor did they gamble out of bravado. They gambled for the same reason as they made love—because they were children at heart and enjoyed it so much; and because they had not the strength of character to stop.

They also made love out of the kindness of their hearts. If they

9

were so weak that they could never say 'no', they were also so warm-hearted and sympathetic that they failed to say 'no' for fear of being unkind. Throughout life they gave as generously of their emotions as they did of their wealth.

Of these delightful sisters it could be said that each failed in the important things in life and succeeded only in the trivial ones. They laughed, they sighed and they played the games of childhood and womanhood. They talked, they danced (Henrietta supremely well) and they gave and received confidences. They loved and were loved in return. They were inconstant, but each was capable of a single, all-consuming love—though in neither case was this given to the husband.

In the final analysis each was a bad wife, a bad mother—and a bad aunt. They spoilt themselves, and then they spoilt their children. Each made resolutions to reform, and neither ever looked like succeeding. They were lax in their own morals and were happy to condone a similar laxity in their husbands. They were creatures of the senses, never of logic.

Each was a product of the Whig aristocracy, and each accepted and enjoyed the extreme permissiveness which this era encouraged. They drifted with the tide and the tide carried them far out of their depth. Their mother, Lady Spencer, was the chief influence in their lives, and yet she never succeeded in controlling them. Throughout their married careers, she was always to be seen in the background, worrying, advising, remonstrating—but to little effect.

Austere in manner, aloof, and rather masculine in appearance, she lacked altogether the gentleness and the charm which so characterized her two daughters. She dressed in a style that was simple and severe; they dressed in a style that was enchantingly absurd, each with a penchant for waving ostrich feathers and outsize hats. She was modest in her demeanour, but they delighted in revealing the charms with which nature had so generously endowed them.

By her own standards, Lady Spencer was a good mother and a good grandmother. She worried about her children's welfare, and about the welfare of her children's children, and particularly about her little grand-daughter, Caroline. But she never really understood her daughters, nor did she ever understand Caroline.

A resolute woman and reluctant to give up her hold on life so long as she could work to protect those whom she loved, she outlived her husband by many years and watched her eldest daughter, Georgiana, suffer and die without being able to do anything to help

10

her. Her husband, John, 1st Earl Spencer, died in 1783, so that the burden of supervising her children in their adult years fell solely upon herself.

Georgiana was the eldest of her three children, born on 7 June, 1757. George John, heir to the title, came next, a year later. Henrietta Frances, the baby of the family, arrived on 16 June, 1761.

The two sisters were utterly devoted, and each was deeply concerned with the welfare of the other. In her youth, Georgiana was certainly the stronger of the two, and the more impulsive. Where Georgiana went, Henrietta followed—often with difficulty, for Georgiana's stamina in youth was inexhaustible, especially when in the pursuit of pleasure, whereas Henrietta was the ailing one, who was never strong. And she, as Rowlandson had noted, was the dreamy one, with her head in the clouds.

At sixteen Georgiana was irresistible. She had the same voluptuous beauty as Emma Hamilton, and the same look of childlike innocence. Men could not resist her, and it was when she was sixteen that she proved irresistible to Frederick Cavendish, 5th Duke of Devonshire. 'She is a lovely girl,' wrote Horace Walpole, 'natural and full of grace; he, the first match in England.'

Thus Lady Spencer's high ambitions for her eldest daughter were fully realized. She could not complain of 'the first match in England', though she had secretly treasured the hope that Georgiana might become Princess of Wales. That title, she decided, could be won by Henrietta.

But now her eldest daughter was to become Duchess of Devonshire, the mistress of Devonshire House in Piccadilly, and of Chatsworth, the finest country estate in all England. And what a duchess she would make! Her hair, as Wraxhall was to note, 'was not without a tinge of red'. It was worn in ringlets that clustered round her innocent, baby face. Her cheeks were pink, her skin clear and white, her chin softly rounded, her lips were red, sensual and full. Her eyes were grey, and dancing with fun.

One would like to record that this was a love match, and that Georgiana had realized at once that here was her fairy prince. This was certainly the story that was put about at the time, but the facts seemed to contradict it. At sixteen Georgiana was still a child; if she had thought of marriage, it was only vaguely, as something still over the horizon. Her pleasures were still those of a child, and her pet hobby was chasing butterflies. But she was a dutiful daugher, and did as her mama advised.

11

The Spencer family had always been great travellers in Europe and especially in France (they were intimate friends with Marie Antoinette) and it had been at Spa, in Belgium, that they had first met the Duke of Devonshire. Georgiana met him there again in 1773, when she was sixteen and he was twenty-five, and it was then that he proposed to her and was blushingly accepted. The wedding day was fixed for 7 June in the following year, which was Georgiana's birthday. But in fact she was married on the 5 June, in order to avoid the crowds that might be expected to attend so fashionable an occasion. It was a Sunday, and she was married at Wimbledon Church between two ordinary services.

The remainder of the summer was spent at Chatsworth, and the Duke did not bring his young wife back to London until the following January. She then began her triumphant reign as queen of the London hostesses and of the Whig coterie at Devonshire House.

It seemed that there was not a cloud in the sky, but in fact they were already beginning to darken the horizon. From the outset the Duke made it very clear to his young wife that the purpose of their sexual union was to give him an heir, and until she had succeeded in that she must consider that she had failed in her wifely duties. It was not a happy introduction to the mysteries of sex for a girl who was eager, passionate and spontaneous in her emotions. As the weeks and months passed by, and there were no indications of pregnancy, she began to worry. A frustrated young woman may turn to a number of diversions under these circumstances. By the spring of 1775, less than a year after her marriage, Georgiana was gambling heavily and was already in debt.

The marriage was never really a success. The Cavendish males were, by tradition, men of solemn mind and careful consideration. It seemed that the sang-froid for which Englishmen were to become so famous had originated with them. It was not that they lacked emotion, or sexual desire; it was that they disliked being hurried. This traditional calm reached its zenith in the person of the 8th Duke, who dozed off whilst making a speech in the House of Commons.

But although the Cavendish males were fascinated by beautiful women (and sometimes even made fools of themselves as a result), they were reserved in the manifestations of their ardour. They tended to be determined but monosyllabic lovers, and they did not pay compliments easily. As a result their wives tended to be vulnerable to the attentions of those who could. This was one of the reasons why Georgiana fell so much under the spell of Charles James Fox, whose

12

eloquence was not limited to speeches in the House. There was no man in London who was better equipped to tell a beautiful woman how much he admired her.

But at the outset Georgiana was contented enough with the bargain that she had made. She had taken to her bed a prosaic and rather dull husband. In return she had been made Duchess of Devonshire. It seemed to her, at the time of their marriage, that he had one inestimable virtue. He was easy-going and tolerant of feminine weaknesses, such as gambling. Georgiana was a compulsive gambler. The rattle of the dice-box was music in her ears.

But time was soon to demonstrate that there was a limit to the calm Duke's patience. There was a limit to how many of his wife's infidelities he would condone. There was also a limit to how much he would put up with before going in search of a mistress for himself. It was not long, therefore, before Georgiana began to realize that she was in competition with one of her own dearest friends, in the person of Lady Elizabeth Foster, who was unhappily married to a dull Irish MP. By the mid-summer of 1782 Georgiana had 'taken up' with Lady Elizabeth with a school-girl's passion. The calm Duke looked upon them with favour, and read them extracts from Shakespeare whilst they were on holiday in Devon, where Lady Elizabeth endeared herself to him by sharing his love of dogs, and indulging with him in the rather whimsical doggy talk which he so enjoyed.

'Dearest Bess' as she was at once christened in the Devonshire family circle, was beautiful, wistful and pathetic, and she quickly became an intimate member of the Devonshire family circle. When Georgiana fell ill, Bess nursed her devotedly whilst she was in bed. In due course she was also invited to attend the Duke when *he* was in bed, but not for the purpose of administering physick. There she was surprised—and gratified—to discover that he was capable of an ardour and energy which he never revealed in public.

Thus there came into existence a *ménage à trois* which gave everyone satisfaction. Georgiana soon realized what was going on, but as she herself was by this time engaged in several escapades of her own, she was in no position to complain. The Duke and Georgiana and 'Dearest Bess' reached a most civilized arrangement whereby they were permitted to change partners at will. Nor did the Duke's activities make any difference to the close friendship between Georgiana and Bess.

It was a great era for nicknames, and the seal of intimacy in the Devonshire family circle was the award of a nickname and the

13

permission to address the members of the family by theirs. Thus the Duke was known in this little triumvirate as 'Canis', presumably because of his dog-like demeanour. Bess, whose melting eyes and anxious, eager face gave her the appearance of some unhappy little animal, was now named 'Racky', which was short for 'Racoon'. Georgiana herself was nicknamed 'The Rat', although the reasons for this were obscure.

Racky was soon entrusted with certain highly confidential tasks, which included being sent abroad to look after one of the calm Duke's illegitimate children, as it was felt that Georgiana was hardly a suitable person to look after it herself.

Georgiana's warm heart was always deeply moved by the sight of children, no matter to whom they might belong. She and her husband were making every effort to raise a family themselves, but the years went by, and still there was no heir to the House of Devonshire.

Henrietta drifted into marriage, with Lord Bessborough's heir, Lord Duncannon, in much the same way as Georgiana had done. She was not madly in love, and indeed her attention at the time was largely taken up with all the exciting things which were going on in London, and in which Georgiana had become so involved. Politics had become a craze for all of them, and Charles Fox was, of course, the idol, whose career had at all costs to be furthered. He was the darling of Devonshire House, and no party there was ever dull when he was in evidence, with his swarthy face and unfailing gaiety. His zest for life was contagious, and his passion for gambling equalled that of Georgiana.

Henrietta's was a good match, although hardly to be compared with that of her sister. Lady Spencer, who had not yet abandoned her hopes of a union with the Prince of Wales, sighed and stifled her disappointment. But Georgiana, writing enthusiastically to her mother, declared that she was so happy about the marriage that she could not express her feelings. 'It is the most charming thing that ever was, in all respects it is the marriage one should have wish'd...'

Lady Spencer replied in a more practical vein. She pointed out that Lord Bessborough could only give £2,000 year to the young couple, plus £400 a year dress allowance for Henrietta; and she contented herself with the prosaic observation that on such a modest income Henrietta was unlikely to become involved in too much frivolity.

'I think I could answer for her that you need not fear the extravagance that has given you so often uneasiness in me,' answered

Georgiana. 'I am sure I need not assure you of my doing ev'ry thing in the world (should this take place) to prevent her falling into either extravagance or dissipation.' A rather muddled comment that scarcely touched the main point, which was that whatever Georgiana did, Henrietta was liable to do also. They were inseparable.

Georgiana's second letter was written on 21 July, 1780. A few weeks later, while at Portsmouth with the Duke, who was in camp, she wrote complaining of an inflammation in one of her eyes. The incident was of some significance. It marked the beginning of her decline in health and of the loss of her beauty.

Henrietta became Viscountess Duncannon without it making very much difference to her. Marriage to Frederick Ponsonby was pleasant enough, but Georgiana remained the first love in her life. She was the more intelligent of the two sisters, was well read, a linguist and enjoyed quite a reputation as a wit. Her husband could in no way compete with her in these matters, for he was no intellectual and all witticisms were far above his head. Horace Walpole viewed the match with some misgiving, declaring that he would not have selected 'so gentle and very amiable a man' as a husband for a young woman who was the sister of 'the empress of fashion' and the daughter of 'the goddess of wisdom'. But Frederick's chief defect, throughout his life, was his inability to control his family and least of all his wayward wife and his excitable daughter.

Frederick married Henrietta when he was twenty-two. He was as inexperienced in the ways of the world as his young wife. His aims in life were simple enough. First to follow—if somewhat cautiously—in the political footsteps of his father. Secondly, to beget an heir to the earldom. He was a conscientious young man, of high integrity and in excellent health, until laid low in middle age by gout. Henrietta had a stronger feeling for her husband than Georgiana had for hers. She felt protective towards him and worried about his gout when it became painful. Georgiana was less concerned when the Duke suffered from the same complaint.

Henrietta was married on 27 November, 1780, and nine months later she gave birth to her first son, John William. He was followed two years later by a second son, Frederick Cavendish. A third son, William Francis Spencer, was born in 1787, by which time poor Georgiana, married already for some thirteen years, had only managed to produce two daughters.

Life for the young couple was very pleasant. The early years of their marriage were spent at their villa, *Mauresa,* at Roehampton,

15

from where they frequently drove up to London for evening parties. But often they remained cosily at home, playing cribbage and chess.

Frederick was a fond and indulgent father, immensely proud of his sons. He asked little more of life than that they should grow up as his companions in their country life and accompany him on his shooting expeditions for snipe and woodcock in Roehampton's fields and woods. He was also a keen horseman, and his afternoons were spent in the saddle.

He was not at home in women's company, nor in Society. A man who was slow in thought and action and without the gift of repartee, he found little to appeal to him in London Society. He was proud of his wife's popularity and of her social position, but when in London he avoided the gaieties and bustle of Devonshire House and spent his time at Brooks's Club, in St James's Street, where Charles Fox was the leading light.

There were times when his young wife's preoccupation with high life made him feel lonely and ignored, but he was a simple soul who enjoyed simple pleasures, and he developed a taste for foreign travel. As the years passed by, they grew ever more apart, and though they both loved to travel, they seldom travelled together.

He enjoyed gambling as much as she did, but like her he enjoyed no luck. And like her he had no sense of the value of money. He paid extravagant prices for prints which he considered to be of exceptional merit and which he was convinced would increase in value, but they never did. He invested a large sum in a shipping business in Liverpool and was certain that this investment would bring him in a fortune, but the business went bankrupt. He was sadly put out by this, and all the more so when he learnt that Henrietta had herself invested in another Liverpool company and that this had also collapsed. It was all very upsetting, and he complained that women had no business sense and should keep out of matters which they did not understand.

But he was forced to admit that Henrietta had achieved all that he could have asked of her by giving birth to three sons, so that the future of the title was assured. After the birth of their second son, however she confided to him that it was her aim to produce two more children, one of which must be a girl.

He did not share her enthusiasm for a daughter, because he felt that boys were easier to bring up and far easier to understand. One never knew where one was with girls. But if she had set her heart on a daughter, he was ready to play his part by making her pregnant, after which it was up to her.

Her wish was granted. On the 13 November, 1785, she gave birth at the Bessborough home in Cavendish Square to a tiny daughter, who looked so fragile that it seemed she could scarcely survive. She was christened Caroline and her mother at once nicknamed her 'Caro'.

Everyone was delighted. That is to say, everyone capable of expressing an opinion was delighted. The small girl herself was unable to do so for several years to come, but when old enough to make a statement she declared that she ought to have been born a boy.

My mother, having boys, wished ardently for a girl, and I, who evidently ought to have been a soldier, was found a naughty girl... My angel mother's ill health prevented my living at home; my kind aunt Devonshire took me; and everyone paid me those compliments shown to children who are precious to their parents or delicate and likely to die.

It was thus that Caroline described her advent into the world. She always wanted to be a boy, she habitually behaved like a boy, and she often dressed like a boy; and she bore a secret grudge against her mother because she was not a boy.

Caroline's birth was probably a routine affair and lacking in the dramatic incidents with which she would have certainly endowed it had she been in a position to remember it. Far more dramatic and pathetic was the birth a year earlier of another Caroline—the illegitimate child of the Duke of Devonshire and his 'Dearest Bess'. Elizabeth Foster's little girl could not enjoy the respectability and comfort of being born at Chatsworth or at Devonshire House. Bess, instead, was forced to withdraw into the decent obscurity of the Continent, there to give birth to her child under the most sordid circumstances in a peasant's cottage in Salerno. It was then given the further indignity of being named Caroline Rosalie Adelaide St Jules, because an accommodating French aristocrat, Comte St Jules, expressed his willingness to accept paternity for the Duke's illegitimate child.

The Duke was not unduly put out by these events and retained his habitual calm, expressing the view that women always made such a fuss over these things. Bess herself recovered surprisingly quickly. Quickly enough, indeed, to allow herself to be seduced within a few weeks by the Russian Ambassador, but she was able to excuse herself on the grounds of his flattery and her boredom.

Caroline Ponsonby may have secretly envied the other Caroline for the melodrama surrounding her birth. How she would have loved to have been born in a dirty hovel in Salerno, under the greatest secrecy and attended by a filthy midwife and a quack doctor! The story could have been recounted a hundred times and embellished at every telling. It was so infinitely less dramatic to be born in the utmost respectability in Cavendish Square, legitimate, a third child—and a girl!

However Caroline's childhood was thereafter eventful and unusual; and she was able to add the necessary decoration to make it seem a period highly charged with emotion. In later years she was to give a pitiful account of this childhood, about which few facts are available. Lady Morgan, who became Caroline's confidante towards the end of her life, had many stories to tell of the manner in which Caroline was brought up until she was nine. Caroline told Lady Morgan that her mother had suffered a stroke when Caroline was four and that she had then been packed off to Italy in the charge of a nursemaid named Fanny, where she remained until she was nine. As a result she grew up in ignorance of the simplest facts of life, never tasted bread or butter, believed the world was peopled equally by dukes and beggars, and supposed that horses fed on beef. She was still illiterate at the age of ten.

When in England she spent some of her time with her grandmother who lived in extreme opulence in a house where there were seventy servants. These were governed by an autocratic housekeeper in hoop and ruffles. Caroline declared that she was often ill-treated and fell passionately in love at the age of twelve.

Fact and fiction were always so inextricably mixed in Caroline's mind that the real truth of her upbringing was never to be discovered. She certainly spent much of her childhood in Italy, where she may well have felt deserted, but was probably never ill-treated. It was true that her education was shamefully neglected and that she was dragged around Europe at an impressionable age, when the instability of her character demanded that she be given a settled and tranquil home life, with parents who were prepared to devote their attention to her upbringing. This was the treatment that she was never accorded, and she carried the scars throughout her life. She was never unloved, but she never knew security.

Her mother was often seriously ill, frequently in debt, and tormented by unrequited love. Added to this was the fact that Henrietta had no aptitude for bringing up children—or certainly not for rearing an excitable and highly-strung little girl. Both mother and aunt were constantly involved in scandal, arising either out of their numerous love affairs or their mounting debts. Thus Caroline's childhood was chaotic and insecure. Her brothers received companionship from their father, but he never understood his wilful little daughter and she could never turn to him for guidance.

Henrietta's chronic ill-health was always frightening to Caroline. She was terrified by the sight of her beloved mama in the throes of one of her dizzy spells; of her fainting away quite suddenly and for no apparent reason; and of her suffering suddenly from the loss of all movement in a leg or arm.

Henrietta's method of escaping from reality was by making frequent trips abroad. This she was encouraged to do by her family's long association with such continental towns as Paris, Aix-la-Chapelle and above all Naples, the favourite resort, where Henrietta would retire to rally her strength before returning to the exhausting routine of the London season.

Within a few years of Caroline's birth both Henrietta and Georgiana were in deep waters, both financially and emotionally. In 1786 Georgiana was asking the banker, Thomas Coutts, to lend her money, and by 1788 she was reduced to begging a loan from a guest at Devonshire House—M de Calonne, a former Finance Minister to Louis XVI—in order to settle her own debts and those of Henrietta.

Henrietta was also distraught. She had not her sister's facility for making light of her problems, and her conscience troubled her. It was in a mood of maudlin self-analysis that she finally decided she was no longer a fit mother for her little daughter, and so decided to send the four-year-old Caro for a time to Naples, where Henrietta had many friends. With this decision Henrietta made her first and biggest mistake. Caroline had reached an age when she was vulnerable to sudden change and separation. But she had *not* reached an age when the problems confronting her mother could be explained to her. The fact that Henrietta paid frequent visits to her little daughter in Naples only made matters worse, for the child was faced with numerous harrowing farewells. Both mother and daughter were highly emotional, and all such farewells were carried out in floods of tears. Caroline was too young to understand what was happening to her, and so she began to build up within herself the conviction that she was being forsaken. Her nerves became frayed and her tantrums increased. She spent her time moving backwards and forwards between England and the Continent.

The rumblings of the forthcoming upheaval in France made little difference to the continental visits of Caroline's relations. The Duke of Devonshire, still calm and unruffled, set out for Spa in the mid-summer of 1789, on the eve of the French Revolution, taking Georgiana and Bess with him. He had been warned not to visit Versailles, but pooh-poohed all suggestions of trouble, and honoured Louis XVI with the ducal presence. He then travelled to Paris, where he pointedly ignored all hostile demonstrations in the streets. When he saw a house being ransacked by the mob and its contents removed, he assumed that an auction was taking place and that the successful buyers were merely removing their purchases.

Indeed the only event in his life that produced any strong manifestation of emotion was the news that his Duchess might yet bear him a son, for it was at about this time that Georgiana announced herself to be pregnant again.

After the Christmas of 1789 the Duke returned to England alone, leaving Georgiana in company with Henrietta in Brussels. On 21 May, 1790, a son was born to Georgiana at Passy, leaving the fashionable world to wonder just why the heir to the dukedom should have been born in France instead of at Devonshire House or at Chatsworth. Various rumours were circulated as a result, one of which suggested that the boy had been born to Bess and not Georgiana, and was therefore illegitimate.

The Duke, however, was delighted and loftily ignored all such comments. Indeed he was so delighted that Georgiana decided to take advantage of his good humour and to confess to him that she was heavily in debt. But her courage failed her in the end, and she only told him a part of the story. In fact she was owing somewhere in the region of £100,000, with little hope of ever being able to repay it.

Henrietta and Georgiana remained in Paris with their mother, Lady Spencer, which was most unwise in view of what was about to occur. It was not until 19 August that Henrietta and Georgiana returned to England, where the good citizens of Dover gazed with awe on the Duke's heir, who was sufficiently un-Devonshire like in his demeanour as to let out a loud yell of protest when stared at in this manner.

Caroline was not with her mother on this expedition, but a year later it was felt that she was old enough to visit France. Georgiana was still devoted to Bess, and Henrietta also came under her spell. It was a curious triumvirate of women, who shared the same weakness for promiscuity, and the same tendency towards unwanted pregnancies. They felt it necessary to keep together and to travel together, for every so often one or other would have to flee to the Continent to give birth to an illegitimate child, or to avoid some scandal.

Such an occasion developed at the end of 1791, when the Duke was informed that Georgiana, Henrietta and Bess, with the two little Carolines—Caroline Ponsonby and Caroline St Jules—were proposing to retire to the South of France so that Henrietta might convalesce there after one of her bouts of ill-health, although a further reason was that the gossip concerning Georgiana's affair with the rising young politician, Charles Grey, had reached such proportions that even the Duke had been made aware of it—and he was usually the last to learn of these things.

Henrietta was certainly far from well, but the dangerous situation which was developing in France should have deterred them. Paris was in turmoil, and Marie Antoinette sent a message to the travellers warning them against attempting any communication with her. They reached the South by January, 1792, went to Nice and then on to Lausanne. Later they moved on to Italy, but news reached them here of the trial in December of Louis XVI who was guillotined on 21 January, 1793.

Now at last the full tragedy of the Revolution was brought home to the English tourists. Bess did her best to tell her little Caroline something of what was happening in France, but Henrietta could not bring herself to discuss such horrors with her daughter, and Caroline Ponsonby was left to dwell in the realm of fantasy which played so important a part in her life, whilst yet realizing that dreadful things were happening in the world.

But all these comings and goings, the air of furtiveness, the secrecy of what was happening to Georgiana, the half-heard and scarcely comprehended whispers of gossip, and her mother's preoccupation with matters about which Caroline understood nothing at all, together combined to make the impressionable child unsettled and anxious. Worse still, they tended to make her feel shut out and even unwanted. Her mother was ashamed of all that was going on, and she tried to hide her own guilty secrets from her daughter either by sending her out of the room when these things were being discussed or—worse still—by placing her in the care of others and sending her away when her escapades were reaching a climax. The jealousies which tormented Caroline throughout her life were born during these formative years of childhood.

21

Georgiana, Henrietta, Bess and the two little Carolines spent most of 1793 in Italy. Henrietta was still suffering from her dizzy spells and the sudden loss of movement in an arm or a leg. They spent the early spring months in Pisa and Florence, and then moved south to Naples, which little Caro already knew so well, and which only reminded her of the periods in which she had been separated from her mother. But by now she was old enough to appreciate something of her mother's distress, and she did what she could to comfort her in her illness. Mother and child might well have come still closer together at this period had not a further disaster now befallen Henrietta—a disaster that greatly increased Caroline's sense of insecurity. Henrietta's husband, Frederick, had remained dutifully in England, looking after their three sons whilst his wife and her sister enjoyed themselves abroad and during this time his father died and he became the 3rd Earl of Bessborough and Henrietta the Countess of Bessborough. It is possible that this was in part a cause of what now happened to her in Naples.

At Naples, late in 1793, Henrietta fell madly and passionately in love. She who had known so many men, and was married, now encountered one who possessed every quality that she admired, good looks and charm that fascinated her and a physical attraction such as she had never previously known. A woman of nearly thirty, she was now overwhelmed by a young man nearly twelve years her junior. She was as helpless to resist him as a young girl in the throes of her first love affair. In his arms she forgot everything and everyone— even her adored little daughter.

This young man was Lord Granville Leveson-Gower, who was the youngest son of the Marquess of Stafford. He was no idle gentleman of fashion, seeking for a new conquest. He was an Adonis, whom the Gods adored. He was gay, he was brilliant, he was charming, he was irresistible. He was 'Granville, adored Granville, who would make a desert smile'. To be in his company was to live and to laugh. He was the very spirit of youth.

He may, when first he met her, have been influenced by her title, by the fact that the Duchess of Devonshire was her sister and that she was the outstanding celebrity in the gay social life of Naples. But he was no snob, this young man, only a little unsure of himself and disconcerted by the way in which women were attracted to him. It was not simply love that he was seeking, nor mere sexual adventure. He wanted companionship and understanding as well. Henrietta's beauty delighted him, but it was the warmth of her nature which

22

captivated him. She brought him ecstasy, and then gave him tranquillity and rest.

She became his mistress after only a pathetic attempt at feminine restraint, for from the outset she would have given him her soul as well as her body; and as the years went by she learnt to hold him with the ties of understanding and true love long after other women had claimed him as their bedfellow and had revealed a greater sensuality than herself.

To be separated from him was misery to her, and she overcame this by writing to him and telling him of all the joys and troubles of her life and by encouraging him to confide in her in the same way, so that he finally began to tell her of his love affairs. She gave him her advice and scolded him gently, even when these stories of his passing escapades were breaking her heart.

The effect of such a transparent and overwhelming passion could only have a harmful effect on Henrietta's adored little Caro, whom she would never willingly have hurt. Now Caroline felt herself forced to compete for her mother's affection, and although she found Granville as delightful and as handsome as everyone else, and could never bring herself to dislike him, she yet knew well enough that he was a rival in her life. The fears which haunted her in childhood over her mother's health were now increased by even greater fears—that her mother might one day transfer all her love for her little Caro to someone else.

Caroline was still a child, but the escapades of her mother and aunt had taught her the importance of sex in human relationships. She knew that sex could even over-ride the love which existed between a mother and daughter.

Henrietta understood the problem but found herself quite incapable of solving it. The butterfly was hypnotized by the flame and could not force herself to escape. She convinced herself that her affair with Lord Granville would prove a lasting romance, and that the best and wisest course to take was not to end the liaison and devote herself to motherhood, but rather to abandon the claims of motherhood on the grounds that she was too weak and already too steeped in folly to be the proper person to look after her child.

Yet she was well aware that her poor little Caro had been dragged around the Continent long enough. She was a child without roots. Therefore she must return to England and go to school.

23

Two

Caro - The Devonshire House Girl

Difficult children, when they are sent to school, usually fall into two categories—those who mope and pine, and those who make a considerable nuisance of themselves.

There was never any question as to which category Caroline would occupy. Small, resentful and defiant, she made her presence felt from the outset. She was a sore trial to those whose duty it was to teach her—and to control her.

For a short while, after her arrival, there were those who looked upon her as fragile and pathetic. They were soon disillusioned. Her tantrums astonished them, and her talent for telling lies quite overwhelmed them. Active in mind and body, quick-witted, intelligent and rebellious to a degree, Caroline was the last person to submit with docility to discipline.

She fought with all the vigour in her small body to preserve her identity. Experience had taught her that the only way to focus attention upon herself was by making a scene. She had no inhibitions about this. When Caroline made a scene, it was not a small one. She gave full rein to her histrionic abilities. No one could scream louder, bite harder, cry for longer, or roll on the floor in a greater paroxysm of temper than Caroline Ponsonby.

A further method of counteracting the real or imaginary injustices inflicted upon her was to exaggerate them, and this she was well able to do. Caroline had a vivid imagination, and an eloquent tongue. Facts were of little interest to her when she was recounting some story of how monstrously she had been ill-used.

The place chosen for Caroline's education was a seminary for the daughters of gentlefolk in Hans Place in Kensington. Here was no Dickensian Dotheboys Hall, in which pathetic pupils were pitilessly ill-treated by sadistic teachers, but this was the vision of it which Caroline carried into later life. She had no desire to go to school, nor had she any intention of liking school when she got there.

The headmistress was a Miss Frances Rowden, who was certainly no fore-runner of Mr Wackford Squeers. A high-minded and
amiable woman, easy-going and sympathetic, she had once been a
governess in the service of the Bessborough family, and had been
well respected by them. She was in the habit of quoting the elevating
thoughts and pious verses of distinguished personalities. She herself had written a poem entitled *The Pleasures of Friendship*, which
she had dedicated to Lady Bessborough. It included such lines as:

Visions of early youth, ere yet ye fade,
Let my light pen arrest your fleeting shade.

Thus she was an admirable headmistress for docile and godly
children, but not well suited to controlling someone like Caroline.

The suggestion that Miss Rowden ever ill-used Caroline is scarcely
worth considering. More important is the question of how much
Caroline ill-used Miss Rowden. Miss Rowden was not accustomed to
dealing with little girls who behaved so badly or who were in the
habit of telling such dreadful lies. At times she was deceived, as so
many of Caroline's associates were to be deceived in the future, by
the child's ability to look pathetic.

Caroline's tantrums made everyone ill, including herself. The main
problem was that no one was able to control her or to discipline her.
Her mother was too weak and ineffectual. The servants were frightened of her outbursts, and since they had no authority over her, they
were reluctant to correct her.

Caroline's grandmother, Lady Spencer, decided to call in the family
physician for his advice. Dr Warren gave it as his opinion that
Caroline was in a highly nervous state, and that attempts to discipline
her might make her much worse. He also considered that her brain
was too fertile and too agile. The child was not a genius, but she was
undoubtedly gifted and even brilliant. If anything, she should be
encouraged to play more and to use her brain less. His view was that
she should be allowed to run wild for a time, and that no attempts
should be made to educate her. The brain should be rested—and the
imagination as well, if this were possible. The great need in Caroline's
life was that she should be taught to relax.

Perhaps Dr Warren was not so very far out in his diagnosis of her
treatment. It was hardly within his scope to prescribe a saner home
life, a less promiscuous attitude in her mother, and an increased
sense of responsibility in both Henrietta and Georgiana. Dr Warren

might have been tempted to express the view held by many child psychiatrists today—*there is no such thing as a problem child, but only a problem parent.*

The result of Dr Warren's advice was that Caroline was allowed to develop not only without restraint, but also without education. She grew up knowing nothing of the world outside her own social sphere, nothing of how the poor lived, nothing of history and nothing of literature other than what she chose to read herself. A good brain was allowed to lie fallow, and a sharp intelligence was never harnessed to any useful purpose. She continued to live in a world of her imagination, and this imagination of hers certainly never suffered from lack of use.

In 1793 Henrietta's father-in-law had died, and her husband had become the 3rd Earl of Bessborough. This increase in her status had made no difference in her attitude to life, and if anything she became yearly more weak and unstable.

Meanwhile she and Georgiana fell ever more heavily into debt. In 1797 Henrietta was actually arrested and fined for gaming at the home of Lady Buckingham, after two footmen who had been discharged had informed on four of the ladies who had been playing at faro.

Henrietta, still worried by her conscience and the realization that she was failing in her motherly duties, was quite distraught over what she should do with Caroline. She felt quite unable to cope with the child at home, and Miss Rowden fared no better with Caroline at the school in Kensington.

The solution seemed obvious to Henrietta. Caroline needed the companionship of other children of her own age who were her close relatives, so that she might grow up in a much more family atmosphere than she had been accustomed to until this time. And who better to give her this opportunity than her much-loved aunt, Georgiana, with her wonderful country estate at Chatsworth and her equally splendid London mansion, Devonshire House, in Piccadilly?

At first sight it must have seemed an excellent idea. Everyone loved Georgiana and Georgiana loved everyone. The warmth of her unfailing good nature seemed just the kind of tonic that a neurotic little girl was in need of, and in the Devonshire House circle everyone lived in the very lap of luxury.

Yet there were obvious disadvantages which Henrietta overlooked. The atmosphere at Devonshire House was dissipated, to say the least. Georgiana had her lovers and the Duke had a regular mistress in

Bess. Many of the guests who visited this splendid mansion were also engaged in adulterous affairs, and there was no restraint on behaviour so long as some outward semblance of propriety was maintained.

Frequent all-night parties were held at Devonshire House, and the menfolk—and notably the Prince of Wales himself—were often so drunk by the end of them that they had to be escorted to their carriages, taken home and undressed and put to bed by their valets.

But there was also brilliant talk to be heard at Devonshire House; and above all there was Charles Fox to make the chatter sparkle with his unfailing wit and outrageous comments.

There was a liberal education to be obtained at Devonshire House, but in many ways it was altogether too liberal for young children. The brilliant conversation was largely over their heads, but Charles, who was so young at heart, would always laugh with the children, and even the Prince of Wales, with all his faults, had a great affection for them.

As for the Duke of Devonshire, so solemn and portentous, he enjoyed lecturing little Caroline on the intricacies of Whig policy whilst helping her to toast muffins before his library fire.

All this was the very essence of Whig philosophy. Laugh at life, defy the conventions, indulge in the pleasures of the senses. Love and make love—and never believe that love is the privilege of youth. Be tolerant of mankind's weaknesses and hate only injustice.

These were the beliefs by which the Whig aristocracy lived and died. It was heady stuff for young and impressionable minds.

When Anne, Countess of Sunderland, the best loved daughter of the Duke of Marlborough and his wife Sarah, lay on her death-bed in the spring of 1716, she wrote a letter to her husband, begging him to look after their children. And she included the admonition, 'To be left to servants is very bad for children.'

It was one of the problems facing the rich during the eighteenth and nineteenth centuries that their children were all too often left in the care of servants. It was not that their parents or guardians did not love them. It was usually that the demands of social life made parental supervision of children impractical, and servants seemed to make it unnecessary as well.

Devonshire House was full of servants, and so was Chatsworth. They were kind-hearted enough, but the children were allowed to run wild throughout the building and the gardens. No one was really responsible for them, and no one was in a position to discipline them. A naughty child just entering its teens might well become the master or the mistress of the house within half a dozen years. Because of their position, these children of the aristocracy had therefore to be treated with servility and allowed to do very much as they pleased.

The position was not so bad for the boys, who were packed off to Eton at just about the time when they were becoming unmanageable. One of the chief functions of the great English public schools at this period was to undo the damage which had been caused by indulgent parents and a servile staff. Spoilt little boys who had been accustomed to scream for what they wanted, and to kick and bite if they did not get it, were knocked into shape by the public schools.

But there were no such schools for girls. The daughters of the privileged classes were in theory well-behaved young ladies who did not need correction. But in fact they were often more undisciplined than their brothers.

Caroline was welcomed to Devonshire House with the utmost warmth by Georgiana, whose tender heart went out to this waif-like little creature with her sad and elfin look. The Duke, too, beamed upon her in his calm and amiable way, and patted her blonde curls. But the 'Devonshire House Girls' were less forthcoming. Shrewder than their mother, and less impulsive, they eyed the newcomer warily and welcomed her less effusively.

Caroline wanted to be liked, but her inherent tactlessness prevented her from lying low for the first few months in her new surroundings. She had already convinced herself, in her short life, that it was necessary to fight for what one wanted in an unsatisfactory world, especially in so far as her own sex was concerned.

Had she allowed herself to be subdued by the occasion, she might well have been popular. But it was not long before she staged her first major tantrum, and revealed herself in her true colours. Not that the Devonshire House girls were unimpressed by her perform-ance. They had been brought up in a Whig world in which it was the custom for both men and women to express themselves forcefully and without restraint, and Caroline's initial performance aroused in them a certain grudging admiration.

They were also impressed by her unscrupulousness and the un-ashamed manner in which she was prepared to exert her charm over men, including the members of the Devonshire House staff. Her capacity for telling lies also impressed them. There seemed to be no limits to her mendacity.

There were two Cavendish daughters, Georgiana and Harriet, and one son—the Marquess of Hartington, who was known in the family circle as Hart, for everyone had to have a nickname at Devonshire House. Harriet, known as Hary-O, was the same age as Caroline and nearest to her in temperament. Georgiana, known as G., was two years older, having been born in 1783. Hart was the baby of the family, born in 1790, and spoilt by everyone. He was a gentle, warm-hearted little boy who immediately fell in love with Caroline, and continued to adore her throughout his life. Her tantrums were never vented on him, and she was always sweet to him. She fought constantly with Hary-O, however, and found her to be an opponent who could more than hold her own when it came to blunt speaking and the pulling of hair.

A further member of this family circle was the other Caroline—Caroline St Jules—the illegitimate daughter of the Duke by his dearest Bess. Her inclusion, which had been skilfully engineered by her mother, was in the true tradition of Whig permissiveness, for it was not considered unseemly for illegitimate children, whether born as the result of the husband's indiscretions or those of his wife, to be included in the family circle.

Thus the Devonshire House family included two virtual 'outsiders' —Caroline Lamb and Caroline St Jules—who were nearly the same age but totally different in character.

Caroline St Jules was gentle, unassuming and amenable. She, too, had known what it was to be dragged around Europe in early childhood, enduring a life of insecurity and lack of affection, but this had aroused no bitterness in her. She was a lovable and warm-hearted child.

The Duke treated her with more affection than he treated his own children, and this was a cause of resentment amongst the others. Far worse was the fact that he treated Bess with more affection than he treated his wife, Georgiana. By now Bess had almost assumed the role of second wife and step-mother in the Devonshire House family, and no one resented this more bitterly than Georgiana's younger daughter, Harriet, who was fiercely loyal to her mother.

Hary-O took after her father in character and in looks. Forthright, solid and unimaginative, with a rather dumpy figure and little charm, she had disliked and distrusted Bess from the outset. Resenting Bess as she did, she tried her utmost to influence the other Cavendish children. Her elder sister, Georgiana, was easy-going and tolerant, but little Hart accepted whatever Hary-O told him. He tried to hate Bess,

29

but found it difficult to do so.

Caroline Ponsonby shared Hary-O's dislike of Bess. She, too, was devoted to her aunt, Georgiana, and described Bess as 'a serpent' who was trying to worm her way into the Duke's affection. Otherwise she had little in common with Hary-O, with whom she usually quarrelled. Caroline did try to be friendly at the beginning, but Hary-O, soured by the situation which existed over Bess, grew up a short-tempered and unattractive child, and it was not until after she had left the influence of what was—to her—a broken home that she mellowed and revealed an unexpected amiability and sense of humour.

The problems of the family were complicated by the fact that Georgiana herself remained devoted to Bess, even after she realized that Bess spent more time in her husband's arms than she did herself. Georgiana had all the Whig's easy tolerance of infidelities in the home.

Bess was in a difficult position. She loved her little daughter, Caroline St Jules, and was naturally anxious that the child should be brought up at Devonshire House. And although she was realistic enough to know which side her bread was buttered, and was therefore anxious to maintain her hold over the Duke, she was not a grasping or ungenerous woman, and she made a real attempt to show affection to the other Devonshire House children and to win them over to her side.

Her chief opponent was Georgiana's mother, Lady Spencer, who had always distrusted her and had never made any attempt to hide the fact. Bess's efforts to ingratiate herself with this formidable woman never succeeded, but she never gave up trying.

Bess had charm and knew how to use it. Gibbon once declared that no man could withstand her, and that she had the power to charm the Lord Chancellor from the Woolsack; but he also made reference to 'the good Duchess of Devonshire and the wicked Lady Elizabeth Foster'.

But wicked she was not. Nor was she basically treacherous, for she and Georgiana had a working agreement in relation to the Duke's sexual desires. At the back of Bess's mind might have been the thought that she might well outlive Georgiana, and would then be able to claim the Duke as her own. But if the thought did exist in her mind, she never wished Georgiana anything but well. She loved Georgiana, as did everyone else.

But it was not surprising that she was resented at Devonshire House, and that rival factions developed there, despite Bess's attempts

30

to be friendly with everyone. She had had two sons, Frederick and Augustus Foster, who also spent a great deal of their time at Devonshire House, although both were several years older than the Devonshire House girls. Augustus, the younger brother, soon fell under Caroline's spell, but was less demonstrative in his approach to her than little Hart. But he, too, found her enchanting. This company of young men was also strengthened from time to time by the appearance of Caroline's three brothers, John, Frederick and William, so that when the establishment was at full strength (including one or two additional young people whose parentage seemed in doubt) it comprised a large and vociferous assembly, in which it was necessary to fight hard to preserve one's individuality. Caroline fought hard, and certainly preserved her own. Hart and Caroline St Jules, however, were forced into the background when any conflict raged.

Theoretically in charge of the schoolroom, but in fact wielding but little authority, was the Devonshire House governess, Miss Selina Trimmer, a cheerful, plain and friendly person who was generally liked but all too seldom obeyed.

Caroline Ponsonby, when she joined the family at the age of nine, made an attempt to settle down amicably but failed, partly because of Hary-O's hostility but largely because of her own failings. Talking incessantly, nearly always about herself, revealing her immaturity by the absurdity of her views but at the same time revealing her intelligence by quoting long passages from Shakespeare which she had learnt by heart, always the ring-leader in any games, ordering about the staff as if she were mistress of the establishment, borrowing the uniforms of the pages and dressing herself up as a boy—quarrelling, mimicking, pinching and pushing, deliberately breaking what few rules anyone ever attempted to impose, and telling one outrageous lie after another, Caroline was not exactly the type of little girl who could be taken easily into the bosom of any family.

She rode bare-back when everyone else used a saddle, she would not go to bed when she was told, she would not eat what she was given, and she remained outrageously precocious and stubbornly self-willed.

But her tantrums were not always effective at Devonshire House because Hary-O was not one to be influenced by them. Hary-O was quite happy to allow Caroline to scream until she was purple in the face, and in the end the two contestants developed a certain mutual respect. They at least shared a dislike of Bess and an adoration of

31

Georgiana, who appeared on the scene from time to time to try and bring peace into her household. But Georgiana had so many problems of her own to contend with that she had little enough time to cope with the bickerings of her children and their cousin.

As the 1790s progressed, Georgiana became ever more a caricature of the glorious young girl that she once had been. As Walpole noted, she was becomingly increasingly coarse in her appearance. Her colouring, which had always verged on the florid, was now becoming garish, and the light auburn tints which still lingered in her hair showed up the cruder red in her cheeks. The trouble with her eye, which had first manifested itself at Portsmouth several years previously, was now growing more serious, and her eye-sight was beginning to grow weak. She also suffered from a swelling in her neck.

Henrietta noted these changes in her sister and wrote despairingly to Lord Granville, giving him a heart-rending account of the drastic remedies that were being employed by the physicians in their attempts to reduce the inflammation.

To Hary-O this was particularly distressing, for Bess remained beautiful and slim, her complexion was still excellent, and her hazel-brown eyes had lost none of their allure. Little wonder that the Duke still looked upon her with such favour, so that it seemed to the child that if anything were ever to happen to her mother, Bess must inevitably take her place.

Caroline, at least, was spared some of this anguish. She had less reason for disliking Bess, who had always been kind enough to her, but the atmosphere of brooding resentment which at times pervaded Devonshire House and Chatsworth did not promote a sense of youthful gaiety and love of life.

Yet despite all these dramas and conflicting loyalties, life still went on for the children in Devonshire House in many ways the same as it went on for those born of less privileged parents. They played and quarrelled, climbed trees and rode horses. They contracted the usual childish diseases and survived them without undue distress. Caroline caught chicken-pox when she was thirteen, felt very sorry for herself and was sent home to be nursed by her mother, probably in order to avoid infecting the others. By now Henrietta was writing almost daily to Lord Granville, telling him of all the problems of her life, and the one in which she discussed Caroline's convalescence gives an interesting side-light into the workings of Caroline's mind. After writing that Caroline was recovering quickly, that she had only two spots and would not be marked, Henrietta went on to say,

'Caroline said this morning, "I suppose Lord Granville would not deign to look at me if I am all pitted with the chicken-pox." I asked her why she thought so; she said, "he seems too fine a gentleman to like ugly people, but I can assure him I would not give sixpence for any body who would not like me as well with a rough face as with a smooth one." I don't know why Caroline supposes you are so governed by looks, but I think you ought to be flattered, as you are certainly the only person she has enquired after.'

Caroline's behaviour in this matter revealed the conflict that was developing in her mind. Although outwardly still very much the tomboy, dishevelled and often grubby, she was already beginning to think about her looks—and about men. Her immature reaction, when dealing with a man whom she knew to be very interested in women, was to adopt a defiant attitude towards him, and to accuse him of thinking her unattractive before he had voiced any opinion at all. The fact that she showed any interest in his opinion, however, suggested—as Henrietta realized—that the matter was of importance to her.

But there was a further undercurrent at work in Devonshire House. Hary-O had developed an ardent love for the handsome young man who was her aunt's lover, and of this Henrietta was vaguely aware without attaching any importance to it. In one of her letters to Lord Granville she wrote, 'Little Harrio cries after you and wants a horse to ride after you, and fetch you back.'

It can never have entered Henrietta's head that Lord Granville might ever look upon any of the Devonshire House girls with anything more than tolerant amusement. But Caroline, with her sharp sensitivity, might have already guessed that he was not so disinterested in these young girls as he seemed. She was jealous of Hary-O, and at this moment—when they were just entering their teens—her determination to outdo her cousin increased.

Caroline, for all her outward assurance and conceit, was never quite sure of herself when it came to attracting men. She realized only too well that her elfin quality, her seeming fragility and her lisp together made men eye her with interest. She did not feel pathetic—indeed the very essence of her nature was defiance—but she was certainly not above putting on a pathetic, little-girl air when men were about. But she was yet not certain of her looks, and her self-confidence was not increased by the rude remarks made about her by her young rivals.

Already the pattern which was to develop throughout her life was beginning to take shape. Males were often attracted by her on sight,

33

but females often disliked her on sight. She could deceive the opposite sex but she could never deceive her own. Her lisp, which in these early days of puberty was probably her strongest asset, could devastate young men but was sneered at by her girl friends. 'Lady Caroline ba-a-a-as like a little sheep,' was the tart observation of one of them. The comment was repeated by Hary-O and the other Devonshire House girls, and it made Caroline blush with fury.

The situation was not improved by the dog-like devotion which was shown to Caroline by little Hart. He was adored by his two sisters, and it was mortifying to them to find him devoting his whole attention to their cousin.

Hart was happy to spend hours in Caroline's company, and he used to tell her solemnly that when he was grown up he would marry her. But Caroline would only laugh, and then kiss him and tell him that when he was grown up he would find someone else whom he would love much better than her. In fact he never did.

As Caroline entered her teens many young men who visited Devonshire House paused to study this little tomboy who was always romping about in the grounds. And not only the young men stopped to eye her speculatively, for it was a period when young girls were very much to the taste of older men as well.

Small and slim, with a boy's narrow hips and with still only the hint of a bust, there was yet something very feminine about Caroline Ponsonby. When she pouted and lisped, as she did often when in men's company, she could look adorable; and her fragility aroused in strongly masculine men an urge to take her up in their arms to pet and to kiss her as though she were a child. She still had baby ways and would impulsively take the arm of a man, or hold his hand, or look gravely up into his face, in a way which made him her slave. To these visiting males she showed only her good side. She did not lose her temper in their company, or scream or sulk.

She could enchant so many different kinds of men, and in so many different kinds of ways. Byron, in the years to come, was to declare that she never really attracted him, for her body was too thin to be seductive, and her face was quite lacking in all the accepted tenets of beauty. Her voice annoyed him, her moodiness infuriated him, and her excitability drove him nearly mad.

He saw her more through the eyes of a woman than through those of a man, which was why he always remained so critical of her. And yet she ever enchanted him.

But the man who was later to become her husband, and who was

34

so essentially masculine, loved her both as a woman and as a child. She touched his heart from the very first moment that he set eyes upon her; and these same eyes would later fill with tears at the mention of her name—even many years after she was dead.

She was no more than a child when first he saw her, running wild with her cousins and seemingly quite oblivious of his glance. He looked and looked again, for the sparkle in a young girl's eyes had always delighted him, and turning to his companion he remarked, 'Of all the Devonshire House girls, that is the one for me.'

She was always the one for him, even though she brought him so little happiness, and so much heart-break and despair.

Three

Caroline - Debut in Society

One by one the Devonshire House girls grew up, made their debut in Society and went out into the world. The fact that momentous events were taking place both at home and abroad did not affect them. *Their* purpose was to marry well and to exchange the tumult of their existence for comparative calm in a home of their own making and with a husband of their own choosing. Being Devonshire House girls they had no reason to suppose that they would be faced with any problems in finding the requisite suitors. Their father had been the first match in England when he married Georgiana Spencer. Now his daughters and his niece were looked upon as prizes well worth the taking.

The nineteenth century opened significantly with Georgiana secretly borrowing £6,000 from the Duke of Bedford at 5% interest. This immediately changed her outlook and improved her health. The fact that she would sooner or later have to repay the money was soon forgotten. She was momentarily relieved of anxiety and became her old, exuberant self.

In the spring her eldest daughter, Lady Georgiana Dorothy Cavendish, was presented at Court. Later a magnificent ball was given at Devonshire House in her honour. The young Georgiana was seventeen and therefore of marriageable age. Her most attentive partner at the dance was the young Lord Morpeth, the eldest son of the 5th Earl of Carlisle. Within the year she had married him.

The younger girls, Hary-O, Caroline Ponsonby and Caroline St Jules were also anxious to go out into the world. Hary-O still treasured her school-girl infatuation for her aunt's lover, Lord Granville, to whom Henrietta was still writing almost daily, but Caroline was more concerned with the problem of staging a sensational entry into Society. She derided Hary-O for her simple loyalty to one man and added wickedly that she might even consider Lord Granville for herself, although of course he was far too old, and anyway the property of her mother.

All three girls, Hary-O, Caroline Ponsonby and Caroline St Jules, were now ready to leave the shelter of Devonshire House's high walls and also to leave childhood behind them. Hary-O and Caroline St Jules showed a certain apprehension about the future. Caroline Ponsonby showed none. Outwardly she remained self-confident and self-satisfied.

The Peace of Amiens was signed in March, 1802, and almost at once a two-way traffic across the Channel developed, with French ladies of fashion hurrying over to England to see the Prince of Wales, and English ladies of fashion hurrying over to Paris to see the macabre relics of the French Revolution and to gaze in fascination upon the First Consul, whose image had by now reached heroic proportions.

Henrietta and Caroline followed in their wake. Now, for the first time in her life, Caroline and her mother were constantly in each other's company and were behaving almost as sisters. Henrietta's health had improved, and she was now more active than she had been for some time. She and Caroline had spent the previous months travelling round England, visiting the country houses at which they were always welcome—Chatsworth, of course, Lady Spencer's home at Althorp, and Brocket Hall, the country estate of Lord and Lady Melbourne.

Caroline enjoyed these visits. She blossomed out and even mellowed. She was by now beginning to look really pretty, with her boyish slimness and unfailing animation. Admittedly she still talked far too much and usually about herself, with the words tumbling out of her mouth in an almost incoherent stream, but she had intelligence and a quick wit. Men of the world scarcely knew what to make of her. Here, it seemed to them, as they gazed on her lissom figure and babyish face, was virginity personified; but from her worldly chatter one might suppose that she had already given herself to numerous lovers. Her attitude was very much that of youthful antagonism to all stuffy codes of behaviour. Her manner was aggressively unconventional.

The place she loved most was Chatsworth. 'Caro Pon: says Chatsworth is Paradise,' wrote Georgiana in one of her letters. But Chatsworth apart, Caroline now found Paris also enchanting. Her memories of it as a child were vague and rather forbidding. Now, with only a scant knowledge of the Revolution, and with Charles

37

Fox's extravagant praise of the revolutionaries ringing in her ears, she was as ready as anyone to gaze in awe upon Napoleon, whom Charles was alleged to have described to his face as 'the greatest man of the greatest nation'.

In Paris they were joined by Bess and Caroline St Jules. Georgiana had remained in England to nurse the Duke's gout, together with that of another acute sufferer, Lord Bessborough, but Henrietta and Bess were not going to miss Napoleon on any account.

Sheridan had offered to bet them any sum they cared to name that they would faint seven times running at their first sight of him; but although Bess was soon writing an excited account of the first meeting to Georgiana, neither woman actually collapsed on first glimpsing Napoleon, whom Bess thereafter referred to in her letters as 'Him', spelt with a capital 'H'.

'It seemed to me to be the most worth seeing of any sight I ever had beheld—this extraordinary Man in all simplicity of acknowledged greatness, the creator—the commander—the head of this and in-numerable other armies...'

The fact that He was the acknowledged enemy of England and might shortly be leading His armies in an attempt to cross the Channel and subjugate the English race did not seem to have any great significance to these dedicated Napoleonists.

However, Bess was able to add a more homely touch to her correspondence by adding that she hoped Hary-O might soon find time to visit Paris, for 'the corsets here are very advantageous to the shape'—which was not the kindest of references to Hary-O's rather dumpy figure.

Georgiana's health was once again a cause for concern, and Bess concluded her letter with some examples of that intimate Devonshire House baby-talk which she reserved for such occasions, 'My dearest, why are oo gloomy? Why are oo vexed?'

Altogether it was not the sort of letter that would endear her to Hary-O.

Henrietta was at the same time busily engaged in writing her impressions of Paris to Lord Granville. She was genuinely concerned about her husband's health and remarked, 'Poor Ld. B.'s gout looks very threatening. He is quite laid up at present.' But by the following January the whole family were together in Paris, Lord Bessborough having come over to join them, and bringing with him his heir, Lord Duncannon. They were presented to Napoleon and were suitably impressed.

By now preparations were being made to present Hary-O at Court as a prelude to getting her married. Lord Aberdeen was already much taken with her, but Georgiana favoured another suitor, Caroline's brother, Lord Duncannon. But Hary-O remained faithful to her first love and still thought of no one except Lord Granville.

In the spring of 1803 the Treaty of Amiens died its inevitable death when it became apparent that Napoleon's aim was merely to keep Britain on the side-lines whilst he set about annexing the rest of Europe. The sightseers in France hastened back across the Channel, and before the summer was out more than two thousand invasion craft had been assembled by Napoleon at Boulogne. There was panic in England, but admirers of Napoleon still held him to be a noble and trustworthy leader, with the good of Europe at heart.

Georgiana's hero, Charles Fox, returned from Paris having suffered some loss of face but remaining impenitent of his actions. His comment that liberty was now asleep in France whereas it was dead in England caused much indignation. He still believed that Napoleon was at heart the friend of England; and even considered that Britain was as much to blame as the French for the resumption of hostilities.

Charles was already a sick man, as his beloved Duchess was a sick woman, but she still managed to retain her sweetness, while he was growing more crotchety each day. Too much drinking and hard living had ruined his liver. Now the doctors were killing him off as they were killing Georgiana off, with their quack remedies and tragic lack of knowledge.

When Caroline made her debut in Society in 1803 and took up a prominent place in the centre of the Mayfair stage, she did so with an outward assurance that deceived many. At no time in her life were the contradictions in her character more pronounced.

She looked self-assured but she was not. She appeared worldly and mature, but she was not. Her defiance of convention, her tendency towards immodesty in dress and her freely expressed opinions on all matters pertaining to human conduct, suggested that she had inherited the lax morals of her mother and her aunt, but in fact Caroline was something of a prude.

She was almost certainly a virgin, and was not only frightened of sex but was also secretly doubtful about her own sexual potential. Her figure was immature and boyish, and bore no resemblance whatever to her aunt Georgiana's full-blown voluptuousness.

She appeared to be well-read, and even something of an intellectual, and she could quote readily from Shakespeare and other great writers, but her reading had in fact been very limited. Nor had she been instructed on how to interpret the classics. Thus she had knowledge without judgement.

She had an excellent brain, receptive and quick, and a considerable talent for the arts, but this talent had been allowed to develop without guidance or purpose. She merely turned her attention to whatever happened to interest her at the moment.

This lack of controlled thinking revealed itself in every aspect of her creative work. She had a flair for writing verse, her prose was vivid and descriptive, although over-loaded with adjectives, and her sketches were delightful. But verse and prose were produced helter-skelter in sudden outbursts of energy, and the sketches were often left unfinished. Her letters were a jumble of different topics, with numerous scratchings-out but with few corrections, which suggested that she seldom read through what she had written.

Today probably the largest collection of Caroliana—diaries, letters and sketches—is in the possession of Lady Salmond, a descendant of William Lamb's sister, Emily, who married Lord Cowper. To sit at Lady Salmond's desk, surrounded by countless items of Caroline's written work, is a curious and an illuminating experience. The words seem to have been poured out onto these faded pages as though someone had seized a dictionary and had tipped them out in confusion across the paper. The scribbled lines zig-zag across the page, and many of the sketches seem to have been added at random.

One point is particularly striking. Melancholy so often intrudes on what is otherwise a happy, carefree mood, and a sudden sadness seems to overwhelm the writer. On one page of her commonplace book is a sketch of a child gazing down in delight upon a basket piled with flowers. But on the opposite page the child is looking sadly on the same basket, in which all the flowers have withered away.

These letters, diaries and scribbles across the page are the work of an immature child—but of a gifted and even a brilliant child, none the less. There is evidence here in plenty of her failings—her impetuosity, her inability to concentrate on any one thing for more than a few moments and her wild flights of fancy. But there is also so much evidence of her lovable qualities—of her warmth of feeling, of her spontaneous gaiety and of the lark that was forever singing in her heart.

But at least it could be said of her that she was conscious of her failings, and of her immaturity. Of herself at the age of fifteen she once remarked, 'I wrote not, spelt not, but I wrote verses which they all thought beautiful.' It was a precocious enough comment, but she then went on to say, 'For myself, I preferred washing a dog or polishing a piece of Derby-shire spar, or breaking in a horse, to any accomplishment in the world.'

Like so many young girls of her age, she was quite obsessively devoted to horses. Riding seemed to give her a sense of freedom; controlling a horse a sense of power; and loving a horse fulfilled the need for giving and receiving affection.

Her attitude to politics was equally immature. She was, of course, an ardent Whig. With her family traditions and with Charles Fox so often a visitor to Devonshire House she could scarcely have been anything else, but she would have been hard put to it to make any knowledgeable statement about Whig policy or the war with France. The Tories were merely the enemy—the opposition who were to be scorned whatever they said or did—and it was her custom to drink damnation to the Tory Party in endless mugs of milk.

Yet in many of these ways she was but typical of her era. Both Englishmen and Englishwomen were going through a very emotional period, and the Victorian belief that a public display of the emotions was bad form had yet to be adopted. Men wept openly and copiously in moments of stress. Gamblers gave way to paroxysms of anguish and frustration when they lost at cards. Discarded lovers openly bemoaned their misfortune.

Yet for all this, times were changing. The dandies, led by Beau Brummell, had adopted the attitude that to show emotion *was* bad form. Fate, they argued, was determined to break a man's spirit in the end, and a gentleman defied Fate by refusing to acknowledge either triumph or disaster. Life in itself was but a bad joke, and one neither laughed at it nor cried over it. Here was the origin of the Victorian demeanour, and of the Englishman's stiff upper lip.

Times were changing in other respects, and the mood of Englishmen was changing with them. The growth of industrialism was changing the face of the country. Idealism was dying amidst the embers of the French Revolution, and war itself was losing its glory.

An age of materialism was being born, and there were those who tried to fight against it. They had little enough justification for doing so. The French Revolution had killed freedom, not given birth to it; and the wishful thinking amongst romanticists which had invested

Napoleon with all the attributes of a hero of old was proving to be a tragic fallacy.

To be a true romanticist it was necessary to turn one's back on reality. This was not difficult for those blessed with a vivid imagination, and least of all those who occupied a station in life which hid from them the miseries of the poor and under-privileged.

Caroline was deeply romantic and the new wave of romanticism which had found its inspiration in the poetry of Wordsworth was something which appealed strongly to her emotional nature. Not that Wordsworth fully satisfied Caroline. He was too simple for her. She longed for something much more flamboyant and dramatic. Coleridge was more to her liking, but at heart she longed for something that had about it a stronger flavour of tumultuous ardour and knightly heroism. She had read *The Taming of the Shrew* and had thrilled to the submission of Katharina. She realized that there was much of Katharina in herself, and was secretly longing to be purged of her own bad temper and lack of control by an heroic male.

But she was becoming quite vain, and the attention which she was able to command when she entered a ballroom was something to be gloried in and exploited to the full. She knew that it was her winsomeness and charm that attracted men rather than any sensuality in her body. She therefore behaved in a way often adopted by girls who fear they may lack sensuality. She began to wear dresses that were unduly revealing after the style which she had seen in Paris, where the brazen immodesty of women such as Madame Récamier and Madame Tallien had shocked even the worldly citizens of Paris.

Her defiance of convention and scornful comments on morality encouraged her listeners to assume that she was in fact both immoral and promiscuous. A certain Mr Hill, whom she met at a ball at Devonshire House, later told her aunt that he found Caroline the cleverest and prettiest girl in London. And Georgiana, who had the delightful habit of repeating the nice things that she heard about people and ignoring the spiteful ones, promptly told Caroline what he had said.

Caroline was much flattered, and her vanity made her seek out Mr Hill in order that she might be told some more. When he repeated his compliments, and then grew bolder, praising her face and figure, and hinting at the tumultuous passions which he detected beneath her youthful demeanour, she was even more delighted and encouraged him still further.

The outcome was described by an outraged Henrietta in one of her letters to Lord Granville, for Mr Hill became so bold as to write a letter to Caroline in which he not only made an open avowal of his ardour, but also suggested that he should bed her. And he added some uninhibited suggestions as to what the pair of them should do when they got there.

Caroline read the letter with dismay. According to her mother, she only read the opening paragraph, and then flung the letter down in disgust, but this seems unlikely. But she showed it at once to her mother who was horrified by its contents. It was, Henrietta declared in shocked amazement, a letter 'filled with every gross, disgusting indecency that the most depraved imagination could suggest, worse indeed than anything that I ever heard, saw or read or could imagine...'

'Poor little soul!' Henrietta concluded, 'She has been quite ill with it. I do think it very hard; there never was a purer, more delicate mind existing than hers. C'est l'innocence de l'enfance même.'

No doubt Caroline *was* shocked, but it was probably the realization that she had made a fool of herself that upset her the most. That she should thereafter have staged one of her famous scenes, and declared the contents of the letter to be so vile as to make her physically sick, was only in accordance with the drama which she felt inherent in the situation.

Despite the artificiality of her manner, and her many exasperating mannerisms, Caroline still remained an attractive and stimulating companion. When she behaved naturally and forgot to pout and to pose, the youthful radiance which was her especial quality still shone forth. At heart she was as unsophisticated as her mother and her aunt Georgiana had been in their youth, but they had never attempted to hide this, and indeed had always been far too simple to do so. They had always submitted without protest to the ardour of their lovers, but Caroline was made of sterner stuff. Her attitude to romance was more decisive than theirs had ever been. They had drifted into marriage in the same way as they had drifted into promiscuity— largely as the result of an inability to say 'no'.

Caroline was determined not to make the same mistake. The picture of her ideal husband was now fixed clearly in her mind. He must be brave, handsome, brilliant and possessive. He must be her knight in shining armour. He must be her hero, whom she could blindly adore.

She had already encountered such a man, when she was still only

43

twelve. She had seen him watching her one day as she had been scampering helter-skelter round Lord Melbourne's estate at Brocket Park, and had noted the quizzical way that his eyes had followed her, half in amusement at her antics and half in admiration of her lissom grace. And she had later heard a whisper of what he had said on that occasion.

'Of all the Devonshire House girls, that is the one for me.'

Her schoolgirl heart had thrilled to the message which she had read in those quizzical, indolent eyes. Of all the men whom she had met in her young life, this was the one for her.

'William Lamb was beautiful,' she said years later, when recalling this schoolgirl love, 'and far the cleverest person then about, and the most daring in his opinions, in his love of liberty and independence. He thought of me but as a child, yet he liked me very much.'

One cannot guess at just what moment this liking was transformed into love. It may have developed over the years, or it may have kindled at this, their first meeting. William loved youth, he loved laughter and he loved the elfin charm in one whom he looked upon as half child and half woman.

Casual, carefree and already drifting aimlessly along the pleasant paths of life, he could smile inwardly at the manner in which this madcap child had already taken possession of his heart.

One day, perhaps, when she had left childhood behind her and had become a woman, he might seek her out again. But could one marry an elf? Might not this butterfly creature prove too elusive to capture and to love?

Time would tell. But of all the Devonshire House girls she remained the one for him.

Four

Caroline - Love, Honour and Obedience

The schoolgirl grew up, the madcap became a girl of enchanting femininity, and with the flowering of loveliness there also developed a feeling of self-confidence, and even of power. Caroline began the London Season of 1803 timidly as but one of many young girls who were taking their place upon the social stage. By the end of 1804 she was nearly in command of it.

Men looked at her not only with admiration but also with a certain calculation. She was undeniably a good catch. As a prospective wife she had much to offer. She had looks, brains—and authority.

Who were the prospective husbands? There were plenty of them, but the majority were socially unworthy of her. A niece of the Duchess of Devonshire could pick and choose. The world was at her feet.

William Lamb, the second son of Lord Melbourne, was eligible, but only just. Had he been the eldest son, of course, and heir to the title things would have been different. As it was, he had not much to offer.

Of course, he was handsome—and also well-connected. He was popular with everyone, and he mixed easily in the highest circles. He had been taken up by the Prince of Wales after leaving Cambridge, and was frequently to be encountered at Carlton House. He was also a close friend of Caroline's mother, Henrietta. He was certainly a woman's man, and very much the swell and the dandy—casual, fun loving and debonair. Very masculine in his outlook, he was forthright in his speech and down-to-earth in his manner, as were all his family, but yet there was about him a curious refinement and sensitivity. Thus he remained a contradiction, outwardly a philistine, inwardly a philosopher. His crude oaths concealed a fastidious mind.

He had wit and intellect, and even a touch of scholarly brilliance. He spoke easily and fluently, dressed casually but in the very best of taste, had abundant self-confidence, and wrote both prose and verse in a rather florid and romantic style. He had impressed Charles Fox, whose faith in this young man's future was such that Charles was happy to quote some phrases of William's when making a speech in the House.

As for William himself, his political hero was Charles Fox, a man after his own heart. His political villain was the parvenu Tory, George Canning. He wrote some sharply satirical verse at the expense of Canning, and the lines were quoted with glee in many of the fashionable clubs and drawing-rooms favoured by the Whig élite, and at parties at Devonshire House. The general view was that here was a young man of considerable promise—providing the flesh-pots did not get him first. His only weakness as a budding politician was his transparent honesty. It was not in his nature to prevaricate, or to adopt a devious course.

During the Season of 1803, which first launched Caroline into the world of high Society, a subtle difference developed in their relationship. She had been meeting William socially for several years, for he was a frequent visitor to Devonshire House, but until this moment she had been the child, gazing with secret adoration upon his dark good-looks, while he had been very much the man-of-the-world, gazing down at her with his lazy, quizzical smile.

Now the balance of power was gradually being altered. She still adored him, but she now knew how to hide this adoration. Moreover, her growing popularity in Society and the admiration which she aroused in so many of the young men of the fashionable set, began to invest her with a touch of arrogance. It was he who was now required to reveal his admiration, in competition with many other eligible young bachelors. His ardour increased, and although hers did not diminish, she certainly kept it secret.

Caroline's mother, Henrietta, had high ambitions for her daughter. She was very fond of William Lamb, but considered that his name must appear fairly low upon the list. At the top she had tentatively entered the name of the Prince of Wales. He was a little old for Caro, being over forty, but this was of no great consequence.

As for Caroline herself, she was in no great hurry to make up her mind. She was enjoying herself immensely, and blossoming daily under the stimulating influence of male adoration. She was warm and friendly towards William, but tended to treat him simply as an old friend of the family.

Nor was she anxious to commit herself. She was well aware of the many pitfalls of marriage, and the physical side of it alarmed her.

She knew of William's reputation as a lady's man—and a vigorous and virile one at that. She was still innocent, and despite her delight in scorning convention, she remained conventional in the matter of sex. Indeed when she had first heard a whisper that some doubt hung over the question of William's parentage, and that Lord Melbourne might not be his father, she was seriously put out.

A point that escaped her, however, was that there were powerful forces at work to bring about a match between herself and William Lamb. Her mother was anxious for her to marry the Prince; but William's mother, Lady Melbourne, had already decided that he should marry Caroline, and when Lady Melbourne decided that something should happen, it usually did. She was a woman of considerable determination.

As for William himself, his increasing adoration for Caroline was in part offset by his growing indolence. He was enjoying himself in London Society, and was reluctant to commit himself either to marriage or to a settled career. Had he been the eldest son, of course, he would have taken up politics. As it was he toyed with a number of possibilities, considered the Bar, and even cast an eye on the Church. With his looks and stature he would make an impressive bishop. And while he was making up his mind he lounged about the town, supped frequently with the Prince at Carlton House, and enjoyed 'a bath of quiet' at his father's country estate of Brocket. It was peaceful in the heart of the Hertfordshire countryside. There was shooting in the winter, horse-riding and horse-racing in the summer, and always there was the tranquil solitude of the library, where he could write verse and think up some new political *bon mot* or lose himself in the world of the classics.

Finally, he bestirred himself sufficiently to take up the law as a profession, and was called to the Bar in the Michaelmas term of 1804. He joined the northern circuit and distinguished himself at the Lancashire Sessions. And so, for a time, he played with the idea of becoming Judge Lamb instead of Bishop Lamb. His splendid presence, his charm and his stalwart integrity would add dignity as well as authority to the ranks of the judiciary. But still he remained unsettled and reluctant to commit himself to any definite course of action. He was still a dilettante at heart.

It was during the year of 1804 that he first proposed to Caroline. How and when is not known. But she refused him. She hesitated, and then refused him. Her reason was that she felt herself unready for marriage, and perhaps even unsuited to it. Her temper, she said, was

47

too violent and she feared that she was incapable of ever settling down. This was a practical comment. It was followed by a wholly impractical suggestion. She offered to disguise herself as a clerk and work for him on the northern circuit.

Then, in January 1805, something occurred which altered William's whole life. His elder brother, Peniston, heir to the title and to the bulk of the Lamb fortune, died suddenly of consumption. William would therefore become the next Lord Melbourne.

To be an heir to a peerage was not something that one could take lightly. The younger sons could go on the loose and dissipate their time and health, but the heirdom to a title—especially if the family were die-hard Whigs—entailed sacrifice and a dedication to political duty. His course was now charted, whether he liked it or not. His immediate destination must be the House of Commons.

It became imperative for him to settle down and to marry; and now he was in a much stronger position to ask Caroline to be his wife. But would she accept him? Caroline, he knew, admired him. But did she love him?

Caroline, once she heard the news of Peniston's death, asked herself the same question. For her, too, the moment for decision had come. If she were to hesitate now, then he might well be tempted to turn to someone else before devoting himself to his political career.

Hary-O had already been commenting for some time on 'an extraordinary flirtation between William Lamb and Caroline Ponsonby' and had noted, a little critically, that they seemed 'mutually captivated'.

William now proposed a second time and she accepted. It was a true love match and each knew that the other was an essential part of life. Whether they could live happily together was something which had yet to be discovered. But they knew that they could not live apart.

His second proposal was made by letter—a letter that was typical of the man. He wrote simply and with deep sincerity:

'I have loved you for four years, loved you deeply, dearly, faithfully,—so faithfully that my love has withstood my firm determination to conquer it when honour forbade my declaring myself—has withstood all that absence, variety of objects, my own endeavours to seek and like others, or to occupy my mind with a fixed attention to my own profession, could do to shake it.'

On the evening on which she received this letter, Caroline and her

48

mother attended a party at Devonshire House. Caroline said nothing at the time, but when they came home in the early hours of the morning, she showed her mother the letter. Henrietta had known that the situation between Caroline and William was reaching its climax and had written a long letter to Lord Granville, in which she spoke well of William but yet expressed alarm over certain aspects of his character. 'I dislike his manners, and still more his principles and his creed, or rather no creed. Yet his behaviour has been honourable...' She also expressed her alarm over Caroline's health. Having refused William once, Caroline had been desperately agitated ever since, unable to make up her mind, but terrified lest she might lose him.

On her return from Devonshire House, Caroline threw her arms round her mother's neck and told her that she loved William better than anyone else in the world except her mother, but that she would give him up if her mother wished her to do so. Thus Caroline avoided making the decision herself. Henrietta, still in doubt but realizing that her beloved Caro was genuinely in love, kissed her daughter fondly and gave her consent.

Her father, Lord Bessborough, presumably gave his consent thereafter although his opinion was seldom considered of any importance. Caroline and William became formally engaged, and Caroline radiated happiness.

'Their love for one another and his behaviour have quite reconciled me to it,' Henrietta wrote to her lover, 'I do believe all her ill health, and all the little oddities of manner and *sauvageries* that used to vex me arose from the unhappiness that was constantly preying upon her.'

Caroline's hesitancy continued for some time after she had accepted William. She asked him not to visit her home for a few days, but agreed to go to the theatre with him at Drury Lane.

The evening started well, but—as so often happened when Caroline was facing a crisis—it ended in tears and hysteria. William greeted her with such evident warmth and affection that Henrietta was quite won over, and told William that he had the blessing of herself and her husband. Whereat he impulsively flung his arms around Henrietta and kissed her.

Unfortunately William's political enemy, Canning, was a witness to the scene, and William was appalled at the misinterpretation that might be put upon it. He ran down the corridor in confusion, while Henrietta went in pursuit of Canning and hastily explained to him why the young man should be displaying such devotion to her. Canning may have been weak, but he was never spiteful and he showed genuine delight at the news of William's engagement.

But worse was to follow. Henrietta and Caroline called in at Devonshire House after the theatre to tell the Duke the news. But before they could do so, he raised a question that had always been dear to his heart. This was the marriage of Caroline to his son, Hart, who had loved Caroline devotedly since childhood and was now, at sixteen, reaching an age when plans for his marriage could be made.

The Duke was jolted out of his usual calm when told of the fact that Caroline had just accepted William. Hart himself was overcome by the news. He had never subscribed to the Devonshire imperturbability, and now he burst into floods of tears, upbraiding Caroline for her infidelity and declaring that she must always have realized that he was intending to marry her as soon as he was old enough to do so.

Caroline for once found herself in a scene in which she was not playing the central part. Hart became ever more hysterical, and in the end a physician had to be sent for—Sir Walter Farquhar, doctor to the Prince of Wales. He administered sedatives and poor Hart was put to bed in a very woeful state. Perhaps his tragedy was more acute than anyone realized at the time. He never married, and on his death the dukedom was inherited by his cousin.

The one person who suffered no anxiety over the engagement was William's mother, Lady Melbourne. She had achieved a considerable coup on behalf of her favourite son, whose character she had shaped throughout his life and whose destiny she had worked so hard to influence. Now he was making a wonderful match, and she was both proud and delighted.

Now the son whom she loved most had become engaged to someone who could only help to further his career and to enhance his position in Society. The greatest ambition of her life had been achieved.

Before her marriage Lady Melbourne had been a Miss Elizabeth Milbanke, the only daughter of Sir Ralph Milbanke, Bart., of Halnaby, in Yorkshire. This was good, country stock, but hardly the stuff of Mayfair and high Society. She had a small, determined and provocative mouth, splendid dark eyes and a rounded and sensual figure of which she was fully conscious.

There was nothing negative about Elizabeth Milbanke; she knew where she was going and exactly what she wanted. Her first aim was wealth, and this she acquired by marrying Sir Peniston Lamb, a vague and inconsequential young man with a love of pretty women and a flair for squandering money, of which he possessed a large amount. Having used his wealth to obtain a peerage in Ireland he became the first Baron Melbourne and thus found himself with a seat in Parliament. He had no political aspirations, however. His main interest in life was gambling: and his spiritual home was Almack's Club in Pall Mall. A tolerant man, he was prepared both to overlook his wife's indiscretions and to pay her bills. Nor had he any objection to her social ambitions. His family treated him with friendly tolerance. He never knew much of what was going on, and was often a little drunk.

His wife dominated his life and she also dominated those of her children, of whom the first four children had been sons, all fine, strapping fellows. She educated them well and gave them every advantage in life. She was a good mother, and they were all devoted to her.

But with so strong an influence in the family life, it was clear from the outset that her dominant personality would play an important part in the union of Caroline and William. She might not always be visible in the foreground, but her influence would always be there behind the scenes. She was a born organizer, above all of matrimonial affairs, whether of her own family or of those of her friends.

The traditional advice that has always been given to a young man who is contemplating marriage is that he would be well advised to make a careful study of his future mother-in-law, because this is what his wife is likely to become. William was happy to act on this advice, for he was very fond of Henrietta and asked nothing better than that Caroline should grow up to resemble her.

Caroline, on the other hand, when adopting the equally traditional advice that a young girl planning marriage should make a careful study of her future mother-in-law, could only find cause for misgiving. William had been dominated by his mother throughout his life, and although his character was by no means weak, he was yet still very much under her influence. She had made him what he was —a young man well able to go out into the world and make a success of his life.

When Lady Melbourne had first come upon the London social scene, some years before the advent of Georgiana, she had made rapid progress. A beautiful woman who enjoyed men's company and knew exactly how to handle them, she had first manipulated her husband and then, after marriage, had turned to bigger fish and had turned her attention to the Prince of Wales.

Early in her social career, she had aroused the sexual interest of the Prince. She had gone out of her way to be friendly with the heir to the throne, and had made it clear to him that although she was some thirteen years older than him that need not be considered a barrier to any intimate association that might develop between them. The paternity of the various members of her family was always in doubt, and her fourth son, George, who was born in 1784 was probably the product of the close intimacy which developed between Lady Melbourne and the future George IV.

The advent of Georgiana into Society came at a moment when Lady Melbourne was riding the crest of the social wave. It was clear to her that the new Duchess of Devonshire would be likely to prove a formidable rival, especially in view of her beauty, which rivalled that of Lady Melbourne, her popularity, which was even greater, and her morals, which were about on a par. Acting on the old adage that if it is not possible to beat them, it is best to join them, Lady Melbourne had at once cultivated Georgiana's friendship. And Georgiana, warm-hearted and uncritical as always, became Lady Melbourne's close friend.

By 1875 Georgiana, in her letters to her mother, was making reference to 'Lady Melbourne, whom I love'; but Lady Melbourne's match-making proclivities, and the materialism of her outlook, later caused Georgiana's ardour to cool.

Henrietta and her mother, Lady Spencer, were never taken in by Lady Melbourne, and they were always conscious of her social ambitions. This was an age when arranged marriages were still common in Society, and a daughter bowed to the wishes of her parents, but although Henrietta was none too happy about this aspect of Caroline's marriage, she was reluctant to oppose it. The matter was finally settled when Lady Spencer gave her consent, although reluctantly.

Once the engagement had been announced, Caroline proclaimed that William was her ideal of all that a husband should be; but secretly she had her doubts about Lady Melbourne. Her instinct told her that Lady Melbourne's fiercely possessive attitude to her favourite son would be unlikely to lessen in the future. Moreover she may well have guessed that she had been chosen as William's bride because she was so well connected and *not* because she was thought to be an ideal wife.

No adoring mother ever considers that her son's wife is worthy of him, and Lady Melbourne had long since decided that it would be necessary to take a firm line when dealing with Caroline. Her only worry was that William was so very much in love, and was revealing an emotionalism which was disturbingly un-Lamb-like. He might well prove too weak with Caroline, and too indulgent of her follies. Caroline had been spoilt all her life. It would be disastrous if William continued to spoil her after they were married.

A further problem was that the young couple were to begin their married life as lodgers in Melbourne House. This was by no means unusual in this period, and since the aristocracy possessed large houses, the arrangement generally worked fairly well. Melbourne House had originally been situated on a splendid site just off Piccadilly (soon to become the Albany), but the Prince of Wales had not only coveted his neighbour's wife, but his house as well.

Lady Melbourne was happy that he should be given both. First of all she presented herself to him, and later agreed that he should also take possession of Melbourne House, in exchange for the Prince's house in Whitehall. Lord Melbourne accepted the change with characteristic resignation, although he would be removed from the immediate vicinity of his clubs. The death of his eldest son had broken his heart. Dejected and largely disinterested, he turned more and more to the bottle in search of consolation.

In the new Melbourne House in Whitehall, which was large and imposing, Lady Melbourne retained the resplendent rooms on the ground floor, and rooms on the upper floors were allotted to the young couple. Thus Caroline learnt that, when married, she would be required to live in close proximity to her mother-in-law. It did not strike her as an ideal arrangement.

But, on the whole, the months preceding the marriage were passed without either emotional upheavals or lovers' tiffs. It is true that poor Hart was still subject to paroxysms of distress at the thought of Caroline's desertion of him, but Caroline contrived to keep her *sauvageries* in check, although Henrietta was conscious of some ominous rumblings as the day of the ceremony approached. The thought of leaving home and her mother was causing the first symptoms of homesickness, and the need for choosing an elaborate trousseau, and then of spending hours in the company of milliners and dress-makers whilst it was being fitted, made Caroline tearful and short-tempered.

53

It was during this difficult period that William acted with the best of intentions, but yet unwisely. He not only paid a great deal of attention to his bride, but also to his bride's mother. This was intolerable to a woman as fiercely possessive of her son as was Lady Melbourne. She bristled with indignation, and she and Henrietta had difficulty in keeping their tempers. 'Yesterday, after various very unpleasant *cuts,*' wrote Henrietta, 'she told me she hoped the Daughter would turn out better than the Mother, or William might have to repent of his choice; and would not (like many Husbands) be made to resent impunement. This was said half joke, half earnest; but there are subjects too sore to bear a joke...I felt hurt and possibly could have retorted, but check'd myself, however; and only said I hoped and believ'd she would prove much better—"especially (I added) with the help of your advice" (I would not say example).'

There were other causes of friction between the two women. With Georgiana's health growing progressively worse, Henrietta had taken it upon herself to bring out Hary-O and to find her a husband, being still unaware of the depth of Hary-O's devotion to Lord Granville. Meanwhile Lady Melbourne had succeeded without effort in marrying off her own very attractive daughter, Emily, to Lord Cowper of Althorps, who was a grandson of Lady Spencer. Emily disliked Henrietta and only pretended to like Hary-O, whom she declared was far too ugly to find herself a husband.

Thus there was far from being an atmosphere of harmony between the Bessboroughs and the Melbournes as the day of Caroline's wedding approached.

In accordance with the Devonshire House tradition, a nickname had to be found for Lady Melbourne, and Henrietta christened her 'The Thorn', because she was so prickly. It had a greater significance than perhaps Henrietta realized at the time.

Almost everything about Henrietta annoyed Lady Melbourne. She found both Henrietta and Georgiana absurdly emotional and unstable in their outlook and she resented the effortless way in which they attracted men. The moral outlook of the two sisters also irritated her. Lady Melbourne herself had no morals, but she had discretion. It was her greatest asset as a mistress. She never publicised her amours, nor did she ever boast of her conquests. 'Anyone who braves the opinion of the world, sooner or later feels the consequence of it' was the slogan by which she lived.

Lady Melbourne believed that one did not *openly* defy the laws of convention; one merely ignored them in private. But Caroline not only took pleasure in defying convention, but also gloried in announcing the fact. There were often moments when Lady Melbourne turned over in her mind how she would have treated Caroline had Caroline been her own daughter. There would have been no tantrums and no sulks. Caroline would have been smacked very hard and then sent supperless to bed.

Lady Melbourne's chief regret was that William showed no signs of agreeing with her when she discussed his marriage with him. Caroline, she warned him repeatedly, had to be treated with firmness. But he only smiled and replied that Caroline was a very sensitive little creature and needed to be understood. As the marriage grew nearer, Lady Melbourne's exasperation grew greater.

The day of the marriage was fixed for 3 June, 1805. The place, the Bessborough residence in Cavendish Square. The time, eight o'clock in the evening.

All the preliminaries were duly completed before this date. On 8 May the Prince of Wales had been informed and had approved; and Lord Bessborough also gave his formal consent. From then on the house was full of milliners, mantua-makers and an endless procession of friends who came to wish Caroline good luck.

'Caroline Ponsonby is to be married tomorrow,' wrote Bess to her son, Augustus, 'She looks prettier than ever I saw her. Sometimes she is very nervous, but in general she appears to be very happy. William Lamb seems quite devoted to her.'

On the evening before the ceremony Caroline formally received her wedding presents. Hary-O gave her a beautiful burnt-topaz cross, and Bess a pearl cross with a diamond in the centre. Her future father-in-law, Lord Melbourne, gave her a set of amethysts, and Lady Melbourne a diamond wreath. The Duke of Devonshire, who had always had a soft spot for Caroline, ever since he had instructed her in Whig politics while toasting muffins, presented her with her wedding-dress; and Georgiana gave her a jewelled wreath.

Fortunately Georgiana's health had improved since the early spring, when she had been very ill with 'an attack of gall-stones'. Sir Walter Farquhar, their physician, had announced that there need be no further cause of worry, and by April she was nearly her old self, although putting on weight.

On Caroline's last Sunday as a single woman, Henrietta took her down to the family villa at Roehampton in order to occupy her mind. William accompanied them, but Caroline remained silent and 'was rather low and frightened'. William looked hurt and Henrietta whispered to Caroline that it was unkind to him to appear so depressed.

In her letter to Lord Granville describing the incident, Henrietta wrote that Caroline then turned to William and said, ' "My dear William, judge what my love must be, when I can leave such a mother as this for you. Girls who are not happy at home may marry without regret, but it required very strong affection indeed to over-power mine." I believe I told you this before, but it made such a strong impression on me from her eager manner of saying it, and the extreme kindness of his answer to her and to me; indeed I am so flattered by my children, it will turn my head.'

In the years to come Caroline was to give a graphic description of her own behaviour at the wedding, in order to illustrate the strain under which she had laboured during the ceremony. She recalled that she had succumbed to a fit of hysteria, had screamed, torn her wedding dress and collapsed in a faint.

Like nearly all of Caroline's accounts of the major incidents in her life, this story of her wedding would seem to have been grossly exaggerated. She undoubtedly was extremely nervous and had to be supported by William, but Bess, when she wrote a description of the ceremony to Augustus, made no mention of any hysterical outburst, and merely remarked that Caroline was very nervous and that William's manner to her 'was beautiful, so tender and considerate'.

The ceremony was performed in the presence of the Bessboroughs, the Devonshires, the Melbournes, Bess and Lord and Lady Spencer. Hart was not present, as it was felt that he was even more likely to create a scene than the bride.

The honeymoon was to be spent at the Melbournes' country estate, Brocket Hall, in Hertfordshire. At nine o'clock the carriage containing the bridal pair set off on its fifteen-mile journey through the leafy Hertfordshire lanes, in the cool of an early summer evening. The setting was a romantic one which could not fail to arouse an answering chord in Caroline's heart. She leaned her head on her husband's shoulder and he placed his arm about her and told her that from then on she need have no worries about anything, for he would always be by her side, to comfort and protect her.

She sighed and closed her eyes. Her dreams had come true and she had married her fairy prince. She would undoubtedly live happily ever after.

Caroline, on her wedding night, was uncertain of herself and of her ability to satisfy her husband. She knew that he had been accustomed to satisfying to the full his physical desires, but this did not shock her. Nearly all the men she knew had lived promiscuous lives before marriage, and she had no wish to marry a man who was lacking in many experiences. It was the thought of her own responses which aroused her apprehension.

In the years to come she was to refer—with complete truth in this instance—to 'the almost child-like innocence and inexperience I had preserved till then'. It says much for William's gentleness and consideration that she suffered no crude awakening on her wedding night. He realized only too well that the woman who lay trembling in his arms was at heart only a child.

Five

Caroline - The Realities of Marriage

In spite of William's tenderness and restraint, the honeymoon was not a success. Caroline had approached her marriage in a mood of tension and apprehension, and this mood continued after the ceremony. Marriage was an irrevocable step. Now she was committed to adult womanhood, and to the responsibilities of raising a family. She felt homesick and missed her mother. Her childhood seemed already very far away.

She confided in her mother that the sexual act had come as a shock to her, and Henrietta wrote to tell Lord Granville of the anguish that Caroline seemed to be suffering. 'I do think it very hard that men should always have *beau jeu* on all occasions,' she wrote aggrievedly, 'and that all pain, *Morale et Physique,* should be reserved for us.' She did her utmost to comfort Caroline in her distress.

Caroline, of course, flitted from mood to mood, and from gaiety to despair which was very perplexing for her husband. Her grandmother, Lady Spencer, drove over to Brocket a few days after the marriage, and she and Caroline drove round the estate in a cabriolet, proudly escorted by William on horseback. Lady Spencer was alarmed by Caroline's demeanour. In a letter to her daughter, Georgiana, she remarked that although she had found Caroline physically well and seemingly in high spirits 'her nervous agitations will grow to a very serious height if they are not checked'.

She had always been worried by Caroline's nervous agitations and now she tried to warn William of the problems which he had to face, but William remained the starry-eyed lover. He was reluctant to admonish his child wife.

Her alternating moods disconcerted him, however, and also the changes in her health. Sometimes she would declare herself to be ill and would retire to her room and refuse to see anyone, not even her husband. But her gaiety would be as suddenly revived. Smitten by a sudden pang of conscience, she would climb on her husband's knee and cuddle him like a child, cooing into his ear and telling him that he was the handsomest man that she had ever seen, and that she loved him to distraction. She flirted with him, never allowed him out of her sight, and gazed in adoration upon him.

The fact that William not only withstood this treatment but even enjoyed it showed that there were other influences within his character besides those that had been implanted by his mother. Lady Melbourne never cooed over *her* lovers. The sight of Caroline fussing and petting William in this way quite revolted her.

But William, of course, was easy-going and lazy; and so for a time, he was quite happy to sit in a chair and be caressed by Caroline. But after a while the treatment palled; particularly so when it was made a substitute for more down-to-earth expressions of love.

He was a man of strong sexual appetite, which was not satisfied by small and tantalizing morsels. As the nights passed and he was left exasperated and frustrated, he suffered from moments of understandable irritability. But the hold which Caroline exerted over him with her child-like qualities and elfin enchantment was still strong. He still loved her deeply.

It is a truism of marriage that a husband should begin as he intends to go on, and in these early weeks William committed himself to a policy of weakness. He failed altogether to take a strong line with his young wife, and although he occasionally sulked in her presence, he never scolded her.

At no time during his life were the curious contradictions in his character more in evidence than during these first weeks and months of his marriage. It seemed then as if he were ready to follow the policy of his father, Lord Melbourne, by giving in to his wife on all points and by making no effort to exert his authority.

Yet there was a considerable doubt as to whether Lord Melbourne *was* his father. Many believed that in fact he had been the product of a union between Lady Melbourne and Lord Egremont. His eldest brother, Peniston, had been born in 1770, when Lord Melbourne was still actively engaged in his wife's bed; but thereafter there had been a curious lapse of nine years before she had again become pregnant. The rumour that had then gone round Society was that Lord Melbourne had quite exhausted himself with attempted acts of procreation and had resigned his position as a begetter of children to others more virile than himself. For years Lord Egremont had been Lady Melbourne's closest and most intimate friend, and there seemed so much of Lord Egremont in William that it seemed probable that

59

he, and not Lord Melbourne, had sired William Lamb.

Lord Egremont was a scholar, a gentleman and an eccentric. The Lambs were notable as a family for their lack of scholarship, and although they had certain gentlemanly qualities they lacked both refinement and sensitivity. But William was a scholar and also a man of sensitivity and of refinement. Moreover, unlike Lord Melbourne, he was a man of vigorous sexual performance. The only quality with which Lord Melbourne had endowed William was an amiable lethargy, and an attitude of easy-going toleration.

One of the curious aspects of the marriage between Caroline and William was the conflicting reports which were made about it. Bess, writing from Devonshire House to her son, Augustus, unhappily established in Washington as Minister to the United States, was able to report that Caroline was 'the same wild, delicate, odd, delightful person' that she had ever been. Even Hary-O, who had always been one of Caroline's severest critics, found her cousin vastly improved by marriage. In a letter to her old governess, Miss Trimmer, she spoke of Caroline being 'most amazingly improved by being as gentle and *posée* as if she had been a matron in the country for 20 years instead of days'.

But by the autumn, when they had returned to London, evidence was mounting that the marriage was not altogether a success. In a letter to her sister, Georgiana, written at the beginning of October, Hary-O described Caroline as looking 'very pale and ill in health, but pretty. I think her grown very fat, but not at all from her situation...'

Caroline was indeed pregnant by this time and inevitably making the most of this dramatic condition. She was walking about the house with exaggerated caution, 'as if one quick step would be fatal', as Hary-O tartly observed, and the news of her pregnancy was already being broadcast about the town.

The Melbourne family, as Hary-O noted with some disapproval, showed neither reticence nor modesty on these occasions, talked loudly about morning sickness and all other such symptoms, and discussed all gynaecological problems in detail and with gusto. They were nothing if not extrovert.

A fortnight after writing to her sister to say how fat Caroline was growing, Hary-O was writing again to say how thin Caroline was looking, from all of which it can be deduced that Caroline was indeed making the most of her interesting condition, and ringing the changes not only on her facial appearance but also on her waistline. In common with many other young wives, she had already convinced herself that she was going through an experience that was well-nigh unique.

Already there was evidence that William was beginning to wilt under the strain of her intense and melodramatic behaviour. Hary-O reported violent quarrels between the two over typically unimportant matters—as to whether the carriage should be open or shut, and whether she could or could not eat the meals that were placed before her. Sometimes she threw things at his head.

On one occasion William stormed out of the house and left her to her own devices, whereat she hurried round to Devonshire House for dinner and afterwards dressed herself up in her aunt's jewellery, 'rouged herself up to the eyes', sent her wedding ring back to Melbourne House to await her husband's arrival and betook herself to the play, which she much enjoyed. But before the end of the evening her mood changed to one of contrition, she wept copiously, condemned herself as a faithless wife and returned to William. In no time she had succeeded in winning him round with her baby talk and child-like caresses, and peace reigned once again on the upper floors of Melbourne House.

Indeed Hary-O was later able to report on a scene of impressive connubial bliss, when she discovered Caroline and William sitting in the same chair and reading the same book. Hary-O was somewhat critical of William, and she may well have been a little resentful of Caroline's exaggerated possessiveness towards him and her outspoken conviction that he was the most handsome man in London. Caroline, she noted critically, had moments when she would not allow poor William out of her sight and would even follow him to the lavatory when he sought for a moment's peace there, or send her maid to wait outside the door until he emerged.

There was a hearty atmosphere at Melbourne House which Hary-O found exhausting, for the Lamb family as a tribe cracked earthy jokes with each other and laughed loudly over the telling of them. George, the largest, loudest and most uncouth of them all, had a leaning towards the theatre. He liked writing plays and then persuading his friends to act in them. At the Christmas of 1805 they all went down to stay with Lord and Lady Abercorn at the Priory at Stanmore, outside London, where George presented his musical extravaganza, *Whistle for It*. Everyone was in immense good humour, except for Georgiana, whose eye was once again causing her pain, and Caroline, who already considered herself in far too delicate a state for cavorting on the stage under George's direction. Instead she was content to sit gazing with adoration on William from the front row of seats.

William was not at home in amateur theatricals. However he was young enough to accept his wife's view that he was a natural-born stage hero. Hary-O viewed his performance with a jaundiced eye and reported that he was 'too much occupied with his beauty and expression of countenance, and makes crooked smiles to the audience when he ought to be attending to his companions'.

Caroline's role of mother-to-be also aroused Hary-O's indignation and she gave it as her opinion that the end product of all this fuss could only be 'a little thing with wings that will fly away as soon as it is born and nobody be able to catch it'.

But despite Caroline's exaggerated air of fragility, she and William contrived, when in London, to go out almost nightly—to the theatre, the opera, to Drury Lane or to the Society balls which were held at Almack's or in private houses. It was a shallow and artificial existence, which not only proved harmful to William, with his growing indolence and lack of purpose, but also to Caroline who was retreating more into a child's world of eternal playtime.

Caroline's child-like outlook on life revealed itself in other ways. She was still obsessed with her belief that she ought to have been born a boy, and was continually appearing in boyish clothes. Above all she loved to appear dressed as a page—preferably as one of her own pages, of which she had a small retinue. These she fussed over and dressed as if they were her dolls; or as though they were a little army of toy soldiers whom she had brought with her from her nursery. Long and detailed instructions were sent to her tailor in London, a Mr Baker, outlining exactly how their uniforms should be cut.

A letter which she sent to him was charmingly illustrated by pencil drawings of a little boy, and roughly coloured in scarlet and sepia. 'The red cloth waistcoat and the drab must have three rows of buttons,' she wrote, 'and the drab waistcoat red down the seams and button holes: they must both be made to button close up to the neck cloth and a drab belt with red seams and buttons made to go to either; the jacket you made is not quite a proper shape, not sloped off enough on the side before, and the belt and waistcoat near an inch and a half too long-waisted, the trousers also too tight at the bottom, and too short, so that they are not concealed as they should be under the belt. This does not signify for what has been done hitherto, but I wish you to attend to it in future.'

But although she enjoyed dressing up as a boy, Caroline was also feminine enough to take a great deal of trouble over her image as a girl. She had a strong leaning towards soft and flimsy materials of crêpe or muslin, diaphanous and floating such as a fairy queen might wear in a gossamer world. The weight of these garments never exceeded a few ounces, and the emphasis was always on a fragile delicacy. A petticoat would be dampened to cling to the figure, and the dress limited to something flimsy and revealing, with a high waist, low bosom and no sleeves. This was all very much in keeping with the period, and certainly very French, but Caroline's tiny figure looked even smaller in such apparel, and her complete indifference to the amount of her boyish figure she revealed shocked Society.

Henrietta noted of her that she was 'so unlike a wife—it is more like a schoolgirl'. Bess, in her letters to Augustus in Washington, continued to emphasize how Caroline remained 'the same wild, delicate, odd, delightful person, unlike everything'.

Augustus, who had once had an eye for Caroline, expressed his doubts about this, but then he was out of tune with life in Washington, where he considered himself to be surrounded by the biggest rogues in the United States, and particularly by those who had come from Ireland.

He had reason to be doubtful about the success of the marriage, and about any suggestion that Caroline would remain unchanged by it. He considered that sooner or later Caroline would be forced to face up to reality.

In this he was right. Throughout the first year of her marriage Caroline continued to live in her world of fantasy. But the year of 1806 was destined to awaken her to certain unpleasant facts which she could not ignore. Before the year was ended she was destined to part with some of her most treasured illusions.

One of the first shocks was the discovery that William, for all his indolence, was reluctant to spend the rest of his life billing and cooing with his young wife and devoting the whole of his attention to her and her alone. After six months of marriage he came to the conclusion that he was becoming bored with his existence, and that it was high time that he took up a political career. He had started out with such high promise—and now he felt the urge to justify his existence by doing something of practical assistance to the community. He was by no means without a sense of duty. On the 31 January, 1806, he was returned as the Whig member for Leominster.

63

On 23 January, only a week before his triumph at the polls, the news of Pitt's death had come as a great shock to him. William had never been a supporter of Pitt, but he was moved by the passing of a great statesman. Only a month previously Napoleon's defeat of the Russians and Austrians at Austerlitz had left Europe largely at his mercy. It was the beginning of a year that was pregnant with disasters for England.

Caroline was a Whig supporter, but the grave facts of what was now occurring in Europe never really came home to her. What happened across the Channel was a long way from England, and still further from the cosy surroundings of the great houses in Mayfair. What did destroy her trust in the dream world which she inhabited was that on 31 January, the day on which her husband became a Member of Parliament, she suffered a miscarriage.

It was a profound shock to her and she suffered physically as well as mentally. The hardships and inconveniences of pregnancy had all been of no avail. Life could never be quite the same again.

Another tragedy was soon to follow. By the beginning of March, Sir Walter Farquhar was being frequently summoned to attend to both Henrietta and Georgiana, but whereas he was able to bring some comfort to Henrietta there was little that he could do to help Georgiana. Tortured by constant headaches, and suffering also from jaundice and bilious attacks, she began to grow weaker, although still convinced that she was making a steady recovery.

'I am certainly much better, tho' very low,' she wrote to her mother on 15 March, 'The jaundice has chang'd from orange to lemon colour. Sir Walter says this is proof of its going off without any danger of gall stone, and indeed that I shall be quite well if I keep myself quiet. Dearest mother, would you once more come to my assistance for a few days, I mean only till Lady day by inclosing me by return of post draft for £100.'

By now she looked so weak and ill that Henrietta had moved into Devonshire House, where she spent nearly all her time in her sister's room. Charles Fox called for news on 25 March and was assured by her physicians that she was in no danger. They prescribed frequent hot baths and administered massive doses of laudanum. They were quite certain that the combination of these palliatives would quickly restore her to health.

A week later she was dead.

Her passing was almost more than Henrietta could bear. The Duke of Devonshire was deeply distressed, but he had his dearest Bess to turn to in his bereavement. Bess herself, although conscious enough that this now left the field clear for her to become the second Duchess of Devonshire, was also deeply moved. In her diary she wrote on the day of her death, 'My angel friend—angel I am sure she now is—but can I live without her who was the life of my existence!—my friend, companion—farewell indeed—yet even the last day she knew me.'

As for Hary-O, her distress was greatly increased by the fear that her father would now be trapped into a second marriage. She knew how Bess loved to organize and she realized that it would not be long before Bess was running the Duke's life for him.

When they told Charles Fox of Georgiana's death he said they had lost the kindest heart in England, and there were many people from all walks of life who were ready to echo his words. And in truth her kindness of heart had been at once her greatest virtue and yet one of her biggest failings, for she had never been able to deny her friends whatever they asked of her.

It was to prove a bad year for England. Charles Fox himself, another person whose generosity had so often proved his undoing, died at the Duke of Devonshire's villa at Chiswick in September. He had lived unwisely and too well, and the pace had told in the end.

His wife, Elizabeth, remained by his bed-side, night and day, and at sunset on the 13th he turned to her and said, 'I die happy, but I pity you.' Then seeing the distress on her face he added, 'It don't signify, my dearest, dearest Liz,' and then was gone.

To Caroline, the news of the death of her hero came as another shock. Her world of fantasy was crumbling about her, and death was taking its toll. Her reaction was to throw herself more resolutely than ever into the gaieties of social life in London.

In her heart she was echoing the last words of Charles. It didn't signify. Nothing signified in life except pleasure and pretence, and a continuing belief in the world of one's dreams. Yet she had her moments of profound melancholy, when she thought of the day when she, too, would be carried away into eternity. 'I am like a vestal who thought of other concerns than the poor flame she hoped Heaven would keep burning,' she wrote in one of her letters. 'Do not condemn me to be burnt alive; wait a little, I shall return to dust without any unusual assistance.' And she visualized the announcement that would appear in *The Times* obituary column—'Lady Caroline Lamb, of the disease called death; her time being come and she being a predestinarian.'

The year 1807 seemed to dawn with prospects of a happier and more tranquil life, although there were still storm clouds in plenty on the horizon.

Caroline was now living a more settled existence at Melbourne House. Her father-in-law she liked, for he was easy-going and generally uncritical of her, so long as she remained cheerful and did not give way to one of her tantrums. An affable man of equable temperament, he had put up with his wife's indiscretions and ambitions for so long that he had grown inured to the junketings that went on at Melbourne House—the coming and goings, the constant entertaining and the chaos of never knowing who anybody was or when he would get his next meal. He accepted the fact that his young daughter-in-law would delight in the same exhausting round of endless gaieties.

He did no more than nickname her 'Your Lavish-ship', because of the lavish way in which she helped to spend his money. Having spoilt his own wife throughout her life, he hardly felt in a position to criticise those who had spoilt Caroline. He was ready to tolerate those who exhausted his bank balance, but not those who exhausted his patience.

The differences between Caroline and her mother-in-law were daily becoming more accentuated and their mutual dislike grew ever stronger. When Caroline discovered that her tantrums had no effect on Lady Melbourne, she became less hysterical but far more rebellious. Thus each watched the other with a wary eye, for each accepted the other as a formidable opponent.

Caroline herself was beginning to grow up. The child-like innocence was beginning to fade and the puritanical streak was being worn down under the influence of her husband's materialism and the extreme sophistication of the social set in which she now mixed. She was now making a serious attempt to educate herself and to learn something of history and of the world. She would write off excitedly to her mother asking for a brief outline of historical events, 'just write me the principal dates and events, wars, risings from Romulus till the time of Constantine the Great—if you are unwell do not do it.'

Henrietta's health was improving and she tried to help, but she was bewildered by the change in her daughter's outlook. Caro, to her, was still a child, but in the circles in which the Lambs moved no one looked upon Caroline as a child any more, and no one called her Caro.

William was also growing up and becoming more politically mature. He had even lost much of his youthful hero-worship of

Napoleon. Just before the Christmas of 1806 he had been chosen to move the Address to the House as his maiden speech, and had carried off the occasion with dignity and eloquence. There had been a commotion at Melbourne House just before he had spoken, as Caroline had suddenly disappeared, but it subsequently transpired that she had dressed herself up in some of her husband's clothes and had been smuggled into the House in order to hear him.

At the general election in the spring of the following year he was returned to the House as the member for Portarlington. Despite his ability as an orator he was content for the most part to remain silent, but he listened and he learnt.

At the beginning of the year Caroline's physician, Dr Pemberton, pronounced that Caroline was pregnant once again, and that the child would be born at the end of August. Pregnancy was a physical state which called forth all Caroline's most melodramatic instincts, and she at once began to make much of her condition, and to express doubts about her ability to sustain the rigours of child-birth without a total collapse. 'Her uncertain health prevents one knowing what is her state, or almost what to hope for,' wrote Bess in one of her letters to Augustus.

Caroline's attention was distracted for a period, however, by the news that Caroline St Jules, her playmate at Devonshire House and the Duke of Devonshire's illegitimate daughter by Bess, was about to become engaged to William's theatrically-minded brother, George Lamb. The ebullient George had revealed quite a talent for the theatre, and his comedy, *Whistle for It*, which he had staged at Stanmore Priory before Christmas, was now enjoying a successful run at Drury Lane.

Caroline had always been fond of Caroline St Jules, but she was woman enough to bristle now because there was talk of this other Caroline joining the family as Mrs George Lamb. People were already beginning to refer to 'Caro-William' and 'Caro-George' to distinguish the two girls and this also was a cause of irritation. Caroline had become quite possessive over George, and she now started to make tart and hurtful comments about Caroline St Jules. This aroused the indignation of Hary-O who rallied to the help of Caro-George and began to disseminate what she referred to as *'contre-poison'*.

There was no doubt that George was falling deeply in love with Caroline St Jules, and she with him. She was a gentle and sensitive creature and he was urgently in need of a steadying influence in his rumbustious life. Even so, she had grave doubts about the moral issues at stake. As was the case with so many illegitimate children of this period, she had never been told the facts of her birth, and did not know with any certainty that the Duke of Devonshire was her father. Was it right, she asked herself, that she should marry George under these circumstances? A simple soul, she had never believed in the gossip which had been whispered that George himself might be illegitimate, and might well be the son of the Prince of Wales.

Caroline remained resentful and jealous of the match, pouted when the romance was mentioned in her presence, and finally lost interest in the whole affair as the time of her confinement grew near. 'I continue very well,' she wrote to her mother, 'though a little disappointed at not having fainted away to-day: I can't think why.'

Henrietta worried constantly about her daughter, and her agitation increased in August when Caroline announced that she was now so weak and ill that she could not stir from Melbourne House. Henrietta became quite distraught, and spent many hours of each day with her, reading aloud and doing her best to comfort her little Caro. The weather was atrocious, and it rained continuously as the fateful day approached.

The day itself was one filled with drama and suspense, for Caroline's labour pains were 'so slow and lingering' that everyone was kept in a suitable state of alarm until she finally gave birth to a boy.

The rejoicing was universal. William was a proud and happy man, and wrote heartily to Lady Holland to tell her the news, 'Caroline was brought to bed an hour ago of a very large boy for so small a woman.'

Caroline gazed down at the infant lying so placidly in her arms and found that one, at least, of her lost illusions had been recovered. Here was the perfect child, a baby prince who would one day grow up into a perfect man.

In her commonplace book she wrote:

> His little eyes like William's shine—
> How great is then my joy,
> For while I call this darling mine,
> I see 'tis William's boy.

Her belief in her son's perfection, however, was not shared by all of those who crowded round the infant's cot. Certainly he was a large and healthy child, but there was yet something about the expression in the face—a vacancy in the look of the eyes—which gave rise to apprehension. Was the child quite as perfect as his mother supposed?

Georgiana and Henrietta (centre) at Vauxhall Gardens — 'dainty and delightful, and looking for all the world like two little shepherdesses who have escaped from a sylvan study by Watteau . . .' A detail from 'Vauxhall' by Rowlandson

'She is a lovely girl, natural and full of grace.' Horace Walpole on Caroline's aunt, Georgiana, Duchess of Devonshire. Sketch portrait of the Duchess by Joshua Reynolds

Henrietta Spencer, Caroline's
mother, later Lady Bessborough.
From the painting by Reynolds

Above Devonshire House, Piccadilly, about 1800. Caroline spent her childhood there. It was pulled down in 1924

Below The gaming table at Devonshire House, by Rowlandson. This was the atmosphere in which Caroline was brought up

Caroline on horseback. From the
painting by Reynolds

Caroline's husband, William
Lamb, whom she married in
June, 1805

Caroline's mother-in-law, Lady Melbourne — the confidante of Byron

Caroline's sister-in-law, Emily Lamb

Caroline's sketch of herself,
William and baby Augustus

Caroline and William decided that the child should be called George Augustus Frederick, and preparations were made for the christening. This was a splendid affair. Caroline floated dreamily amongst her guests, looking pale and fragile, and describing the ordeal which she had miraculously survived, and everyone who was anyone in London Society was present.

The Prince of Wales had graciously consented to stand as god-father for Augustus and arrived in seeming good health, although complaining frequently, according to Bess, of a pain in his head and in his eye. He certainly had no intention of allowing Caroline to steal all the sympathy.

The party began at six in the evening, and the Prince showed such a marked reluctance to leave that it was still in progress at two the next morning.

The child was toasted again and again, and the sound of these revelries must have reached up to the nursery which was situated at the very top of the house, where Augustus lay, vacant-faced and undisturbed. From time to time Caroline stole up to look at him and wondered why he seemed content to spend so much time in sleep.

'We hear of nothing but the beauty, strength and size of Caro's boy and her rapture at its birth,' wrote Hary-O critically. 'She succeeds in nursing it and seems to be as well and prosperous as one could wish her.'

However in a later letter she noted that the advent of the child had not cured Caroline 'of her absurdities'. She was still much pre-occupied with her little regiment of pages, and on one occasion she took one of them to the theatre with her, and they sat together in a box, thereby causing a considerable stir amongst the audience.

The baby had to be dressed up and paraded for public adulation. When at Brocket she would lead a procession through the Park and out onto the high road, with herself on horseback at the head, with the baby elaborately clothed in her lap, and a page in full livery holding her mount's bridle. She would be followed on foot by her maid and by a retinue of nurses, and thus would proceed in regal cavalcade, to the vast amusement of the men on duty at the turn-pike. Stories of her 'oddities' were recounted over the dinner tables in Mayfair, and everyone was eager to learn about her latest escapade.

At this period Hary-O revealed yet again what her earlier correspondence had shown—that Caroline could change from day to day, looking healthy, vivacious and gay on some occasions, and pinched, thin and bad-tempered on others. Certainly her moods continued to vary remarkably, and William was hard pressed to keep up with them. She still quarrelled with him violently when feeling out of sorts and would stand in the corner of the room flinging cups and saucers at his head.

Such conduct brought down upon her head the wrath of the Lamb family. There was, as Hary-O noted, 'much spite in them against her' and the hearty George announced that she was impossible and that her baby was the most frightful creature that he had ever seen. Hary-O could criticise Caroline but no one else was allowed to do so in her presence, and she flared up at this and told George that he was talking nonsense. He reddened and looked flustered; and she was able to elicit from him the admission that William's sister, Emily, had been the first one to sneer at the child, and had encouraged him to do the same.

The problems of nursing and rearing a child did not provide Caroline with very much to occupy her mind. There were nursemaids in plenty to look after her son as he grew slowly larger and more apathetic, and she was free to occupy herself in whatever way she wished. She continued to ride frequently and scorned the use of her carriage, but she was a married woman now and the days of riding bareback like a boy were over. She was very fond of sketching, and her pictures of her husband and other members of the Melbourne household were well conceived and credible likenesses.

She was not unhappy, but she was not happy. Her chief problem was that she was bored; and not only bored, but resentful.

By now William was losing some of the signs of adoration which had so characterized his behaviour at the time of his wooing, and he did not dote on Caroline quite so openly as he once had done.

'I could not help remarking the difference between a husband and a lover,' Caroline remarked sadly after they had formed a party to go to the theatre and George had fussed over *his* Caroline while William had failed to put in an appearance until the play was half over.

It was not that William had ceased to love her. She knew well enough that he had not. He had merely relapsed into his normal way of life, which was that of any ordinary husband. He did not notice if his wife looked pale, and he always had to be told if she had a headache.

The remainder of the family had no great love for Caroline, and showed it. She was often referred to as 'the little beast', and when she complained about such treatment to William, he merely laughed and told her to ignore all these cuts.

Caroline was sensitive to atmosphere and to any suggestion of hostility. William remained quite oblivious to them. He contented himself with teasing his young wife and laughing at her serious views and her strongly held convictions. He tried to laugh her out of her moods and poured cold water over her illusions. A devout, religious and generally rather prim young woman such as Caroline was to him a person in urgent need of awakening to reality.

Finally his habit of shocking her often caused her a real distress, and he failed to appreciate the fact when he was wounding her. He began to talk of his previous love affairs—which had been numerous enough—and to relate to her the bawdier aspects of his adventures. When she showed her embarrassment, he laughed at her.

She, for her part, irritated him by her primness and her prudish outlook. It annoyed him to discover that although she talked so glibly of freedom of expression and the need to rebel against convention, she was herself highly respectable at heart.

The process of drifting apart in marriage can be slow and imperceptible. It need not imply any fundamental decline in affection. Often it springs from little more than a difference of interests. Two young people find themselves growing up, and at the same time growing apart.

As the years passed William became more dedicated to his work. At first he had entered the House simply because this was the done thing for the heir to a title. Soon the inherent goodness, and indeed nobility, in his character made him view his political work as part of his duty to the nation.

He found little difficulty in making progress. After all, he had been brought up in the heart of Whig politics, and he knew everyone. The leaders of the Party were only too anxious to encourage this promising young man. Gradually he began to lose the pose of supercilious indifference and to reveal instead a genuine maturity.

By 1807 Lord Holland was asking his advice on the choice of a leader, and William was in the habit of attending the informal discussions at Holland House, which were dominated by his host and Lord Grey—that same Charles Grey whom Georgiana had so adored as a young woman. But Charles was very different now. He was in his forties, and had become a serious-minded politician; he had been made Foreign Secretary and leader of the House after the death of Charles Fox, and was developing vigorous and progressive views.

The Whig party were going through a period of stagnation and were sorely in need of new blood. William fitted their need exactly. He was young but had never been handicapped by that hot-headed idealism which had sent Charles Fox tilting against windmills in his fiery youth. William had his feet firmly planted on the ground.

Thus William had everything in his favour, and his political future seemed assured. His charm and friendliness were an immense asset. Even his political enemies found it hard to dislike him. He was married—happily, as everyone assumed—and he had settled down, with his wild oats behind him.

'William Lamb,' wrote Lady Holland, 'is certainly one of the most rising men in politics.'

The development of William's character was reflected in his approach to politics. He believed in progress, but was reluctant to upset the old way of life. Democracy had a fine-sounding name, but he had yet to be convinced that it was workable. He was in favour of legal and penal reform; but he opposed parliamentary reform. He called himself a Whig but in truth he was by now too near to the middle of the road to carry a political label.

Nor had he any stomach for rival factions, and the bitter feuds which politics could arouse. He hated the flashy type of professional politician, with his opportunism, his calculated rhetoric and his love of intrigue. It was for this reason that he despised Canning, whom he looked upon as a charlatan and the worst type of Old Etonian. But although he despised the man, he did not reject many of the things which Canning believed in, or that he advocated; and so William was happy to join the Canningites, with their Tory outlook, although Toryism was still an anathema to him.

Thus William was happy to follow a middle course. Not through any deviousness of mind but because he found extremes of political thought extravagant and rather vulgar. Indeed he had no great love for extremists in any sphere, or for those who adopted a rigid outlook. He himself had a natural inclination towards compromise, as being so often the best way out. At Eton, when challenged to a fight, he would go through a round or two to sum up his adversary; and if he considered him to be stronger, and therefore liable to win, he would hold out his hand and offer to call the whole thing off.

There was much of the dandy in him, and although he had rather despised Brummell at Eton, and held him to be an ass, the dandy's lofty disdain in the face of adversity was something after William's heart. He could believe, with the dandies, that to show emotion of

72

any sort was the height of bad form.

Eton had left its mark upon him, and he was in so many ways a typical Old Etonian, with his languid air and his bored look, carefully contrived to hide a sensitive nature and an enquiring mind. Ostensibly he was an atheist, and he detested all manifestations of smugness and of ostentatious piety. Pompous sermons he could not abide in Church, and in fact he seldom went there; but he enjoyed shocking those who did. He would make flippant comments about sacred matters, and on one occasion, after being taken to Church and hearing a long sermon on the lusts of the flesh, he had observed that things were coming to a pretty pass if the influence of religion were allowed to invade private life.

He distrusted sentiment, yet he could never quite determine how far sentiment should be despised. It could make a fool of a man, and it could impair his judgement. Therefore the realist should fear sentiment in himself and should be ready to mock all evidence of it in others.

Sentiment was a human weakness, like a love of beauty, which was so palpably absurd, for beauty had no practical value. And sardonic as ever, and objectively intrigued by the many paradoxes of life, he could yet smile his quizzical smile at the realization that he, too, could be betrayed by sentiment and embarrassed by evidence of his own tenderness of heart.

At times he envied those who charged so recklessly into the battle of life, never pausing to consider where their impetuosity might lead them. But he comforted himself with the thought that it was better to sit on the sidelines, watching the battle ebb and flow. Thus he withdrew into himself and lived in his own private world—a hedonist who could smile at the absurdity of human existence.

This was Caroline's husband as he changed from an ardent lover who watched her every move and foresaw her every wish into a practical man of the world who seemed to have outgrown his romanticism as he had outgrown his youth.

He loved her still, she knew that. Nor had she any rival to his affections. She knew that also. And gradually she began to look upon him not as a lover, but as a manifestation of permanency in a shifting world. William would always be there to protect her and to smile his whimsical smile at her absurdities and her indiscretions. He was her haven in times of distress. But this very solidarity irked her and made her impatient with him. She loved being treated as a

73

child, and yet she resented it. What right had he to look down upon her as a foolish impetuous little girl? When would he learn to treat her as an adult—a mature woman of passion and emotion?

The manner in which he laughed at her innocence exasperated her. She still read her Bible and still liked to go to Church, but William would no longer accompany her. She had been confirmed in the company of Hary-O and Caroline St Jules in the spring of 1799, when she was thirteen. The confirmation had taken place in Westminster Abbey, and they had worn plain white dresses and white head bands.

The ceremony had impressed her deeply, and she had returned to Devonshire House subdued and silent. Caroline was not one to take her vows lightly. She had besought her Maker to direct, sanctify and govern both her heart and body, and it distressed her when William laughed at her beliefs.

She still remained sexually immature and her husband warned her that no man would want her as his mistress, because she was so lacking in ardour. The rebel in her made her long to disprove this, by seeking out some lover and overwhelming him with her passionate embraces, but the puritan streak within her made her hold back from any such adventure. Instead she tried to assume an air of sensuality by talking openly of sex, which deceived only the more gullible of her admirers.

Her life became an endless round of gaiety and self-indulgence. The illusion that she had given birth to a god-like child who would grow up into a perfect man was slowly being destroyed by the child's listless air and clumsy apathy. The dull eyes gave back nothing when she kissed him goodnight. The body was healthy and strong but the mind developed not at all. She had given birth to no more than a soulless lump of humanity. But she refused to face up to the possibility that the child was abnormal. She merely thought of him as perhaps a little backward.

As the years passed she made further efforts to have children, but without success. After a second miscarriage she gave up hope of ever again becoming a mother.

In the October of 1809 occurred the event which Hary-O had always foreseen. Her father took Bess as his second wife, and she became the Duchess of Devonshire. It was scarcely a union of two young lovers, for he was sixty-three and she was fifty-two. Yet they had shared a close intimacy for nearly thirty years, and she had proved a great comfort to him.

Caroline, Hary-O and Hart remained vigorously opposed to the match and the two girls did their utmost to stir up trouble. Caroline wrote indignantly to Hart, warning him against Bess and accusing him of being taken in by her. 'Oh, she is a deep one! She has flummeried up a certain young Marquis from his cradle.' Hart replied indignantly that he was as much opposed to the marriage as any of the others. And he stoutly denied that Caroline had ever seen him 'fawn upon this crocodile'. Bess was deeply hurt and did her best to win over Hart at least, for whom she had always had a real affection. She wrote him a sad little letter, begging him to visit his father and herself at Chiswick, and adding, 'For myself I can say nothing—my heart must ever be full of gratitude to him as of affection for you all, as it has been from your cradles.'

Surprisingly enough, the first person to weaken, and to show Bess some consideration, was Hary-O. She herself visited Chiswick quite soon after the marriage, and by November was writing to her brother to tell him that he might be pleasantly surprised with the way in which things were going.

This sudden mellowing was the outcome of events that were in no way connected with Bess's marriage. Lord Granville—her adored Lord Granville—had come to visit the Duke and Bess at Chiswick at this time, and on the evening of 14 November he had taken Hary-O's hand and had asked her to marry him.

The news of this unexpected engagement came as a surprise to all their friends and as a terrible shock to poor Henrietta. She had always known that Lord Granville had enjoyed affairs with other women, but that he should now choose to marry Hary-O was inconceivable. Seventeen years of unselfish love were to be discarded as though they had never existed. The man whom she had worshipped 'almost to idolatry' was now demonstrating that he had loved her 'least of all those that professed to do so—though once I thought otherwise'. It was a bitter, bitter blow and she never recovered from it.

Caroline, loyal as ever, rallied to the side of her mother and denounced Hary-O and Lord Granville for their treachery. However she agreed to attend the wedding which took place on the Christmas eve of 1809, at which Hart, George Lamb, the Duke of Devonshire and his new duchess were also present. 'Everything went off perfectly well,' wrote Bess in her diary, 'and they are gone to Walmer. May she be as happy as I wish her and believe she will be.'

Caroline alone maintained an attitude of unrelenting hostility towards Bess, and remained, as Hary-O was to remark, 'like a volcano on the subject'. There was a hard streak in Caroline, which was ultimately to degenerate into vindictiveness.

In the December of 1810 William was selected to move an amendment to the Regency Bill. His speech was warmly applauded by Canning. The period of the Regency had now begun, and poor, befuddled old King George III had been pronounced incurably mad. In 1811 his eldest son, Prince George, who had been waiting impatiently for so long to step into his father's shoes, became the Prince Regent, and an era of self-indulgence and extravagance engulfed Society.

The Tories were now in power, and the Prince Regent, although he had always been pro-Whig, felt it right to abandon many of his old Whig friends who were tainted with the party's anti-monarchial sentiments. But William had been a close friend of the Prince's for a number of years and Caroline also knew him well. Thus the Lambs still remained very much a part of the Regent's circle.

Although Caroline was seen frequently in the company of her cousins, Georgiana, now Lady Morpeth, and Hary-O, now triumphantly Lady Granville Leveson-Gower, they were not her close friends. She was making the mistake of choosing for her intimates older women with a wide experience of life in Society and with none too savoury a reputation. Chief among these were Lady Wellesley and Lady Oxford.

Lady Wellesley was of French birth, and her morals, even judged by the permissive company in which she mixed, were held to be deplorable. Lady Oxford, who was some thirteen years older than Caroline, was very much a woman of the world. In her youth she had been exceptionally attractive—'that beautiful and accomplished woman,' as Gronow had described her. She had married Edward Harley, the 5th Earl of Oxford, in 1794, when she was twenty-two, and had at once taken a close interest in politics and men, being happy to embrace both the Whig principles and the better-looking males who supported them.

True to the tradition of the age, whereby the wives showed all the spirit and initiative and the husbands were content to remain in the background, she had quickly made a name for herself in Society. Her large family were known as 'The Harleian Miscellany', because they were sired by such a miscellaneous band of her admirers.

At the time when she took up with Caroline she was in her late thirties and a little *passée*, but still hotly in pursuit of men. To innocents such as Caroline she seemed a fascinating person, and her stories of her love life were both uninhibited and sensational.

Lady Oxford soon realized that Caroline was still sexually immature, and it amused her to educate her. But unlike William, she never laughed at Caroline for her lack of experience, but rather suggested to her that she was missing one of the most pleasurable sensations of the body. And being a pseudo-intellectual, she indulged at length in the customary talk of freedom of expression, a woman's right to live her own life, unfettered by moral or social convention, and other such generalizations calculated to break down Caroline's puritanical defences.

Caroline pretended that she had indulged in numerous affairs herself, but Lady Oxford was not deceived, and neither was Hary-O, 'Caroline seems to have more faith in theory than in practice,' she noted acidly.

It was bad company that Caroline was keeping, and her husband, her mother and her mother-in-law were equally shocked. Henrietta was bewildered and distressed. Lady Melbourne was sharply condemnatory, accusing Caroline of degrading not only herself but also her husband. William himself lectured Caroline on the need for preserving some sense of decorum, but he understood her well enough to know that this behaviour was only bravado and that Caroline was pretending to be something that she was not—a woman of the world.

When she came to him with her stories of wild parties and of the amorous advances being made to her by would-be lovers, he refused to believe her. He could not accept her in the role of *femme fatale*, and when she tried to shock him out of his complacency by hinting at secret love affairs, he only laughed.

What she would have liked was for William to have been deeply outraged. He should have displayed an uncontrollable jealousy and forbidden her ever to look at another man again. And he certainly should have hit her. She would have screamed hysterically if he had administered a sound spanking, but she would have respected him.

William would never have raised his hand against her, even had he been convinced that this was psychologically the right course to pursue. He remained quite exasperatingly certain that his wife would never be unfaithful to him.

Caroline, defiant as ever, decided that he must be taught a lesson. A lover must be found and bedded in as dramatic a fashion as possible. William could then be confronted with her infidelity and thus be forced to suffer the fearful pangs of jealousy.

At the back of her mind was still the fear that she might prove herself to be an inadequate partner in the sexual act, and she therefore decided to select someone whose own wide experience of seduction would remedy any defects on her part. Moreover the affair had to be sensational and the chosen lover a man with a notorious reputation.

Her choice fell upon Sir Godfrey Webster.

It was a short and inglorious escapade. Sir Godfrey was certainly a rake, but he was unused to the habits of women such as Caroline. Caroline, as always, over-played her hand. Her inexperience was such that she failed to realize that whilst signalling her willingness to her chosen lover, she should at the same time reveal some outward semblance of restraint.

Sir Godfrey was the son of Lady Holland by her first marriage. Born in 1789, he had begun his professional career as a soldier and taken a commission in the 18th Light Dragoons. He fought in the Peninsular War and distinguished himself sufficiently to earn a commendation from Lord Paget, the commander of cavalry under Sir John Moore, but his regiment was brought home in 1809.

His introduction to Caroline occurred soon afterwards, when he still fancied himself as something of a military hero, and so did the ladies of Society. He was a coarse and dissolute young man, much given to gambling, drinking and the pleasures of the flesh. It was his habit—as an ex-cavalry officer—to carouse for most of the night and never to go to bed before dawn. He was amiable enough in his way, bucolic and rather stupid.

It would have been hard to imagine a personality less likely to attract the attentions of a romantic and sensitive person such as Caroline, for Sir Godfrey's penchant was for uncomplicated women of easy virtue, but once Caroline had decided that this was to be her chosen lover there was not very much that he could do about it, except to follow obediently in her wake and wait for the moment when he was invited into her bed.

The scandal caused by this association was considerable, but how far they went, and how near Sir Godfrey came to Caroline's bedroom door, was open to question. Caroline's demeanour, however, her flirtatious displays in public and her brazen attitude together suggested that they were indulging in orgies of sexual abandon, which prompted her husband, and several others who knew her well, to conclude that probably nothing was happening at all.

But once the scandal had been created and she found that her reputation had been seriously damaged, she began to have second thoughts. Bravado demanded that she should confirm the allegations that were being made against her; but her natural modesty, and her very genuine affection for her husband, made it desirable that she should deny everything. Being Caroline, she did both.

Once again she found her conduct being loudly condemned by her husband, her mother and her mother-in-law. To this trio was added Lady Holland, whilst in the background Hary-O voiced her caustic comments.

Ever an impetuous—and largely incoherent—letter-writer, Caroline now poured out a flood of explanation to Lady Holland, in which she babbled about irresistible attraction and overwhelming passion at one moment, and then spoke of her unassailable virtue at the next. Her aim was to play the roles of *femme fatale* and faithful spouse simultaneously. William, she declared, was the only man whom she loved or could ever love. Sir Godfrey was the only man who could sweep her off her feet and render her powerless in his embrace.

Lady Holland hit back by expressing her strong disapproval of Caroline's conduct, but accepting Caroline's declaration that intimacy had not taken place.

Caroline was incensed. 'As to the gnats and mites that dare to peck at me,' she wrote, 'let them look to themselves. If I choose, you shall see them lick the dust I tread on.'

It was a masterpiece of mixed metaphors and muddled thinking.

Lady Melbourne proved a more formidable critic. Backed up by the full weight of Lamb family opinion, Lady Melbourne thundered her denunciation. Caroline had brought discredit upon the family and disgrace upon herself. 'A married woman should consider that by such laxity she not only compromises her own honour and character but also that of her husband—but you seek only to please yourself.'

Caroline replied in the one way calculated to infuriate her mother-in-law still further. She blamed the whole affair on William. Had he not been so cynical and worldly in his outlook, and had he not sought to rob her of her girlish ideals, she would never have been brought to the state in which she now found herself. He had destroyed her innocence.

By this time Lady Melbourne was beginning to realize that in Caroline she had met her match. Bitterly resentful, she withdrew from the contest after having written a long letter of condemnation in which she used the phrase by which she was later to be remembered,

'When anyone braves the opinion of the world, sooner or later they will feel the consequences of it.'

Referring to Sir Godfrey she added, 'You seem to delight in everything that recalls him to you and to nourish and foster those disgraceful feelings which have caused so much embarrassment to those who ought to be dearest to you...Only one word more—let me alone! And do not drive me to explain the motives of cold civility that will from henceforward pass between us.'

Thus she withdrew from the engagement, leaving the field to Caroline. Caroline, however, had already grown tired of the affair, as well as of her bucolic lover, and was herself seeking a means of withdrawing from the stage. Clearly some melodramatic incident or gesture was called for, whereby she could renounce Sir Godfrey for ever.

At the outset of the affair, Sir Godfrey had presented Caroline, as a mark of his undying passion, with a small bracelet and a rather snappy little dog. Caroline, by way of acknowledgement, had ostentatiously worn the bracelet, especially in the presence of her mother-in-law, and made a great fuss of the snappy little dog.

Now the dog repaid her by extricating her from her predicament. In one of its frequent moods of irritation, it bit her little son, Augustus.

To Caroline, this was an omen. Or rather it was an instrument of God, designed to bring her back to her senses. The child, she confidently predicted, would shortly succumb from rabies; and she saw herself in deepest mourning, grieving over the tiny grave, with William's strong hand on her shoulder to comfort her in her affliction. But if the child should be spared, then she would repay her Maker with a ceaseless devotion to her husband in the future.

It was a most satisfactory way out. Her abject contrition impressed everyone except Lady Melbourne, and William once again basked in his wife's adoration. The baby recovered, the dog was banished, the bracelet was returned to her jewellery box, and she once again immersed herself in the theory, rather than the practice, of romance. She resumed her reading of the Greek poets: sex as described in the ancient legends and myths was so much more satisfying than that practised by William, or by Sir Godfrey, with his large hands and coarse embraces.

Her avowals of good behaviour were for a time carefully implemented. No one could be more endearing than Caroline when in one of her simple, child-like moods.

Her reformation, she declared, was such that she would be 'Silent of a morning, entertaining after dinner, docile, fearless as a heroine in the last volume of her troubles, strong as a mountain tiger...you should say to me, *Raisonnez mieux, et repliquez moins'*.

Her eagerness to defy convention was now channelled into the innocuous pastime of dancing the waltz. An importation from Germany, it was being widely frowned upon by Society in general as it was held to be indecorous, and indeed immoral. This was enough to make it attractive to Caroline, and she staged dancing classes in the ballroom of Melbourne House. Small, dainty and nimble, she soon showed herself to be adept at the new steps, and the lilting refrains transported her into a world of joyous, carefree youth.

Then for a time she lost her interest in the activities of Society and went off for a family holiday to the Isle of Wight with her son, Augustus, and with her husband. At Cowes, playing on the sands or wandering along the shore, she was the perfect little mother, and after William had been forced to return to London she wrote to him to tell him, 'I have been playing all day with that pretty little Augustus of yours. He is the dearest child I ever saw, and shows where you are gone by pointing to the sea.'

This chastened mood continued, but it was not in Caroline's character to remain subdued for very long. The breach with William was not fully healed. As the months passed he became less vulnerable to her cajoling and more impatient with her outbursts of temper. She could still win him over with her child-like embraces, but William was becoming more wary of her.

He hated outbursts of temper. It was not in his nature to lose his own temper, or to blaze out in fury. Violent scenes exhausted him and left him feeling bitter and resentful.

Anything for a quiet life was now his philosophy. When Caroline was in one of her moods he avoided her and allowed her to take it out on the servants, who were paid to suffer her hysteria.

Caroline was intelligent. But she could not argue rationally, and so easily took offence. Arguments then developed into bickerings and she would seek to win her point by spiteful personal comments.

He might have been excused at this time had he found consolation with some other woman. But loyalty was the corner-stone of his character. Loyalty and honour. She was his wife and he remained conscious of his marriage vows. He resigned himself sadly to the knowledge that his marriage was not a success, and that there was little that could be done about it. He was still unable to arouse himself sufficiently to throw himself whole-heartedly into his political career. He was happiest in his library, surrounded by his books, or riding in Brocket Park, or shooting or going racing.

His family were also aware that the marriage was not working out well. Their sympathies were wholly with him. His mother was grieved to see her son unhappy and suffering from the selfishness of his foolish young wife. But she was aware that his loyalty made it difficult for her to criticise Caroline in any way.

Caroline also realized that her marriage was not proving a success. She knew at heart that she was largely to blame, and so she blamed William. She found his refusal to quarrel with her altogether exasperating, and when incensed she returned again and again to the charge that he had ruined the ethereal quality of their romance by his crude approach to sex, and attacked him for 'instructing me in things I need never have known'.

When at Brocket she turned to riding as a means of escape, galloping madly around the estate with the wind in her hair and a look of defiance on her small, determined face. William, for his part, found consolation in spending long hours in his library, deeply absorbed in the classics. This was *his* form of escape.

Caroline was discontented and resentful. Her life seemed to have become pointless and dull. She longed for excitement and drama, and for the intoxication of some wild escapade. It was at this critical moment that she was given the proofs of a book of verse that was shortly to be published, and was asked to give her opinion on it.

The book was called *Childe Harold*. It was by an unknown young poet named Lord George Byron.

Six

Byron - The Adulation

The overwhelming effect which Byron's poetry, and later Byron himself, had upon Caroline is not difficult to understand, for he came into her life at the moment when she was most vulnerable to his influence. Had she met him five years later or five years earlier, the whole story of her life might have been different.

They had much in common. Both were deplorably indiscreet, and both were destined to suffer social ostracism as the result of their ill-advised behaviour and their writings. Both had infinite charm, and both could be quite insufferable at times. Both were handicapped in their adult life by ill-health, excitability, and alcoholism.

Byron's greatest failing was his conceit, but curiously enough this did not extend to his work. He considered his profile magnificent, but he would never have used this adjective in relation to his verse. Thus the instant acclaim which was accorded to *Childe Harold* took him by surprise. He revelled in his sudden notoriety, but he never foresaw it.

It was not Byron's first work. In the spring of 1807, at the age of nineteen, he had produced a book of verse entitled *Hours of Idleness* which was singularly lacking in merit. This had been followed up two years later by *English Bards and Scotch Reviewers,* which was substantially better. But he required inspiration for his vivid imagination and his love of adventure, and in the summer of 1809 he had embarked on a grand tour of the Mediterranean and the Aegean Sea. This had provided the inspiration which he needed. The tour lasted two years and his adventures on it provided the basis for *Childe Harold.*

Some of these adventures had certainly been remarkable. Pirates, brigands and cut-throats of every description were still to be encountered in these waters, and he sought them out. At Malta he had fallen madly in love with a Mrs Spencer Smith, whose own life had been far from tranquil, for she had been seized by Napoleon's licentious soldiery and only rescued in the nick of time by a chivalrous Italian nobleman.

From then on his exploits became increasingly bizarre. In Albania he was honoured as a patrician by the terrible Ali Pacha, who was in the habit of roasting his enemies on a spit. He was then almost drowned while travelling in a Turkish warship which foundered in a storm; was shipwrecked and then befriended by bandits; fell under the spell of Greece, so that the country's liberation from the Turkish became an obsession with him; and gazed in awe upon Mount Parnassus.

He fell in love with three young Greek girls, each of whom was under fifteen; emulated the feat of Leander by swimming the Hellespont from Europe to Asia; visited Ephesus and Constantinople; lodged in a Capucin monastery near the Acropolis in Athens; fell in love with a young Greek boy named Nicolo Giraud; met the formidable Lady Hester Stanhope (in itself quite an adventure); became desperately ill with fever, brought on by the chill winds from Missolonghi, and was saved by his faithful attendants who told his doctor that he would be massacred if the patient died.

He then spent a period of meditation in a monastery cell and devoted his time to mastering Italian; added an Islamic fatalism to his already morbid philosophy of life; learnt to despise the lack of imagination in his fellow Englishmen; and finally returned to the prosaic atmosphere of Reddish's Hotel in St James's Street, in the heart of Mayfair, where the staff looked askance at his luggage, which contained four Athenian skulls, a phial of poison and some live tortoises.

Altogether it had been quite an adventure, and his friend and fellow writer, Robert Charles Dallas, hurried round to the hotel to find out what literary or poetic work it had inspired. Whereupon Byron produced a paraphrase of Horace's *Art of Poetry*, and announced that this represented the major portion of his literary effort. Dallas read through this material and then plaintively enquired whether Byron had written anything else.

There was something else, it transpired, but Byron attached no value to it. It consisted of no more than a few short poems and a large number of stanzas that described the highlights of the voyage. Dallas was at liberty to do what he liked with them, but was advised that the work was largely autobiographical and was written in semi-narrative form. The hero, Childe Harold, was Byron himself.

Dallas read through the jumbled pages and found them filled with melancholy. The mood was romantic, erotic, somewhat decadent, and charged with a sense of fatalism. The legends of the past had been recreated with vivid descriptions of Nature's violence and man's cruelty to man.

Byron soon withdrew from the tedium and decorum of Reddish's Hotel, and returned to his ancestral home of Newstead Abbey, in Sherwood Forest, near Nottingham. It was here that he deposited his tortoises in the Park and added his four Athenian skulls to a similar prized possession—the ancient skull of a monk, which he had dug up in the grounds of Newstead and which he had fashioned into a drinking goblet.

His mother died at the beginning of August, 1811. She had been hysterically inclined throughout her life and had been half mad for several years. Her treatment of him had always been unbalanced, for she had doted on him at one moment and reviled him the next. But she was his mother, and he felt the loss deeply. 'I had but one friend in the world,' he moaned as he gazed upon the corpse, 'and she is gone.'

Further tragedies were to follow. Within two days they brought him the news that his brilliant Cambridge friend, Charles Skinner Mathews, had been drowned while bathing in the Cam. Soon after this came the news of a further death—that of his friend of his schooldays at Harrow, John Wingfield.

This triple blow would have come as a shock to even the most normal and well-adjusted of individuals. To Byron, already weighed down by his sense of foreboding, the effect was to produce a mood of deepest fatalism.

Meanwhile Dallas had been left behind in London with the discarded manuscript of *Childe Harold*. He gave it to publisher John Murray, who shared his enthusiasm for it, and printing of it was at once begun.

Had Byron been able to re-write it at this period, he would no doubt have loaded it further with his sense of gloom and foreboding. Instead he began to add prose notes to the proofs as they arrived, and shocked poor Dallas with the cynicism of his observations on religion.

By February 1812 he was back again in London and deeply involved with the plight of the unemployed and especially those in the vicinity of his home near Nottingham. The majority of them were hosiery workers, who were now being displaced by modern machinery. Starving and desperate, they had on occasions resorted to smashing up this machinery which was robbing them of their livelihood, and the Government had reacted by sending units of the cavalry

85

to restore order. The suggestion was being made that 'frame-breakers' should suffer the death penalty.

Byron delivered a moving speech in the House, which included the reference to the workers as 'men liable to conviction on the clearest evidence of the capital crime of poverty'. It was dramatic, hard-hitting stuff which appealed strongly to the Whig faction. He was at once admitted to their circle and made welcome at Holland House. Lady Holland had it in her power to make the reputation of any aspiring young politician or writer, and the young Lord Byron was made to feel that he had arrived.

There were other reasons for the interest which Society took in him at this moment. John Murray was well aware that the best way to publicise a book was by word of mouth, and he had been busy for some time spreading abroad the news that he was about to produce one that was certain to cause a sensation.

Others had formed the same opinion as Murray. Chief amongst these was Samuel Rogers, himself a literary lion with ready access to all the fashionable drawing-rooms. He was an unattractive little man, witty and spiteful, but he was shrewd, for he had been raised in the banking profession and knew a great deal about finance as well as about verses. Murray had given him proofs of the work in the January of 1812, when they had first become available, and Rogers had been at pains to entertain the young author.

He was surprised to discover that the author, who was very hand-some, inordinately vain and a practised *poseur*, was yet unaware of the poem's potential. The situation was intriguing. What, he asked himself, would be the reaction on this young man if his poem were to cause a sensation?

Not that Rogers considered that it would be well received. He had read the poem aloud to his sister and had formed the opinion that its mood of arrogant discontent, its theatricality, and above all the strong suggestion of decadence and sinfulness in the hero, would result in its being disliked and condemned. Even Murray had asked the author to tone down one or two of the more decadent inferences.

Byron himself, as the date of publication drew near, had grown ever more apprehensive about *Childe Harold*. He felt that he had given away too much about himself. He had refused at first to have his name on the title page and only relented with reluctance. The whole enterprise seemed to him to be fraught with danger. Above all, its publication just at the time when he had made a name for himself as a serious speaker in the House of Lords could only harm his political reputation.

In order to test out the reactions of Society to this unusual work, Rogers distributed proof copies to a few people whom he felt had the intelligence and literary sense to make a serious judgement on it. One of these was Caroline.

Rogers was a member of Caroline's set. He had been at pains to praise her in the past for her elegance, vivacity and her intellect; but he was also aware that discretion was a quality in which Caroline was singularly lacking. So when he lent her the proofs and asked for her opinion, he also warned her that this was a confidential matter and asked her to keep her opinions to herself. In this way he ensured that the contents of the book would be widely discussed in Society before publication.

Everything about *Childe Harold* was calculated to excite Caroline. The secrecy, the confidential nature of her assessment of it, and the intoxicating melodrama of the narrative combined to arouse in her the strongest emotions. She was out of tune with her husband who was proving unromantic and materialistic. She needed a hero figure to invigorate her life and she found one in *Childe Harold*. More exciting still was the realization that here was no character of fiction. *Childe Harold* was autobiographical. The Childe really lived and breathed. Rumours were already spreading about this young man, who was said to be strangely fascinating and astonishingly handsome. She told Rogers that she must meet him and asked what Byron was like.

'He has a club foot and he bites his nails,' replied Rogers, who was somewhat irked by her enthusiasm.

'If he is as ugly as Aesop, I must see him,' was her reply.

Not long afterwards, *Childe Harold* was published and became an instant success.

'I awoke one morning and found myself famous,' Byron observed on 10 March, 1812, after the publication of *Childe Harold*.

For a time he was puzzled as to why this should be so, but it was not long before he knew the answer. The very reasons why he and Rogers had viewed the work with suspicion were the reasons why the reading public, and above all the women, had become fascinated by it. The hero of *Childe Harold* was a proud young demi-god who was tormented by a sense of foreboding and who was prone to nameless vices. Byron had lifted the curtain on the Eastern world where the infamous practices of the ancients were still to be witnessed, and indeed still to be experienced, and he had suggested that these vices

87

could still be savoured with relish. He was known to have based his poem on his own, first-hand knowledge of brigands and perverts, and the only anti-climax would have been for him to have revealed himself, in person, as someone totally different from the tragic Adonis of his verse.

Yet in fact he was even more arresting in his appearance than was Childe Harold on the printed page. And once Byron realized that he had a part to play, and a character to live up to, the actor in him thrilled to the challenge. Now his brooding melancholy could be turned to rich advantage. Now his vanity could be satisfied by countless seductions. He had been given little enough reason in his life to think with gratitude of women. Here was his opportunity for revenge. And being a snob and anxious to command a place in Society, he was delighted to discover that Society women—both young and middle-aged—were eager to become his slaves.

Caroline was already infatuated by his image before ever she met him. Byron knew this before he first set eyes on her.

Both rehearsed in their minds the scene that would take place when they came face to face. Caroline imagined herself sweeping into a room where the tragic hero stood lonely and aloof. Their eyes would meet and their souls entwine.

To Byron the vision was somewhat different. He imagined himself turning with lofty nonchalance to accept the instant devotion and mute adoration of one of Society's most famous and most beautiful young women.

In fact the meeting, when it came, proved something of an anti-climax for both of them. It occurred at Lady Westmoreland's house. Byron was standing in the centre of the room, magnificently posed, listening with exquisite politeness but with more than a hint of boredom whilst the guests circulated round him and the young women hung on every musical syllable that fell from his lips.

Caroline at once found herself at a disadvantage. Her god was already bespoke and all thoughts of overwhelming him with her own presence had to be abandoned. Her reaction was one of pique. Instead of joining the throng of admirers, she turned her back on him with the tart observation, 'Mad, bad, and dangerous to know,' which was her way of saying that as she could not have him to herself, she had no desire to have him at all.

Byron, for his part, was equally non-plussed. He had been fully conscious of Caroline's arrival and had awaited her supplication. Instead she muttered something that was clearly uncomplimentary and had walked out of the room. It gave his vanity a jolt.

The next move was therefore with him. However, since it was quite obvious that neither party would ever apologize, the best method was to attack. Two days later he was presented to her at Holland House. He was invited by his host to meet her and said, 'This offer was made you the other day. May I ask why you declined it?'

He then delivered what he well knew to be his *coup de grâce*— his 'under look' which he had already spent much time in perfecting. This was an upward glance from the magnificent eyes, delivered with telling effect from beneath the magnificent eyelashes, and suggesting an intense and smouldering passion.

Alas, poor Caro! She had as much chance of resisting that glance as a rabbit hypnotized by the weasel's beady stare. That night she confided in her journal, 'That beautiful pale face is my fate.' The comment was tragically prophetic.

It was an era when pallor was deemed to be highly attractive, suggesting as it did that the wearer was a tragic creature in the last throes of consumption. Everyone who was anyone in Society sought to be pale. Caroline certainly set out to be. Rouge was no longer being bought, and instead lotions were being marketed which promoted in women a lily-like look of fragility.

Byron had unfortunately suffered in his youth from almost rosy cheeks. This disadvantage he had been able to overcome by the excessive use of laxatives. Because of his nervous and excitable temperament, he suffered from indigestion; and because he was frightened of losing his figure, he ate too little but drank too much. All of which helped to promote the necessary pallor, but were not conducive to an equable temperament.

Caroline was too romantically-minded to wonder why Byron was so pale. She assumed it was but a reflection of his anguished soul. And now that she found him challenging her boldly for having ignored him at their first meeting, and the beautiful pale face was wearing the 'under look', she succumbed immediately. She who had held William at bay for so long whilst wondering whether or not she should marry him now succumbed to Byron without the semblance of a struggle.

'Mad, bad, and dangerous to know.' The observation, had Byron realized it, might have been applied with equal truth to Caroline herself, who in this moment of abject submission was certainly a little mad, and—as events were later to prove—most dangerous for him to know. But she was not bad, of course, and neither was he, although it was a quality on which he prided himself.

It was the spring of 1812. Caroline was not yet twenty-seven, and very young for her age. Byron was just twenty-four, and also young for his, despite his foreign adventures. Neither was of the type to behave with maturity, or even as a rational human being.

Caroline became instantly infatuated with him because she was a romantic. Byron was strongly attracted to Caroline because he was vain and she worshipped him; because he was a social climber and she was highly born; and because there was something about her elfin looks and child-like eagerness which he found at times irresistible.

Yet in many ways she represented almost everything that he most disliked in women. He did not like thin women, and Caroline was slim to the point of being skinny. He did not like possessive women, or neurotic women, or women who liked to show off, because he liked showing off himself. He did not like women who sought for the limelight, because the limelight—as far as he was concerned—should always be focussed on himself. He did not like over-sexed women, or women who pretended to be over-sexed. He did not really like young women, nor outspoken women. Indeed he was already reaching a stage in his life when he did not like women at all—except, perhaps, those who were older than himself and who flattered him but who did not make many demands upon him.

He looked at Caroline and saw a person who was intensely feminine and yet was half a boy. This in itself was an attraction, yet he sensed that although the body was almost that of a lissom young man, the mind was very much that of a woman; and that type of woman of whom he was most afraid. A woman who would adore him whilst he loved her, but one who would persecute him once he ceased to do so. He had suffered much at the hands of women in the past, and here was one of whom he had every reason to be afraid.

But Caroline, for her part, looked upon him and found no flaw. He was her Adonis. Physically he was her ideal of a man, with his sad, pale face and his athlete's body. And mentally? Mentally she could only judge him by what he had written. He was *Childe Harold*. That was all she wished to know.

In his face and figure she saw what others saw. His was a striking appearance; and he effortlessly commanded whatever company he was in. He was of medium height and strongly built, with as yet only a hint of the corpulence that was to come. The head was magnificent, the hair of reddish chestnut, with a profusion of curls that clustered over the smooth, wide forehead. The nose was straight and of classical line, with the nostrils sharply defined. The eyebrows were arched, the eyes brown yet dissimilar, the ears small and well-shaped but without lobes. The mouth was wide but well formed, the lips full and sensual, drooping at the corners. The chin was massive and strong, in contrast to the refinement and delicacy in the upper part of the face. The skin was clear and smooth, but of marble pallor. The hands were small and white, like the hands of a woman, but were yet the hands of a capable boxer. The expression in the proud and arrogant face was of melancholy, hinting at deep sorrows nobly endured. The voice was low and musical, with a caressing quality that was almost tangible in its seductiveness. The clothes were elegant and elaborate.

This superb specimen of manhood was marred by one deformity. The left leg terminated in a club foot. This prevented him from moving easily or quickly, and certainly made dancing impossible. Thus the lithe suppleness of the upper half of the body was in contrast to the halting and clumsy movements of the lower. It was as though Nature had set out to create the perfect man and had then spoilt the image by a single, cruel joke.

This was a handicap of which the god-like creature was acutely aware. Yet those who studied him with a cynic's eye could not fail to notice that the actor in him was able to rise above this handicap and indeed turn it to advantage. The superb body commanded feminine admiration; but the club foot could be used to arouse feminine sympathy. The sudden tightening of the lips to indicate suffering bravely borne, the proud dignity with which the disfigurement was ignored.

Byron had chosen to play the part of the tragic hero and he played it to perfection.

The effect of all this on a simple, impressionable girl like Caroline was overwhelming. She had neither the sense nor the experience to cope with such a situation. After a lifetime spent in dreaming about her ideal hero, he had suddenly materialized before her eyes, more splendid and more glamorous than she had ever imagined.

Her only hope of escape would lie in the hero's refusal to take advantage of her defencelessness. A gentleman, when he has a young innocent at his mercy, is restrained by feelings of chivalry towards her. Byron was no gentleman. He was not bad, nor wicked, nor mad. But he was socially ambitious and he was vain and weak. The girl was for the taking and so he took her. He was not then to know that having sown the wind he would one day reap the whirlwind.

Caroline was woman enough to take pleasure in parading her 'conquest' before Society. Everyone was seeking for an introduction to the young poet, and it was gratifying to reveal on what intimate terms she was with this much sought-after celebrity.

Their courtship proceeded along theatrical lines. Within a short time of confiding his troubles to her, and admitting to his chronic state of penury, she had offered him all her jewels to sell. He had replied by sending her a single rose, with a note that read, 'Your Ladyship, I am told, likes all that is new and rare—for a moment.' From the outset she revealed her unwise impetuosity and he displayed his worldly cynicism.

Her first ploy—which had been that of displaying a seeming indifference towards him—had proved instantly effective, for it had stung his vanity, but she was too inexperienced to maintain this attitude. When he paid his first visit to Melbourne House she had just returned from a ride in the Park and was dusty and dishevelled. Their mutual friend, Samuel Rogers, was with her, and she had been chattering away to him, quite unconscious of her appearance. As soon as Byron was announced she jumped up and fled from the room, appearing in due course looking cool and exquisite.

Byron was intrigued, and hinted to Caroline that he had been hoping to find her alone. She whispered to him that he could come back later in the evening, and this he did.

Having mis-played her hand from the start of the affair, Caroline moved from one major blunder to another.

On receipt of the letter which accompanied the single rose, she at once concocted a fulsome and over-demonstrative reply which must have made him wince as he read it. She compared herself to a sunflower which 'having once beheld in its full lustre the bright and unclouded sun that for one moment condescended to shine upon it, never while it exists could think any lower object worthy of its worship and admiration'.

Byron's capacity for wallowing in adulation was almost limitless, but this was going a little too far. There were moments when she almost grovelled before him, and this offended his sense of propriety. It also stimulated a sadistic urge in him. He saw in Caroline an opportunity to revenge himself on the female sex. Even quite early in their association when he was on his best behaviour, he could not resist the temptation to snub her, or to withhold the compliments which would have brought her so much happiness.

At the outset, however, the affair progressed in such a way as to give reasonable satisfaction to both parties. Byron would arrive at Melbourne House at eleven in the morning and would then be shown up to Caroline's boudoir, where she would receive him coyly, blushing with feigned modesty as she discussed with him what dresses she would wear during the day. The child, Augustus, would then be brought down and Byron would go through the motions of dandling the apathetic infant on his knee and playing the part of the jolly uncle. It was not a very convincing performance and he soon grew tired of it.

Writing later of this, his first major conquest in London Society, he observed that Lady Caroline was 'young and of the first connexions', and went on to make the patronizing comment, 'she possessed an infinite vivacity of mind, and an imagination heated by novel-reading...I was soon congratulated by my friends on the conquest I had made, and did my utmost to show that I was not insensible to the partiality I could not but perceive. I made every effort to be in love, expressed as much ardour as I could muster, and kept feeding the flame with a constant supply of *billets doux* and amatory verses.'

Caroline was wholly taken in by these advances, refused to consider for one moment that the *billets doux* were anything but sincere, and soon convinced herself that not only had she captured the literary lion for herself, but that she had also become deeply involved in a genuine love affair. She displayed her new conquest with the pride of a child, hung on his arm when they were together in public, and gazed triumphantly on her rivals.

Sometimes Caroline would dress up for his benefit, and the performance which she most enjoyed was that of dressing up as one of her own pages, and appearing as a boy. This was a part she had always enjoyed playing, and she could look very youthful and endearing in the silks and laces of the little regiment of small boys with whom she surrounded herself.

To her surprise she found that it was in this mood, and in this garb, that she seemed to attract him most, so that a genuine passion seemed to kindle in his eyes. But for the most part he remained moody and difficult to understand: whilst at one moment he was ready to pay close attention to her, at others he scarcely seemed to notice her.

It came as a shock to her when he began to show interest in her mother-in-law, Lady Melbourne. Byron was twenty-four and Lady Melbourne was sixty-three, and it was incredible to Caroline that the man whom she had envisaged would be her lover could yet be so obviously attracted by a woman old enough to be his mother. This was something beyond her comprehension; and she also became aware that he would often be most critical of her after he had spent some time in Lady Melbourne's company.

Gradually the truth dawned upon her. Lady Melbourne was not only trying to capture Byron for herself, but was also sabotaging her daughter-in-law's chances at the same time.

If Caroline played her cards badly at this time, Lady Melbourne played hers with practised skill. She was still a handsome woman and still attractive to men, including the Prince Regent. Moreover she knew how to handle men and how to please them in their different ways. Byron needed an easy companionship rather than a flamboyant affair. Her first step had been to appear aloof and to intimidate him with a feigned hostility. She had then relented and had started to flatter him by accepting him into her circle and treating him as a man of the world with whom she could discuss worldly affairs. Her attitude had been to keep their association ostensibly platonic, with the implication that he need not pretend with her, as she was too old for his attentions; but she yet contrived to suggest that he would be far happier with a mature woman such as herself than ever he would be with an excitable and neurotic child like her daughter-in-law.

Caroline continued to blunder. If Byron was as immoral as his reputation suggested, she assumed that he would be impressed by a brazen display of her body. Her dresses became ever more revealing and her talk more outrageous still.

She made the further mistake of thinking that as he was a poet and a writer, he would enjoy hearing her reading or quoting from the works of other poets and writers. In fact the majority of literary lions, and certainly Byron himself, take little interest in the work of anyone except themselves. If poems are to be read, then it should be their own. Furthermore, if there was reading to be done, Byron preferred to do it himself. He could listen for hours to the musical cadences of his own voice.

But at least Caroline had the good sense to realize before long that her obsession with the waltz was now ill-advised. Byron, with his lame foot, was quite unable to dance and it was therefore his custom to sit in the corner of a ballroom, looking upon the dancers with a haughty disdain, or else adopting a wounded deer look of infinite pathos, suggesting that—had he only been made as other men were—he would have been one of the most graceful performers on the floor.

For weeks past Caroline had been entertaining her young friends to her waltz parties in the ballroom of Melbourne House, where they had gathered together in a noisy, happy throng—parties that had gone on for most of the day and often far into the night. Now, in deference to Byron's scowling disapproval, the waltz parties were discontinued. She had discovered to her surprise that he considered the waltz unlady-like and shocking.

Instead he required her to spend the morning and afternoon hours with him alone, when he would read to her in his exquisite, musical voice and she would gaze up at him with that look of utter adoration which at once flattered and irritated him.

She found an unexpected and wholly unintentional ally in her mother, Henrietta, who now sought to discourage Byron by warning him that Caroline was in fact deeply in love with another man. She told him that he would be well advised to give her up, as he had no hope of winning her affection. This in itself was enough to arouse his interest, which would have been even more strongly stirred had Caroline supported this allegation and hinted at a rival for her affections. But poor Caroline was in no state to do anything but worship and adore. She assured him that he was the only man in her life and that he always would be.

There were moments when he warmed towards her and moments when he pitied her. He called her Caro—the nickname of her childhood—and this, at least, made her believe that he had some real affection for her. In public she held his arm, gazed into his face, and delighted in exchanging little intimate asides with him to suggest that theirs was a union of complete understanding.

He was flattered. He could not fail to be. Only a few short weeks previously he had been a nobody. Now he was London's most envied celebrity—a young man of genius and supreme good-looks who had captured the heart of a married woman who was a leader of the Devonshire House set. And so, for a time, he encouraged her in her pretence of a deep and highly emotional intimacy, so that they were treated as though they were an engaged couple.

But as the weeks went by he found himself, time and again, withdrawing early from her presence when visiting Melbourne House and pausing on his way down from the upper floors which William and Caroline occupied to look in on Lady Melbourne. Here, in the presence of this sophisticated and sympathetic woman he felt both soothed and stimulated. He would of course suggest from time to time that he was on the point of seducing her; and she would then laugh and imply that of course she was *far* too old for such a thing, and they could then settle down together for a frank and intimate discussion without the need for him to attempt the part of the great lover.

At times she would scold him gently when he became too demonstrative, and suggest that he should go upstairs again to Caroline if he was in need of something more than friendship. And the look which she gave him then would tell him that he was far better off where he was.

In the years to come he was to write of Lady Melbourne that she was 'the best friend I ever had in my life, and the cleverest woman. If she had been a few years younger, what a fool she would have made of me had she thought it worth while.'

With Lady Melbourne the emphasis was always on friendship; and when, at moments, he showed signs of a great ardour, she skilfully quietened him with teasing admonitions that he was forgetting himself, especially when he declared dramatically that it would have been better had they never met.

'I cannot see why you should wish that you had not known me,' she wrote to him after one of these outbursts. 'It cannot lead to any regret and if circumstances should not stop it entirely our Friendship will be very pleasant to both as any sentiment must be where all is sunshine—and where love does not introduce itself, there can be no jealousys, torments and quarrels...'

The allusion to Caroline was scarcely veiled. Caroline, as she well knew, was already beginning to torment her would-be lover with her jealousies, and he was beginning to find them exhausting.

But he was not above staging scenes himself. Caroline had some male admirers to whom he took exception, notably little Lord John Russell whom she had known since childhood, but it was William who became the chief target of his animosity.

Caroline remained loyal to her husband, even during her infatuation, and she often referred to him with admiration and affection. This would produce an outburst from Byron. When she spoke with pride of William's many virtues, Byron would seek to ridicule him as a paragon, and he emphasized that if William were a saint, then he, the wicked Lord Byron, was a devil. Sometimes he would even go so far as to force her to swear that her love for himself was greater than her love for William; and once, when she hesitated over this, he thundered out, 'My God, you shall pay for this! I'll wring that obstinate little heart!'

William's many undeniable good qualities were a source of much resentment to Byron; and he soon found that the best way of countering these good points was by referring to the many advantages which William had enjoyed as a young man, with a happy home life and a wise and understanding mother. He would then plunge his head in his hands and bemoan his own wretched childhood; and these memories would in turn lead to his favourite theme—that of the curse of the Byrons, who were condemned to go through life bringing misery upon themselves and upon all whom they loved.

The curse of the Byrons! It preyed upon his mind. And although the curse was an integral part of his role as the doomed hero, he yet believed in it, and had good reason to do so. His melancholy was not simply the product of a melodramatic mind and a bad digestion. It sprang from the unhappiness of his childhood, and when he spoke of this he found a sympathetic listener in Caroline, who would watch him wide-eyed as he told her of his tragic family history.

This was the story that he had to tell.

Seven

Byron - The Taint of Wickedness

The name of Byron was an ancient one in English history. By tradition it was one of shame.

But it did not become accursed until the monks of Newstead Abbey were dispossessed by order of Henry VIII and the building was sold to Sir John Byron in 1540. The monks had occupied Newstead for three hundred years, and their eviction had been sudden and ruthless. They had been rendered homeless by the militia, but not before they had thrown their founder's charter, their lectern and their other treasures into the lake.

Their cells were left empty, but their ghosts, so the local folk believed, soon returned to haunt the ancient monastery and the grounds in which so many of them had been buried.

Sir John Byron was warned that a curse had been placed on anyone who came to occupy the monastery, but he laughed at such tales and bought it from his sovereign for £800. His family had come over with the Norman conqueror and were rich and powerful. By tradition they feared no one, least of all the pale shadows of long dead monks flitting through the deserted cloisters.

The family motto was *Crede Biron,* written in the French style and meaning 'Trust in Biron', but this they had never honoured, for they trusted no one and no one trusted them. Sir John Byron rebuilt the Abbey into a fortress, and a century later these fortifications were put to the test when Lord Byron of the day supported Charles I against the Roundheads. He commanded a regiment of cavalry and displayed great courage and gross stupidity at the battles of Edgehill and Marston Moor, for on each occasion his arrogance and conceit made him charge too soon. Prince Rupert's comment at the time was, 'by the improper charge of Lord Byron, much harm was done.'

Thus one of the first of the Byron traditions was established. They showed courage but lacked discretion. They were impetuous and unwise.

It was during the reign of George I that the 4th Lord Byron took as his third wife, Frances, the younger daughter of Lord Berkeley of Stratton and this introduced a new strain of eccentricity and profligacy into the Byron family character.

The curse of the Byrons thereafter manifested itself in two forms—lust and extravagance. If they did not ruin themselves by the one, they did so by the other. The males were cruel, promiscuous and spendthrift. The women whom they enslaved were made to suffer.

By the advent of the eighteenth century the phantom of a black-cowled monk had become an accepted part of the ancient corridors, and the Byron family began to believe that they were accursed. They were paying for the sins of their ancestors.

The climax was reached with the two sons of the 4th Lord Byron. His heir, the 5th Lord Byron, killed his cousin and neighbour, William Chaworth, in a duel in a London club in 1765. True to the Byron tradition the duel was not fought over a matter of honour, but was the outcome of a drunken quarrel over a point of no importance. Lord Byron was sent to the Tower, and at his trial before his fellow peers he pleaded not guilty. He was acquitted of murder but found guilty of homicide, which was tantamount to an acquittal.

He showed no evidence of remorse, hung the sword with which he had murdered his kinsman on his bedroom wall and continued to live a life of viciousness and depravity.

A terrible legend grew up around him. He built a small fortress in the centre of the lake at Newstead—that same lake into which the monks had thrown their treasures—and here he was believed to stage bizarre and revolting orgies. He had a violent and uncontrollable temper, and grotesque stories were circulated about him. One was that he had shot his coachman dead in a fit of anger and then forced his wife to sit with the corpse while he drove the carriage home himself. Another was that he had tried to drown his wife by throwing her into the lake.

Whether or not these were true, his treatment of his wife became so cruel that she was forced to leave him and her place was taken by a servant girl. She became known as Lady Betty and proved herself as crude and vicious as her former master. By now he had been nick-named 'The Wicked Lord', a title in which he gloried. By now he had also begun to reveal all the symptoms of mental decay—due, in all probability, to syphilis—and when his son and heir married against his wishes, he became obsessed with the desire to squander his fortune and to thus ruin his descendants. He cut down the noble oaks which had stood for centuries, and massacred two thousand seven hundred head of deer in the park. He took an infantile delight in committing acts of childish vandalism on his property, and also became revolting in his person, running insect races up and down his naked body.

His younger brother, John, who had been born at Newstead in November 1723 inherited the Byron trait of lust and the Byron ill-luck. He distinguished himself at school by his courage and athleticism, but was expelled at the age of sixteen for seducing the girl who made his bed. He then entered the Royal Navy as a midshipman. At Plymouth, where he first lodged, he at once seduced his landlady, who was a widow, but he was sent on foreign service before he could marry her.

He accompanied Commodore Anson on his voyages to the South Seas and his ship, *Wager,* was wrecked off the coast of Patagonia in 1741, where he and his shipmates suffered such privations that they were forced to eat the ship's dog before they were rescued by the Spanish authorities five years later. It was this disaster at sea which made his companions at first look upon him as a Jonah. He certainly had a remarkable flair for attracting rough weather to himself. It was only necessary for him to set out of harbour for a gale to spring up almost on the instant.

It was his custom to retire periodically from active service and to settle down to the pursuit and seduction of young women living in the vicinity of his home in the west country. However in 1764, after one of these periods of rest, he was appointed commodore of an expedition to the South Seas. He travelled extensively in his ship, *Dolphin,* discovering a number of small islands but overlooking the larger ones, such as Australia. During this time the chroniclers of his adventures were able to record that whilst the desire to discover new lands remained his principal purpose, he yet was able to make the further discovery that 'the queens and princesses of the islands were ever partial to Englishmen'. Furthermore it was noted that 'nature and politeness prompted him to return their civilities'.

But his unfortunate effect upon the weather had by now earned him the nickname of 'Foulweather Jack'. On the first occasion he put to sea to engage the enemy the storm which his departure from port precipitated caused one of his ships to sink and others to suffer so badly that the enemy were not called upon to inflict any further damage.

On the second occasion that he set out to face the foe, he revealed another unfortunate family trait; like his ancestor at Edgehill, his arrogance and bravado caused him to attack too soon, and his ships were badly mauled. However his career progressed well enough and he was made a rear-admiral in 1775 and a vice-admiral in 1778.

These were the stories that Byron told to Caroline when he visited her at Melbourne House, or when she visited him in his rooms. Her eyes would widen at these terrible anecdotes of his long dead ancestors and of the curse that lay upon Newstead.

The stories filled her with horror, as they were intended to do, but it was when he told her stories of his own birth and childhood, and of the miseries which he had suffered as a little boy, that her heart was deeply touched.

She began to realize that whatever his faults, he had reason for them. The curse of the monks of old might well be no more than a winter night's tale, but the curse of a broken family life and of a bitter childhood were all too real. Her own childhood had been unhappy at times, but she had always been supported by the devotion of her mother. But Byron's mother had been mad and so had his father.

Foulweather Jack had had two sons. The elder was John Byron, nicknamed 'Mad Jack', and this was the poet's father.

It seemed that Mad Jack had inherited the sins of his uncle, 'The Wicked Lord Byron' and of his father, Foulweather Jack, for he had the vices of the former and the ill-luck of the latter. His own special contribution to the Byron tradition was charm. Of this he had an abundance, and it was something that women could not resist.

He had been born at Plymouth in February 1756, and was educated at Westminster School. He might well have gone into the navy, but his father decided that the curse of bad weather had best be avoided by sending his eldest son into the army. To this end he was sent for a time to a French military academy, and his father then bought him a commission in the Guards.

This form of education produced a soldier and a rake. In France he learnt to speak French fluently and he also learnt the arts of seduction in the permissive world of pre-revolution Parisian society. Even before he went into the Guards he was an accomplished and prolific seducer, an obsessive gambler, a spendthrift, and a heavy drinker.

His commission in the Guards led to a period spent with the British forces in America, but at the age of twenty-two, and with the rank of Captain, he decided to retire from the military arena and to live on his wits and his looks. He gambled heavily and cheated whenever possible. It was the done thing in those days and nearly half a century was to pass before the English sporting spirit was to become a feature of the English character.

Mad Jack now looked around for a really wealthy and influential mistress, and his challenging gaze was met by one that was equally challenging.

Lady Carmarthen, the wife of Francis, then Marquis of Carmarthen, and afterwards 5th Duke of Leeds, was a clever and beautiful woman who was bored with her kind but ineffectual husband. She openly revealed her interest in Captain Jack Byron from the moment when she first met him—on a picnic to Coxheath—and replied to his verbal assaults and witticisms with practised skill, making him 'the constant butt of her wit and pleasantry'.

The young Captain became quite outrageously indiscreet, as did the woman who became his mistress. News of their affair reached Lord Carmarthen in Yorkshire and he came hurrying back to London to put an end to it, only to find that the couple were once more experiencing the delights of picnicking, this time at Barrow Hedges.

The Marquis instituted divorce proceedings, and Lady Carmarthen and her lover went to live in her house in Grosvenor Square.

In due course the divorce came through and Captain Byron married his heiress on 9 June, 1779, the bride being already eight months pregnant. However the scandal developed such proportions that they had to emigrate to France.

But despite her wealth, they soon fell on hard times. Mad Jack became a member of the fast set in Paris, gambling and drinking, and paying less and less attention to his wife, except to make her pregnant from time to time. In the four and a half years of their marriage she gave birth to three of his children, but only one of these, the last, survived beyond infancy.

This was a baby girl who was born in Paris on 26 January 1784. Her mother died in childbirth, and the father had little use for her. He would have much preferred the child to have died and the mother saved—not because of his devotion to her, but only because of his devotion to her substantial income, which unfortunately died with her.

There was nothing for him to do but to hasten back to England in search of another heiress. This he did, leaving his infant daughter behind him in the care of one of her relatives. Her future seemed unimportant at the time.

She was named Augusta Mary and she was destined to become the most important factor in shaping the career of her future half-brother, George Gordon Byron.

On his arrival in England, Mad Jack decided to follow the precedent of 'Beau' Nash and set out to seek his fortune in Bath. Here he met a Scottish heiress who was plump and rather plain. He realized that there was more than a hint of passion beneath her prim exterior, but failed to realize that there was also a hint of temper.

She was of ancient lineage and even more proud of her breeding than he was of his. She was an orphan, with an estate valued at around £25,000 and she loved him to distraction.

There were minor problems to overcome before they married. Her canny Scots relatives were conscious that she would be a target for adventurers and they were of the opinion that if ever they had set eyes on an adventurer, it was Captain Jack Byron. But the young girl, whose name was Catharine Gordon of Gight, was both head-strong and determined. She announced that she was going to marry her gallant Captain, and there was nothing that they could do about it.

The marriage took place on 13 May, 1785, at the parish church of St Michael. After a short honeymoon they went to live at the bride's home town of Gight. It was explained to the young man that in Scotland it was custom, after a wedding, for the husband to adopt his wife's surname, and he happily became Captain Byron Gordon. From his young wife he learnt of the ancestry of the Gordons of Gight and was surprised to discover that not only were the Gordons as old a family as the Byrons, but that their family history was, if anything, more replete with acts of violence.

Mad Jack's extravagance in everything exhausted Catharine physically and ruined her financially. Much of her fortune was swallowed up by his outstanding debts, and it was not long before he had squandered the rest. By March 1786 they were forced to move to England after the estate of Gight had been sold to the Earl of Aberdeen. She made some effort to protect part of this sum from falling into her husband's clutches.

Her situation rapidly deteriorated. Her husband carried her off to France, where he soon fell in with his old associates.

She did her best to maintain a home for him and she also looked after his little daughter, Augusta, whom he had previously abandoned in Paris. For a time the child was very ill and seemed on the point of dying, but Catharine nursed her devotedly.

Her husband continued to treat her badly and to desert her for long periods at a time, but she still could not resist his charm. As the result of one of his rare visits to her, she became pregnant in the mid-summer of 1787. This in no way altered his habits. He came to see her only when he wanted to get money out of her.

She was determined that her child should be born in England, and having handed over little Augusta to the care of the child's maternal grandmother, Lady Holderness, she crossed the Channel. She had no friends in England and took cheap lodgings off Oxford Street, in London. It was in these dreary surroundings that she was delivered of a son on 22 January, 1788. He was born within a caul—and with a malformed foot.

The child was given the names of George Gordon Byron when he was christened at the Marylebone Parish Church on 29 February. Mad Jack was not present. However he continued to appear from time to time thereafter to ask her for money. She had been able to invest a sum of £3,000 to bring in £150 per year, which was just enough for her to live on and to maintain her son, her nurse and herself adequately, but only after much pinching and scraping.

She went to live in Aberdeen, where her son grew yearly more like his father, with the same charm and the same good looks. He was intelligent and very affectionate, but he had inherited his mother's moodiness and quickness of temper.

Meanwhile a feud developed between Mrs Byron and Lady Holderness, who had adopted little Augusta. Lady Holderness decided that Mrs Byron was not a fit person for Augusta to meet, and for the next twelve years George Gordon and his half-sister were kept apart. When finally they did meet, the results were destined to be far reaching.

Augusta grew up knowing only that she had a half-brother, who lived in Scotland, and a father whose name was seldom mentioned and whom she never saw. In her imagination she tried to picture each of them, wondering what they might be like.

Mad Jack's son also grew up with his imagination filled with thoughts of the father whom he seldom saw and whose presence invariably provoked terrible scenes in the household. He, too, fell under the spell of this dashing, romantic man. His father became a hero in the son's eyes.

In the years to come, when he met Augusta and became devoted to her, one of the bonds that united them was the memory of this allegedly heroic figure.

Caroline would listen with fascination to Byron's stories of his father —of how handsome and brave he had been, how irresistible to women. Then his mood would change and he would speak of the bitterness he had suffered by his idol's desertion of him. The loss of his father, as he explained to Caroline, was a wound which he suffered from all his life—like the physical wound of his crippled leg, which had been discovered and treated at much the same time as his father's desertion.

'In separation,' he would say, 'the one who goes away suffers less than the one who stays behind.'

The loss of male companionship in childhood and the loss of the father figure in his youth affected him profoundly. It made him search more anxiously for male friendships than for female.

Mrs Byron struggled on in poverty in Aberdeen. But she had other problems besides an erring husband to consider. Her little boy, the idol of her life, revealed ominous signs of lameness in the left foot as soon as he tried to walk. His feet looked normal and the two small legs seemed of the same length, but when he put his left heel on the ground, his ankle collapsed. The local doctors prescribed special boots and blamed the injury on Mrs Byron's behaviour during the birth, when it was said that her modesty prevented the proper delivery of the infant.

As the boy grew up, his mother grew more unbalanced. He was often rebellious and naughty, and she would then fly into a rage with him, scolding him vehemently whilst declaring that he was as bad as his father.

In 1791, Mad Jack was in Paris, destitute. On 21 June he dictated his will from his sick bed to two French lawyers. It concluded with the Byronic phrase, 'I appoint my son, Mr George Byron, heir to my real and personal estate, and charge him to pay my debts, legacies and funeral expenses.' Thus the torch of insolvency was handed down from father to son.

He died on 2 August. When the news reached Mrs Byron she had an immediate relapse and her shrieks of misery could be heard throughout the locality. She was twenty-six and her son was three and a half.

He was just old enough to realize that he would never see his father again and that his mother was going mad.

An event which occurred three years later was of little interest to him, but of great interest to his mother. In 1794 she learnt, quite by chance, that the grandson of The Wicked Lord had been killed by a cannon ball in Corsica. As a result her son, George, became heir to the title. This was a dramatic change in the family fortunes. The Wicked Lord was old and senile. It could not be long before George became Lord Byron and the master of Newstead.

Meanwhile the boy's earlier education followed that laid down by the stern Presbyterian code. The heavy mantle of Calvinism was thrown round him. He was taught that the fall of Adam had laid a curse upon mankind. Even a babe in the womb was the victim of this curse; and in a child were already implanted the seeds of evil. The vilest of all sins were the sins of the flesh, and above all the sin of lust.

According to his own story, recounted in graphic detail to a wide-eyed Caroline, he was made aware of this lust when he was still a young boy. His mother employed two young maid-servants, Agnes and May Gray, who together looked after him in his infancy and childhood in Aberdeen. May Gray exerted a strong influence over him throughout these early, formative years. She was deeply religious but also deeply aware of the lusts of the flesh, and they proved too strong for her. The contemplation of the young male body that she was required to bath and dress finally overwhelmed her. Byron told Caroline that when he was only nine years old May Gray entered his bed and there initiated him into some of the most evil manifestations of sexual desire. These bouts of sensuality would alternate with lectures on the wickedness of carnal knowledge and acts of fiercely executed corporal punishment.

Caroline had no means of knowing what truth lay in these stories. She may have felt that Byron was seeking to justify himself for his subsequent behaviour in life; but she was too innocent to comprehend the implications behind these lurid stories of his corruption.

But there was one thing about him that she was able to understand and that was the mixture of fascination and detestation which women seemed able to arouse in him. She realized that he was at heart deeply romantic and idealistic, and that these ideals had been violated by his mother, who had failed to give him the maternal love for which he yearned; and by his early experiences with women, from whom he had learned that love could be coarse and obscene.

He also hinted to Caroline of a form of love which she did not comprehend. He told her of his school-days at Harrow, where he had been popular and happy. He was a fine athlete, something of a rebel, and a dashing figure who had been looked up to and envied. The warmth of his nature, and his longing for affection, had led him

106

into several intimate associations with younger boys. He spoke of these friendships with an ardour which she found hard to understand. It was almost as if he was speaking of love affairs that had brought him both spiritual and physical joy. This was something that Caroline found bewildering to her, but she attached no great significance to it.

He spoke with tenderness and nostalgia of boys whom he had known at Harrow, such as Lord Clare and Lord Delawarr. 'My school friendships were with me *passions*,' he said. 'That with Lord Clare began one of the earliest and lasted the longest. I never hear the word "Clare" without a beating of the heart even *now*.' It was evident to Caroline that this friendship with Lord Clare had played an important part in his life.

His stories of calf love were equally dramatic and most poignant. He told her that his first love affair had occurred when he was very young. In Aberdeen he met a little girl named Mary Duff, who had hazel eyes and dark brown hair, and was a distant cousin. She was very pretty and sweet, and all he wanted to do was to look at her and to caress her.

'I recollect all we said to each other,' he wrote in his diary, 'all our caresses, her features, my restlessness, sleeplessness...I certainly had no sexual ideas for years afterwards; and yet my misery, my love for that girl, were so violent, that I sometimes doubt if I have ever been really attached since.'

He suffered in a similar way when some years later he became infatuated with another cousin, Margaret Parker, whom he described as 'one of the most beautiful of evanescent beings...My passion had its usual effect upon me: I could not sleep, could not eat; I could not rest; and although I had reason to know that she loved me, it was the torture of my life to think of the time which must elapse before we could meet again.'

She had later died of tuberculosis, thus confirming his belief in the curse that fell upon those whom a Byron loved.

Finally came the most fervent of his boyhood love affairs—his obsession with Mary Chaworth, another distant cousin, heiress to Annesley, a neighbouring property to Newstead, and a descendant of the Chaworth whom The Wicked Lord Byron had murdered in a duel. By now he was fifteen and she was two years older, a slim, exquisite young woman who was flattered by his attentions and encouraged them without ever seriously considering him as a lover. She did not reject him by declaring him to be the enemy of her family and proudly disdaining his advances. This he would have understood. Instead she only confirmed his belief in the perfidy of women, for she led him on, walked with him through the woods, allowed him small intimacies and gave him hope; and finally destroyed him with a remark that was not even addressed to him, but which he chanced to overhear, 'Do you think I could care anything for that lame boy?'

The story as he told it made Caroline blaze with anger. It was inconceivable to her that any woman should have shown such cruelty. To the passion which she had developed for this troubled young man was added a deep sense of pity.

Here, as she now understood full well, was a human being craving for love. But having been spurned in love, he was now suspicious of it. He had been hurt too often and too deeply. And so he escaped into a world of cynicism and scorn, seduced merely to gratify his sexual desires, believing after he had done so that he had in some way revenged himself upon the sex which had crucified him in the past.

His mother's circumstances had been eased to a certain extent in the spring of 1798, when news had reached her that The Wicked Lord had died at Newstead and that her son was now the 6th baron. This had meant the end of their days in Aberdeen, and she and the 6th baron, now aged ten, had packed their bags and set off for the ancestral home at Newstead.

They had arrived at the Abbey expecting to find a noble mansion, but instead were faced with a house that had fallen into decay. The Wicked Lord had died as he had loved—in confusion and in squalor—and it had been hard enough to raise funds enough to bury him. Indeed the corpse had lain for nearly a month in Newstead before it was finally put away in the family vault in the church at Hucknall Torkard, near Newstead.

At Cambridge, where Byron went in October 1805, his passions continued. He fell in love with a fifteen-year-old choir boy named John Edleston, with an ethereal face and a beautiful voice. Here again, as he explained to Caroline, the younger boy gave to him a devotion which was untainted by feminine guile and which he returned with all his heart.

'His friendship, and a violent, though *pure*, love and passion,' he said, 'were the then romance of the most romantic period of my life.'

Caroline, when she listened to his account of this Cambridge friendship, was perplexed by his frequent references to the purity of his love for this young boy. She assumed that it would have been pure; she did not then realize that he was seeking to imply that not all his friendships had been pure, and that in this case he was doing what Caroline herself had so often done in her youth—sublimating sex and placing the loved one on a pedestal and above all earthly desires.

Then there had been his romance with the fifteen-year-old Greek boy, Nicolo Giraud, whom he had met on his Mediterranean tour. Here again he described the abject devotion on the part of the boy and the more lofty and ethereal attitude on his own part.

Both these boys were of humble birth, and they fulfilled the classic romance of the young lord and the simple shepherd boy. Years later his wife was to make an observation that had more truth in it than ever she realized when she said of Byron that he had suffered in his life from a classical education.

Caroline listened to his descriptions of these beautiful young boys but failed to appreciate their significance. Nevertheless, instinct told her that she would prove more attractive if she appeared sometimes to him as a boy herself, and since she had always longed to be one, she was happy to dress up as a page for his amusement and pleasure. Yet she was non-plussed when she discovered that the change back from masculinity to femininity sometimes irritated him; and that his interest in her seemed to lessen after it had been effected.

Yet she was given no indication of any physical aversion on his part to women. On the contrary, it was not long before he was boasting to her of the women in Society whom he had seduced, or was about to seduce. Thus she was persuaded that his sexual desires were quite normal and assumed that his stories of these conquests were told to her in order to arouse her jealousy and to promote her own willingness to become his mistress.

There were other aspects of his love life of which she was vaguely conscious but yet could not understand. One of the most curious was the way in which he seemed emotionally attracted to women who were his relatives. Each of his first three love affairs with women had been with his cousins. It was almost as though he were reluctant to commit himself outside the family circle.

When Caroline listened to Byron's constant boastings of how women could not resist him, and of what a magnificent lover he was, she set out to prove to him that she was as wanton and passionate as any of her rivals. She began to adopt towards him the same brazen approach she had adopted with Sir Godfrey Webster.

It was another blunder. She failed to realize that there was a strong puritanical streak in Byron, and she failed to understand that although he was flattered by women who threw themselves at his head, he was secretly shocked by their lack of restraint.

In some ways she found him quite obsessively prudish and fastidious. He enjoyed the sexual conquest of a woman, but he warned Caroline that the thought of having to share his bed with a woman throughout the night was offensive to him. He told her that he did not even enjoy sharing a meal with women, because their eating habits, no matter how refined, were often distasteful to him.

He was shocked by evidence of sensuality in women. His conception of the sexual act was that the proud and dominating male overcame a woman's reluctance by the force of his personality, his charm and good looks, and that she then gave herself to him as an act of submission.

She discovered that his attitude towards women was confused and contradictory. At one moment he could be the true romantic, speaking of their exquisite beauty and placing them on a pedestal. At the next he could be the cynic, reviling and despising them. In a young man he sought for physical perfection, and its contemplation gave him an exquisite pleasure. But with women he was far less discriminating. His physical tastes in women tended towards an earthy voluptuousness. Thus he liked the women of the East, with their sensuous bodies and rounded curves. But he also demanded small and dainty feet.

He liked submissive women who allowed him to fulfil his desires quickly and expeditiously and who did not talk whilst the act was being performed, nor lie back and discuss it in retrospect after it was over.

With a cynicism which would have delighted Wilde, he observed, 'One must make love mechanically, as one swims. I was once very fond of both, but now, as I never swim unless I tumble in the water, I don't make love till almost obliged.'

He also compared himself to Napoleon.

'Like Napoleon, I have always had a great contempt for women; and formed this opinion of them not hastily, but from my own fatal experience. My writings, indeed, tend to exalt the sex...but I only drew them as a painter or statuary would do—as they should be... They are in an unnatural state of society. The Turks and Eastern people manage these matters better than we do. They lock them up and they are much happier. Give a woman a looking-glass and a few sugar plums, and she will be satisfied.'

He was at pains to inform Caroline that physically she was not his type. He told her that thin women were like butterflies or spiders and that he found them slightly repulsive. Her figure, he said, was genteel enough but it was sadly lacking in 'that roundness which elegance would vainly supply'. None of which was calculated to bolster her self-confidence, or to encourage her in the belief that he found her attractive.

This did not prevent either of them from making a show of their affection in public. It flattered him to have captured so high-born a prize, and it flattered her to have aroused the interest of such a celebrity. Both were therefore anxious, during the blossoming of their affair in the spring of 1812, to suggest that the liaison was an intimate one. Caroline was aware that the gossips were suggesting that she was altogether too thin for Byron's tastes, and he, for his part, was aware that Caroline was believed to be reasonably happy in her marriage and that her waywardness would stop short at any flagrant act of infidelity. Both were thus happy to imply that they were indulging in a passionate and uninhibited affair.

In public they behaved like lovers, exchanging intimate and meaningful looks. Society in general assumed that they *were* lovers, but there were some, more cynical than the rest, who formed the opinion that their behaviour constituted much ado about very little.

The extraordinary innocence which characterized Caroline was constantly in evidence in her relationship with him. Here was a woman whose mother and whose aunt had each lived lives of quite exceptional promiscuity and who had herself, at this time, been married for several years to a man who was by no means lacking in virility. Yet there were times when she reacted to Byron's embraces with the modesty of a young girl. Nor was this a pose. She was ashamed of her innocence and her modesty but could not conceal them from him.

'But was I cold when first you made me yours?' she asked plaintively in one of her earlier letters to him. 'When first you told me in the carriage to kiss your mouth and I durst not—and after thinking it such a crime it was more than I could prevent from that moment—you drew me to you like a magnet and I could not indeed I could not have kept away—was I cold then—were you so?'

It was a pathetic letter in its way, revealing how vulnerable she was and how incapable she was of understanding the man who had

111

stirred her emotions so deeply. And she told him, 'Never while life beats in this heart shall I forget you or that moment when first you said you lov'd me—when my heart did not meet yours but flew before it—and both intended to remain innocent of greater wrong.'

Inevitably she suffered greatly from jealousy, and her increasing lack of decorum angered him. She did not seem to mind how badly she behaved in public or before the servants. If she attended a dance at which he was present, she would never take her eyes off him; and if he attended a dance to which she had not been invited, she would wait outside for him until he appeared, mixing with the link boys and the coachmen without any sense of the embarrassment which she might be causing to him or to his host and hostess.

Sometimes, as he was driving away, she would jump on the step of his carriage and lean with her body half way through the window, talking to him in the most intimate manner.

There were moments, of course, when the violence of their disagreements resulted in scenes of melodramatic intensity. Samuel Rogers used to find them in his garden, quite played out, having quarrelled violently all day. Byron enjoyed scenes, but not too violent ones and certainly not those in which he was robbed of the principal role. In any shouting match it was Caroline who showed the greater stamina, and she was prepared to maintain a mood of hysteria for a surprising length of time.

He had already told her in one of their first encounters that she had a mind over-heated by novel reading; and he warned her that she was, to him, one of that tiresome breed of women who shouted when they should have whispered.

During their first amatory exchanges he had stimulated her desires by sending her *billets doux,* which came easily to his facile pen. Caroline, who fancied herself as both a poet and novelist, replied to these with enthusiasm, and inflammatory notes were showered upon him.

Byron could not resist either the colourful phrase or the flamboyant gesture, and Caroline used to maintain that there had even been a moment when they had gone through some curious form of 'marriage', when they had exchanged rings and written down mutual vows in a book which they signed 'Byron' and 'Caroline'. But at least he had the good sense to display some reticence in the written pronouncements of his affection, whilst Caroline displayed none at all. It was his policy to praise in one sentence and then to strike a less

112

laudatory note in the next, just in case she should become too sure of him.

'Your heart, my poor Caro (what a little volcano!),' he wrote soon after she had first thrown herself into his arms, 'pours lava through your veins...I have always thought you the cleverest, most agreeable, absurd, amiable, perplexing, dangerous, fascinating little being that lives now.' But lest she might become too elated by this, he then added, 'I won't talk to you of beauty; I am no judge. But our beauties cease to be so when near you, and therefore you have either some, or something better.'

There was little that Caro could make of such observations as this, other than that he found her attractive, but not wholly so. The references to her imagination, and its over-heated state as a result of reading novels, was cruelly derisive.

Eight

Byron - The Separation

The first two cantos of *Childe Harold* were published on 29 February, 1812. Caroline discussed them with Byron at a waltzing-party at Melbourne House on 25 March. Two days later she wrote to him her first love-letter. By mid-summer their affair had reached a crescendo. By the autumn it was over.

During this short period many other events occurred which were to shape the future destinies of Caroline and Byron, and during this period there were other players who were about to make their entrance. In the centre of the stage stood Byron himself, resolutely commanding the limelight. In the wings were two of the leading ladies in the melodrama, waiting to make their entrance.

Caroline also occupied the limelight for a time, and did so with relish. One of the things which irritated Byron so much about Caroline was that she was always ready to steal his thunder.

It was Byron's purpose to live up to the traditions of his family at all times. The Byrons had ever been martyrs to bankruptcy, and now the 6th Lord showed a talent for insolvency which could eclipse even that of his most illustrious ancestors. His debts were rapidly mounting, and his family seat at Newstead was falling into disrepair.

One of the most significant events in his life was the encounter which took place at Lady Melbourne's waltzing-party on 25 March. It was here that Caroline monopolized his attention and first began to lay siege to his affections, but there were other guests at this party who also caught his notice. Amongst those present were the Reverend Sydney Smith, Lady Jersey, Lord and Lady Kinnaird, Miss Margaret Mercer Elphinstone, red-haired and flirtatious, the dashing young Lord Palmerston and—very much in the background—Lady Melbourne's niece, Miss Anne Isabella Milbanke, who was generally known as Annabella.

Annabella was William's cousin and therefore well known to

Caroline. She was very much the country cousin, for she lived with her parents, Sir Ralph and Lady Milbanke, at Seaham, a bleak fishing village in the north of England. Far from being impressed by the ultra-smart set in which she found herself, Annabella remained aloof and disinterested. Social chit-chat had no attraction for her and celebrities bored her.

It was Byron's habit, whilst occupying the centre of the stage, to keep a close observation on the reactions of his audience. He appeared indifferent to the waves of feminine adulation which threatened to engulf him, but he was always on the look out for those members of his audience who were not applauding.

Whilst accepting the attentions of Caroline, who fluttered round him so excitedly, he was also well aware of the presence of the haughty young woman who stood in a corner of the room and viewed him with obvious disapproval. He made use of his 'under look' in her direction, and was surprised to find that it had no effect upon her. So turning to his friend, Moore, he asked whether this frigid creature was some lady's companion.

'No,' answered Moore, 'She is a great heiress. You should marry her and repair Newstead.'

He looked at her again and sized her up as was his wont. The figure was undeniably good, round and comely. The hair was dark, the eyes likewise. The complexion was excellent, the cheeks rosy and fresh, the nose slightly snub. The expression was disdainful and rather smug; her general demeanour suggested a young woman of intelligence and strong character.

Byron questioned Caroline about her and planned his method of approach. The haughty Annabella must be brought to heel, but clearly this could not be accomplished by playing the literary lion with her, by adopting the role of the wicked Lord Byron, or by making a bold assault upon her virtue. But he was nothing if not versatile, and so he settled for the part of the shy and sensitive young poet who was secretly disillusioned by the loose company in which he found himself.

Annabella was an intellectual, with an outstanding flair for mathematics. She was shrewd and a good judge of character. But she was also unsophisticated—and only twenty. She was in part deceived by Byron, but not wholly. She knew his reputation and was clever enough to see through him—up to a point. But her femininity was not fully proof against his wiles.

Byron was not accustomed to dealing with frigidity or chastity, and these qualities in Annabella presented a challenge to his vanity. The resentment which he felt towards the female sex made him view with some relish the possibility of depriving so obvious a virgin of the chastity which she valued so highly. She had one further attraction for him. She was very rich.

And what of Annabella? What had been *her* reactions to this first meeting?

Caroline's initial verdict on Byron had been 'mad, bad and dangerous to know'. Now Annabella reached a very different conclusion when she came to make her first entry in her diary about this wicked lord.

'His mouth continually betrays the acrimony of his spirit. I should judge him sincere and independent...It appeared to me that he tried to control his natural sarcasm and vehemence as much as he could, in order not to offend; but at times his lips thickened with disdain and his eyes rolled impatiently.'

Later she added, 'My curiosity was much gratified by seeing Lord Byron, the object at present of universal attention...It is said that he is an infidel, and I think it probable from the general character of his mind. His poem sufficiently proves that he *can* feel nobly, but he has discouraged his own goodness.'

These were the comments of a woman who was already picturing herself in the role of the saviour of a human soul. The final comment made his ultimate fate inevitable, 'I made no offering at the shrine of Childe Harold, though I shall not refuse the acquaintance if it comes my way.'

Byron's assessment of Miss Milbanke was as informative as hers was upon him.

'There was a simplicity, a retired modesty about her, which was very characteristic, and formed a happy contrast to the cold artificial formality and studied stiffness, which is called fashion. She interested me exceedingly.'

Caroline was fascinated by Byron because she believed that he was wicked. Annabella was fascinated by him because she suspected that he was good. It was a curious situation, the irony of which would have delighted him had he then realized how things were developing.

One of the secrets of Byron's character was his intense desire for companionship and sympathy. He enjoyed playing the literary lion and the tragic hero, but he had a longing to be himself; to behave naturally in the company of someone who knew and understood him so well that he never had to play a part in their presence. He was still in search of the mother-figure to whom he could bring his troubles.

Now, in this critical period of his life, he found at last what he had always craved for—a gentle and uncomplicated woman who understood him perfectly. This was his half-sister, Augusta.

Augusta had been brought up by her grandmother, Lady Holderness. Lady Holderness had always strongly disapproved of Byron's mother, whom she rightly considered to be vulgar and half mad, and she had discouraged all association between Captain Byron's two children.

After Lady Holdnerness' death in 1801, Mrs Byron succeeded in making contact with Augusta, who was then seventeen. She felt a natural affection for the girl, whose life she had saved as an infant, in Paris; but she was also much influenced by the high society in which Augusta had been reared, for Augusta was related on her mother's side to the Duke of Leeds and Lord Carlisle.

Byron and his half-sister shared a strong feeling for family unity, and each had been delighted to 'discover' the other. Byron was at this time at an impressionable age, a schoolboy at Harrow and eager for some romantic liaison. To find himself quite suddenly possessed of an attractive elder sister appealed to him, and the two began to correspond.

'I hope you will consider me not only as a *Brother*,' he wrote to her, 'but as your warmest and most affectionate *Friend,* and if ever Circumstances should require it, your *protector*. Recollect, My Dearest Sister, that you are the *nearest relation* I have *in the world both by ties of Blood* and *affection*.'

Augusta's warm and simple heart was moved by such letters. She, too, had always longed for a close relative to whom she could turn, and in whom she could confide. To her he became at once her beloved 'Baby Byron'.

The correspondence which now began was filled with warmth on both sides; Augusta had fallen wildly in love with her cousin, George Leigh, a colonel of dragoons, and now she asked Byron's advice. Speaking then as a worldly sophisticate, he wrote back to warn her, 'love, in my humble opinion, is utter nonsense, a mere jargon of compliments, romance and deceit.' He added, 'For my part, if I had fifty mistresses, I should, in the course of a fortnight, forget them all.'

There were no secrets between the two, and he was soon discussing

117

his emotional problems with her, and even hinting at his homo-sexual attachments. Augusta was a simple and innocent girl, who could not comprehend these difficulties, but her 'Baby Byron' could do no wrong in her eyes. If he was distressed it was her duty to comfort him.

Byron first met Augusta in 1804, and then not again until the spring of 1805, when he was seventeen and in his last term at Harrow. She was then twenty. Although she was not beautiful, she was attractive, tall and slender, with a small head, a long, delicate neck and dark brown hair. She had a small, pert nose, slightly uptilted, her mouth was wide and generous, and she had excellent teeth. Her complexion was clear and healthy. There were freckles on her face. But her greatest asset was her warmth of heart.

When they met they found themselves instantly in accord. He admired her charm and she was immensely proud of his good looks and his talents. But the quality in her which mattered to him most was that with her he could relax. She could soothe him in a way that no other women had ever done before (or was ever to do again) and in her company he was natural and at ease. He never pretended with her, never struck a pose nor played a part.

As the years went by he found that he needed her most when he was depressed; and the melancholia which settled upon him from time to time caused her great concern. At Cambridge his extrava-gance and dissipation soon placed him heavily in debt, and when she tried to remonstrate with him, and then offered to lend him money, he quarrelled with her. He told her indignantly that she was not to interfere, and said that he did not wish to have anything more to do with her.

Augusta was heartbroken. She said of his bitterness towards her, '*Time* seems rather to increase than remove it, and to have lost his affection and esteem appears to me a still more severe affliction than his Death would have been.'

But by now she had other matters to concern her. In the summer of 1807 she married her dashing hero, Colonel Leigh. He was un-deniably good-looking, but had little else to recommend him, for he was a rake.

Byron refused to attend the ceremony, and did not even send her a present or his good wishes. He was jealous of this man who had displaced him in her affections.

Byron had now left Cambridge and had gone to live at Newstead, where—rumour had it—he was trying to prove himself as wicked as its previous owner by staging orgies. These were attended by his more undesirable Cambridge friends who frolicked with 'Paphian girls'. By now he had become immersed in studies of Gothic horror, and, inspired by the traditions of the Hell-Fire Clubs of the previous century, he staged obscene ceremonies after the manner of Sir John Dashwood at Medmenham Abbey, dressing himself and his friends in monk's garments and indulging in devil worship and satanism. His mind was by now in a very unhealthy state and the knowledge of this caused Augusta much unhappiness.

The breach between Augusta and Byron was not fully healed until after the tragic events of the summer of 1811, when he lost his mother and two of his best friends. Augusta wrote at once to console him, and he wrote back to tell her that he was proposing to include her in his Will. The letter was affectionate, but included the usual worldly observations. He announced that he was thinking of getting married if he could 'find anything inclined to barter money for rank'. At the same time he announced that he was proposing to return to his friends, the Turks, and to wipe the dust of England off his feet.

Later he returned to the question of a marriage of convenience with the comment, 'As to Lady B., when I discover one rich enough to suit me and foolish enough to love me, I will give her leave to make me miserable if she can. Money is the magnet; as to Women, one is as well as another, the older the better, we have then a chance of getting her to Heaven.'

The publication of *Childe Harold,* and Byron's subsequent acceptance into high society as a literary lion, caused him to forget about Augusta. He was by now so famous—and so popular—that he no longer felt the need for her comfort and sympathy. He had sent her a copy of *Childe Harold* and had written on the fly-leaf 'To Augusta, my dearest sister, and my best friend, who has ever loved me better than I deserved, this volume is presented by her *father*'s son, and most affectionate brother, B.' But apart from this he put her out of his mind.

Augusta's problems were multiplying. She had two small children to look after, with a third on the way, her husband was hopelessly improvident, and she was desperately worried about money. Her husband had by now quarrelled with his benefactor, the Prince of Wales, and her future looked grim indeed.

But if he had ceased altogether to worry about her, she was still worrying about him. News reached her of his association with

Caroline, and she realized that nothing but harm could come of this affair. She pondered over his problem and, in her sisterly way, came up with the only solution. He must marry some good woman who would look after him and keep him out of mischief.

The summer of 1812 was a period of deterioration in the characters of both Caroline Lamb and Byron. She grew ever more frustrated and neurotic under the stress of their affair. He became ever more selfish and conceited as the result of his lionization by Society.

The urge to play a part, and to dramatize every act and emotion, steadily increased. Both behaved badly, but of the two Caroline was far more vulnerable than her partner. He was in danger of both a financial and a physical breakdown, but his brain remained active and creative. She, however, was in danger of a mental breakdown that could bring her to the verge of insanity. Her marriage was in danger, her child sub-normal and her behaviour was causing distress not only to herself but also to those who loved her, notably her husband and her mother.

William had never been impressed by Byron. He despised the man and found his vanity ridiculous, and because he found him ridiculous he refused to take Caroline's affair with him seriously. He treated her infatuation as just another of her silly impulses, which would quickly pass and be superseded by some other interest. He could not convince himself that she could be seriously in love with such a peacock of a man.

Henrietta took a much more serious view of the affair and warned him that they might elope. William pooh-poohed the idea. 'They neither wish nor intend going,' he said, 'but both like the fear and interest they create.'

This was certainly true. Caroline was enjoying the excitement which her behaviour was causing in Society. She did everything possible to promote the belief that she and Byron were lovers without actually making a public declaration of their union. Yet throughout all the publicity-seeking and the ostentatious indiscretions, there was evidence of a real affection in Caroline's looks, her words and in her letters. That beautiful pale face exerted an extraordinary fascination over her.

'How very pale you are,' she wrote to Byron, 'a statue of white marble, so colourless, and the dark brow hair such a contrast. I never see you without wishing to cry. If any painter could paint me that face as it is, I would give anything I possess on earth—no one has yet given the countenance and complexion as it is.'

When in his company, however, she soon discovered that her tragic hero could be selfish, arrogant and unromantic. She was further frustrated by the knowledge that she had numerous rivals. There were many attractive women eager to become his mistress, and as many eager to become his wife.

She realized that he might soon marry and tried to adopt an impersonal attitude. And she wrote to him, 'Do not marry yet, or if you do, let me know it first. I shall not suffer, if she you choose be worthy of you, but she will never love you as I did.'

Lofty sentiments with which she deceived herself for a time. But she was convinced of his infidelity to her, and took to spying on him.

'In order to detect my intrigues,' he wrote, 'she watched me and earthed a lady into my lodgings, and came herself, terrier like, in the disguise of a carman. My valet who did not see through the masquerade, let her in, where to the despair of Fletcher, she put off the man and put on the woman. Time 9 in the even. It was worthy of Faublas.'

There were times when even Byron felt twinges of conscience about her husband, William Lamb. He had no more liking for William than William had for him, and he had found it amusing to make a cuckold out of such a typical English gentleman, who never imagined that his wife would ever do more than flirt. When seeking for some justification for his behaviour towards Caroline, Byron was in the habit of blaming William, whom he said had treated her passion as a joke.

Apart from William, the rest of the Lamb family were hostile to Caroline. They felt that she might ruin his life and were already of the opinion that the sooner he sent her packing the better for all of them. But for the meanwhile their aim was to separate her from Byron.

Caroline's affair with Byron had started in late March. By the end of May he was quite worn out by it, and decided to flee to Newstead, where he might discover a little peace amongst the ancient trees and Gothic corridors. He was still basking in the praise that was being showered on *Childe Harold*, which also increased his prestige in the House of Lords. He was now listened to with more attention and his views were seriously appraised. But his enthusiasm for politics was already on the wane. He now had so many other matters to occupy his attention.

Newstead offered a welcome retreat from importuning women. He had tried half-heartedly to break with Caroline, telling her that they must make a united effort to bring back sanity to their relationship. 'This dream, this delirium of two months must pass away' had been his final admonition to her.

Carolinne was not easily rebuffed, however, and she despatched one of her pages to Newstead with letters filled with her usual effusive endearments.

The possibility of an elopement had been discussed between them quite seriously not long before, and although Byron had by now realized the extreme foolishness of such a step, she still had not abandoned hope of it, and it still amused him to refer to it.

His delight in London Society was too strong for him to remain more than a short time at Newstead, and by the middle of June he was back in his lodgings at 8, St James' Street, where he resumed the mantle of being the most eligible bachelor in Mayfair.

By now he had added another confidante to his select company of older women who flattered him and discreetly encouraged his indiscretions without embarrassing him with their forwardness. Lady Melbourne remained the chief recipient of his confidences, but he now found a more openly seductive admirer in Lady Oxford.

Lady Oxford was, of course, a close friend of Caroline's, for she had taken the younger woman under her wing when Caroline had first entered Society. This flamboyant and rather absurd woman had the worst possible reputation, and when she and Caroline had first become intimates, William had warned his wife against such undesirable friendships.

Lady Oxford was forty. Formerly a great beauty and still very attractive, she had progressed from bed to bed in Society, including that of the Prince Regent, and it was therefore flattering for Byron to find himself being invited to join a club that could boast such distinguished members.

Caroline, with her usual flair for jumping to the wrong conclusions, especially where Byron was concerned, assumed that Lady Oxford was merely his friend, and remained friendly with Lady Oxford herself. She knew Byron to be a snob and assumed that his association with Lady Oxford was due in part to his desire to meet the Prince Regent.

He soon discovered that one of the chief advantages of being on intimate terms with Lady Oxford was that she invited him to stay at her country house, Eywood, in Herefordshire, where the hospitality was lavish. At Eywood he could enjoy good food, aristocratic company and as much sexual gratification as he might require. She was still on intimate terms with Caroline, but he soon discovered that when he was staying in her house she had no intention of sharing him with anyone. Caroline dared not therefore intrude upon them.

Caroline herself retired to Brocket Hall, accompanied by William. His political career was not going well and he had lost his seat in the House on account of his support of Catholic emancipation. Caroline gave him little comfort and no consideration. She could think of nothing else but Byron, and was either filled with moments of elation, when she believed that he might yet alter his mind and agree to elope with her, or moods of the deepest despair, when she felt that he no longer loved her.

William felt genuinely sorry for her. He still could not find it in himself to treat this Byron affair seriously, although by now he was forced to consider the possibility that she had been unfaithful to him. His estimate of Byron was that the man was a rake without a moral to his name, and one who took a delight in seducing married women and then abandoning them. Caroline, he well knew, had not a hope of holding him, so that her threats of an elopement could be ignored. But although her obtuseness and her tantrums were exhausting to William, he could not bear to see her so unhappy, and he was still ready to offer her his shoulder to cry upon whenever she felt in need of comfort. His love for her was still strong, his loyalty unshaken. In a way this only increased her resentment. She would have respected him the more had he ordered her out of the house and told her to join her lover.

Brocket was an estate which had been bought by William's grandfather in the middle of the eighteenth century. There was a deer park and excellent facilities for riding. Both William and Caroline were devoted to horses and both were accomplished riders. Riding brought to each of them a sense of freedom and of release from their worries. Both were happy in the country and William, in particular, was always ready to desert the London scene for the peace of the Hertfordshire countryside.

June and July passed in relative tranquillity, but William had long since learnt to fear any prolonged periods in which Caroline appeared peaceful and relaxed. She was only conserving her strength for another emotional outbreak.

One day at the end of July, Byron was entertaining his friend, Hobhouse, in his rooms in St James' when they were disturbed by a commotion outside in the street. Someone began hammering on the door, and a small crowd collected to see what was going on.

When the door was opened, the figure of a young man, heavily muffled in thick clothes, was revealed. On closer inspection the caller proved to be Caroline, in one of her disguises. She was brought in, and when the absurd outer garments were removed she was seen to be wearing her page-boy uniform. Byron tried to reason with her and she was finally persuaded to go into the bedroom and to change into the clothes of one of his female servants. But having done so, she refused to join him in the sitting room.

The faithful Hobhouse ordered her to leave immediately. She then emerged from the bedroom, took up a knife and made as if to stab herself. Byron seized hold of her and took the knife away from her. Hobhouse was then able to persuade her to return to his own lodgings. Later he escorted her in a coach to the house of one of her friends. But she only consented to do this if Byron promised to see her again before he left London.

Hobhouse was shocked by the whole incident and felt that the time had come for a complete separation. He was still frightened lest Caroline might persuade Byron to elope with her. Byron, despite his avowed hatred of Caroline's 'scenes', was still capable of enjoying them. His vanity would not allow her to end the affair. He would tell Caroline that they must never see each other again and then would consent to see her a short time later.

A fortnight after her invasion of his rooms she sent him, as a souvenir, a curl of her pubic hair. This was a typically Carolean gesture, suggesting daring, intense passion and a defiance of convention. Admittedly a lock of hair was then very much in favour as a present from a young lady to her swain, but only very seldom was it one cut from this particular part of her anatomy.

Accompanying this present was a letter which read, 'I asked you not to send blood but Yet do—because if it means love I like to have it. I cut the hair too close and bled much more than you need—do not you the same and pray put not scissors points near where *quei capelli* grow—sooner take it from the arm or wrist—pray be careful...' The letter was signed, 'Your wild antelope.'

Whether or not Byron answered this letter, and sent his own souvenir in return, was not revealed. It was the sort of correspondence which would have appealed to him, with its melodramatic overtones and vows signed with blood. But coming as it did, so soon after the scene in his lodgings, the wording of the letter must have convinced him of something of which he had been becomingly increasingly aware during the summer. Caroline was a little mad, and there was no knowing what she might do next. She had already injured herself with a knife, and later with a pair of scissors. It could only be a matter of time before she threatened him with a knife and possibly with scissors as well. A great lover is seldom a great hero when his safety is threatened by a discarded mistress, and Byron had no stomach for shedding his blood in such a cause.

By no stretch of the imagination could he believe that Lady Oxford, for example, would ever behave in such a fashion. He had by now been a literary lion in Society for three months, and was growing tired of the extravagant attentions of his frustrated young female admirers. He realized that there would be no peace for him so long as he and Caroline remained in London. He must leave himself and do his best to persuade Caroline to leave also—and the further away from him she went, the better that would be for both of them.

Henrietta had already come to the same conclusion. Her aim throughout this summer was to persuade Caroline to remain with William at Brocket and there to try and rebuild her marriage. It was clear that the Lamb family were by now united against her, and Henrietta feared that it might not be so very long before William's own patience became exhausted. His forbearance was certainly remarkable and could hardly be expected to last.

Poor Henrietta was never so ineffectual as when the need was for a cool head and a tactful approach. Now she fluttered distractedly from one party to another, trying to soothe Caroline, trying to persuade Byron to give her up altogether, and trying to stem the growing animosity that was building up at Melbourne House over Caroline's wild and immodest behaviour.

She succeeded with none of them. Caroline would not listen to reason and Byron remained indifferent to her pleas. He had never had a very high opinion of Henrietta, whom he nicknamed 'Lady Blarney'. Her agitation merely irritated him and he snubbed her. As for the Lambs at Melbourne House, their opinion of Caroline could in no way be altered. They looked upon Caroline as a tiresome, vindictive little hussy. They made it clear to Henrietta that they considered the fault was partly hers for never having controlled her daughter.

Matters were finally brought to a head by Caroline herself, who precipitated a family crisis by staging the biggest tantrum of her married life. So big, in fact, that even Lord Melbourne became involved and was reduced to creating a scene himself.

The incident was suitably described by Henrietta in a succession of letters to Lord Granville, in which she poured out the whole story and begged for his advice.

The first reference to the catastrophe was contained in a scribbled note which Lord Granville received from her on the morning of 12 August.

'Oh G!' it began, 'Caroline is gone! It is too horrible. She is not with Byron, but where she is, God knows!'

A full description of the incident reached him the same evening. It began, 'Oh G., I have suffered terribly today, but she is found.'

He was thus prepared for a description of an incident that caused the physical collapse of at least three of the parties involved, whilst those on the fringe of the catastrophe suffered mental contusions and abrasions.

Quite early on the morning of the 12th, Henrietta left her home in Cavendish Square and set out for Melbourne House, in Whitehall. Her purpose was to try and persuade Caroline to leave London. The plan was that Caroline would first of all accompany her mother to the Bessborough villa at Roehampton, where they would shortly be joined by William. They would then all depart for the Bessborough estate in Ireland, where they would spend the remainder of the summer.

Henrietta had set out in some trepidation, because she expected Caroline to prove difficult. Her worst fears were soon confirmed.

Caroline was in a mood and received her mother with pursed lips and a frown. They began to argue acrimoniously, and in the middle of this Lord Melbourne entered the room and took it upon himself to reprimand his daughter-in-law for her childish behaviour. Caroline promptly lost her temper and answered him back so rudely that Henrietta fled in search of Lady Melbourne, whilst Lord Melbourne gazed at her in mounting indignation.

When the two women came hurrying back up the stairs they were passed by Caroline and then stopped at the top by Lord Melbourne, who was shouting to the servants that Caroline must not be allowed to go out.

Caroline, however, was too quick for them and she ran out into Whitehall before anyone could prevent her. She then disappeared.

When the normally placid and undemonstrative Lord Melbourne had been calmed down, he was able to explain what had happened after Henrietta had left the room in search of assistance. Caroline

126

had rounded on him and told him to mind his own business. She warned him that she would leave the house and go to Byron.

According to Henrietta's rather garbled account, Lord Melbourne had 'bid her go and be —'. And had then added sarcastically that hers was but an empty threat as Byron would never take her, even if she offered herself to him.

This parting shot was altogether too near the mark for Caroline. She ran screaming from the room, down the stairs, out of the house and into Whitehall.

Henrietta summoned her coach and, in her own words, 'drove up and down Parliament Street in every direction' in search of her missing daughter. But Caroline was nowhere to be found. London had swallowed her up, and there seemed little that could be done apart from raising the hue-and-cry, or starting to drag the Thames for the body.

However, good sense prevailed in the end and Henrietta and Lady Melbourne went round to Byron's rooms to ask his advice, and to find out whether he was sheltering Caroline. Their dramatic story filled him with alarm, and he promised to do what he could.

No news was forthcoming for the rest of the day, and that evening Henrietta went to dine with Caroline's faithful admirer, Hart, and to pour out her story in his sympathetic ear. While at dinner a package was brought by messenger from Byron. The package contained letters for Henrietta from Caroline, in which she told her mother that she was leaving Byron for ever and that no one would ever see her again.

The package had been given to Byron by the hackney coachman whom Caroline had employed for her escape. Fortunately Byron, showing more common sense than anyone else had done during the emergency, had at once seized hold of the man and by means of threats and bribes had forced him to drive to the address at which he had previously deposited Caroline.

This proved to be a surgeon's house in Kensington, where Caroline had been granted shelter after telling a piteous tale of how she had been cruelly rejected by her loved ones and forced to flee from them for ever. Byron entered the house, told the surgeon that Caroline was his sister and then half carried and half dragged her to the coach. He then drove her to the Bessborough home in Cavendish Square.

Here she showed no signs of repentance, and it was only with difficulty that Henrietta later persuaded her to return to Melbourne House.

127

In due course Henrietta learnt the full story of what had happened. Caroline, it seemed, had run out of the house and up Pall Mall, where she hid herself in a chemist's shop. She sold a ring in order to raise some money and then hired the hackney coach and told the coachman to drive her to the first turnpike off the stones. Then she pledged another ring, an opal one, for twenty guineas, for the purpose of travelling to Portsmouth. Here she planned to board the first ship she saw and sail in it for whatever foreign port it might be bound. She had actually gone so far as to book her seat in the stage coach for Portsmouth before Byron caught up with her and took her home.

Henrietta invariably collapsed on these occasions, and this happened now. 'I have for the last hour spit up so much blood,' she wrote to Lord Granville, 'that I think some little vessel must have broken...I do no good to anyone, and am grown rather a burthen than a pleasure to all those I love most.'

Caroline remained stubbornly unrepentant. She continued to resist all efforts made to persuade her to leave London. She plunged herself into the wildest displays of grief over the trouble she had caused and the injury she had done to her beloved mother. At one moment she was declaring that if anything happened to Henrietta she would destroy herself at once; and at the next proclaiming that if Byron moved out of London she would either go with him or else flee alone.

Finally she played her trump card. She could not possibly travel now to Ireland, she declared, nor even to Roehampton, for she had just made the discovery that she was pregnant.

'She has declar'd she believes herself to be breeding,' wrote Henrietta distractedly to Lord Granville, adding, 'the travelling will certainly make her miscarry, and W. is so anxious to have another Child that she has nearly persuaded him that it will be best not to go.'

However at this point Henrietta found an unexpected ally who was willing to try and bring Caroline to her senses. Her housekeeper at Cavendish Square, a Mrs Peterson, took it upon herself to upbraid Caroline for the distress that she was causing to her mother.

'Cruel and unnatural as you have behaved, you surely do not wish to be the Death of your Mother,' she wrote. 'I am sorry to say you last night nearly succeeded in doing so. She had fallen in a fit at the bottom of her Carriage, and with the utmost difficulty her footmen got her out...She was perfectly senseless and her poor mouth drawn all to one side and as cold as Marble we was all distracted even her footmen cried out *shame* on you for alas you have exposed

128

yourself to all London—you are the talk of every groom and footman about Town.'

Caroline was overcome with remorse. She wrote to her father, admitting that she had been responsible for her mother's breakdown, and assuring him that she was prepared to go with the family to Roehampton. However, she declared that she could not possibly leave for Ireland for at least ten days 'for particular reasons, and I am certain my nerves are so shaken, and I have been so ill these three days, that to hurry off immediately will make me quite so.'

But she added that if, as she feared, her dear father distrusted her motives for remaining for ten more days in England, then she begged him to 'lock me up if you choose during that time, but do not refuse this to your own child, your only daughter, who with all her faults, loves you dearly'.

The purpose of this ten days of rest was not apparent. She swore that she never wished to see Byron again, but could not travel immediately. She could be very devious at times, and there was no knowing what she was planning at this moment.

To her mother she wrote, 'I do promise, upon my honour, and soul, that at all events, whether you grant it or not, I will not see Lord Byron...Trust in me at least at this moment; all deceptions are over now; you may see my whole heart if you please.'

It was not easy to refuse Caroline anything when she was in this mood of pitiful contrition, and she was allowed to stay on in England for a further ten days.

Byron had so far come reasonably well out of this tumultuous affair, but now he reverted to type. First of all he assured Lady Melbourne, in one of their intimate chats, that he was happy to sever all connections with Caroline, and that in truth he never wished to see her again.

But when Caroline, despite all her protestations of never wishing to see him again, began writing passionate letters to him, he was quite willing to answer them—*not* with an ultimatum that their association must now be ended, but with further avowals of his love. And he offered the excuse that any outward signs of coldness that he might now show her would only be for the purpose of deceiving her relations.

The truth of the matter was that although he did not want her, he was reluctant to give her up. Her sensational behaviour, and her wild flight to Portsmouth, bound for an unknown destination across the seas, had become the talk of London, and it was gratifying to know that he was the cause of it all.

He knew Caroline well enough to guess just what was going on in her mind. He had only to crook his little finger and she would come running back to him. Not even his father, Mad Jack, nor his ancestor, The Wicked Lord, had enjoyed such a triumph of feminine capitulation.

The whole matter might yet have been brought to a satisfactory conclusion if only William had been prepared to take some positive action. But William still refused to deal severely with his wife. He could not believe that she had any real love for Byron, or any real intention of running away with him. He therefore convinced himself that it was all just another example of her tempestuous nature and chronic wrong-headedness.

He suspected, also, that the birth of a son who was mentally retarded, as well as two miscarriages, must have had an adverse effect on her mentally as well as physically. Perhaps he realized that not much more would be required to produce a state bordering on insanity, and so he shrank from taking any harsh steps to restrain her.

All his instincts warned him that her story of pregnancy was just a pretence—another of her childish tricks to get what she wanted—but he dared not take the risk. If he insisted on her travelling immediately to Ireland, and she did suffer a further miscarriage as a result, he would feel that he alone was to blame.

Of the other interested parties in the Caroline affair, Lord Bessborough, as was his wont, did nothing, and Lord Melbourne, after his one outburst of temper, relapsed into his former state of lethargy and turned his attention once again to gambling and alcohol. He contented himself with giving the Prince Regent a full acount of the explosion which had taken place in Melbourne House. Caroline, he said, was driving him mad, and Byron was driving the rest of his family mad, for they seemed unable to resist the fellow. His wife was fascinated by him.

'I never heard of such a thing in my life,' said the Prince, 'taking the Mothers for confidantes!'

Throughout the year it had become increasingly apparent to Byron that his financial problems could only be solved by the sale of Newstead, or by marriage—or by both. Newstead was a substantial property and might be expected to command a good price. His own handsomeness and fame could be expected to command a similarly high figure in the marriage market. In August Newstead was offered for auction. He rejected the bids made, however, and on the following day a Lancashire lawyer offered the very large sum of £140,000 for the whole property. The offer was accepted, and almost immediately was in part withdrawn.

Byron remained outwardly unperturbed, but inwardly he was becoming increasingly depressed. He realized now that the sale of Newstead was imperative if he were to remain solvent. His debtors were beginning to harass him and his pleasant way of life was now seriously threatened by them.

Once before, when he had become depressed by his mounting debts, he had declared that marriage or suicide offered the only solutions to the problem. 'I suppose it will end in my marrying a *Golden Dolly* or blowing my brains out.'

Now that he was famous and idolized, the idea of blowing his brains out no longer appealed to him. His thoughts turned once again to the possibilities of marriage, and the question of approaching Annabella occupied his mind.

But it was still high summer, and he felt that such mundane matters could be shelved for the time being. Society was already beginning to migrate to Cheltenham, there to gossip and take the waters, and he decided to follow. At Cheltenham he could enjoy himself with Lady Oxford, who was already staying there. Amongst other advantages, Cheltenham was a long way from London—and from Caroline.

As for Caroline herself, London or Roehampton were no longer of any interest to her once the prey had flown. She learned that Byron had left for Cheltenham, but saw no sinister purpose in his departure, other than that he needed a holiday.

She had no suspicions about his relationship with Lady Oxford, nor of his intentions towards Miss Milbanke. It never entered her head that he could be attracted by someone as demure as Annabella.

When the question of a holiday in Ireland was raised once again, she agreed to the suggestion. She also announced that her fears of pregnancy had proved groundless.

There being no further obstacles in the path of true repentance, she arrived in Ireland on 7 September, cheerful and seemingly in her right mind. It was as though Byron did not exist, and the attempted escape to Portsmouth had never taken place.

But once in Ireland, where she had gone for rest and recuperation, Caroline soon displayed all the symptoms of the latent hysteria which had been building up inside her over the previous six months. Outwardly she appeared neither heart-broken nor depressed. Indeed she entered into the social whirl of the community with an exaggerated bravado and became the life and soul of every party which she attended. If dancing were suggested, then Caroline danced with more vigour than anyone else in the room, threw herself with untiring exuberance into Irish jigs, and tossed her seductive glances into every corner of the room.

But these moods of gaiety—whether forced or quite spontaneously created—were followed by tantrums or moments of deepest melancholy. At one moment she might be screaming in frustration on the floor, and at the next be lying crouched in a corner, a pathetic bundle of pathos, the tears streaming down her cheeks.

At one moment her fears would be for her own broken heart and her longing for her absent lover. At the next they would be for the husband whom she had betrayed, or else for the beloved mother whose health she had ruined. But whatever the cause, they flowed unrestrainedly.

She quickly exhausted those who were with her; Caroline vivacious and excited was often more exhausting than Caroline angry or depressed.

She remained basically a very unhappy young woman, the force of whose emotions was gradually destroying her mental stability, and there was little that could be done to halt this process of disintegration.

The main burden of her hysteria fell upon her husband. A strong man physically, and one whose own emotions were strictly controlled, he yet suffered from the wear and tear of trying to calm her when she was hysterical or plunged in melancholy and self-pity. He should have disciplined her from the outset, as her mother should have done, but now it was too late. Nor could there be any real hope for her in the future. Byron had become an obsession, and Byron had no intention whatever of doing more than trifle with her affections.

To William Caroline's obsessional love was something beyond his comprehension. All he could do was to watch his much loved wife tear herself slowly to pieces. He realized sadly that there was an element of exhibitionism in her displays of wifely affection and that she was never so loving towards him as when someone was watching. Their neighbours were much impressed by the touching little cameos of domestic fidelity, and whispered to each other that William Lamb was indeed a lucky fellow to have so devoted a wife.

There were times when Caroline was genuinely overwhelmed with a sense of guilt. She knew that she was treating William shamefully and wounding him deeply. But these feelings would be obliterated by a sudden surge of passion for Byron, which overcame all other emotions. Then she would become drugged with exhilaration at the thought that she might yet recapture him for herself alone.

The estate of Kildalton, in southern Ireland, had been conferred upon Sir John Ponsonby by Oliver Cromwell, and he had named it Bessborough as a tribute to his second wife, Elizabeth.

Not far away was Lismore Castle, the property of Caroline's cousin, the Marquis of Hartington—and Hart still cherished his old love of Caroline. It was September and the warmth of summer was still in the air. There was much entertaining, much going to and fro, much friendship and—for Caroline—some moments of rest and happiness.

Henrietta was already looking much stronger and William threw himself determinedly into the outdoor activities of the Irish community. Strong men in good health and with sound digestions usually sleep soundly and eat heartily, even when they are worried and depressed, and William now did both.

Caroline could never understand this, and she felt it showed lack of sympathy. It was her habit to pick at her food and declare that she was tormented by indigestion, and to bemoan the fact that she never enjoyed a full night's sleep. Indeed she would wake William up in the middle of the night to tell him of her discomforts, and then would fall asleep again once he was thoroughly roused. During the daytime she hated him to be out of her sight, and when he proposed to spend a few days in Dublin she accused him of deserting her in her moment of need. William sadly abandoned his trip to Dublin, and for three nights in succession he stayed awake until daybreak, holding Caroline's hand and comforting her.

She had arrived in Ireland looking miserably ill, so that even Hary-O had been moved to pity at the sight of her. Although she had always been irritated by Caroline's behaviour, she was yet fond of her.

When Henrietta and Caroline had first arrived, Hary-O noted that Henrietta had made a remarkable recovery from her illness and that she looked stout and well, but that Caroline looked quite the opposite.

'She is worn to the bone, as pale as death and her eyes starting

133

out of her head. She seems indeed in a sad way, alternately in tearing spirits and in tears. I hate her character, her feelings and herself when I am away from her, but she interests me when I am with her, and to see her poor, careworn face is dismal, in spite of reason and speculation upon her extraordinary conduct. She appears to me in a state very little short of insanity, and my aunt says that at times it has been decidedly so.'

Nine

Byron - The Betrayal

Whilst so much was going on in Ireland and Caroline was growing ever more unbalanced and distraught, the cause of all this commotion was enjoying himself in England—chiefly in the company of Lady Oxford.

Byron's first action, when he learnt that Caroline had left the country, was to breathe a sigh of relief and then to tell his friends, and especially his women friends, how glad he was to be rid of her.

His second notion was to sit down and write a long letter to Caroline, telling her how much he missed her.

His duplicity was really remarkable. When in company, enjoying the adulation of Society at Cheltenham, he played the part of the irresistible lover who had successfully freed himself from a tedious devotee. But once he turned his attention to letter-writing, he became the magnanimous but honourable lover, whose sad duty it was to bid a much-loved mistress a long farewell—by letter, of course and not in person—and to assure her of his own distress. Her memory would ever remain green.

Yet in a strange and contradictory way this was true. By now he hated the sight of Caroline, but the thought of her could still arouse moments of nostalgia. Selfish, and extravagantly vain, Byron was nevertheless kind-hearted—and soft hearted as well. The thought of this pathetic girl, so vulnerable and so weak, aroused in him a sense of compassion which overcame him in his moments of loneliness, but which he quickly forgot when in the company of other women.

Of him Caroline was later to write, with surprising insight into his frailties, that his seeming infidelity and disloyalty could be rationally explained. 'Like the wheels of a watch, the chain of his affection might be said to unwind from the absent in proportion as they twined themselves around the favourite of the moment, and being extreme in all things, he could not sufficiently devote himself

135

to the one without taking from the other all that he had given.'

'Our love is not given,' wrote Kipling many years later, 'but only lent.' Nor does it come from a bottomless store. There are those who have just so much love to give and therefore must take some back if the need arises to love someone else.

In nothing was his duplicity more clearly revealed than in a letter which he wrote to Caroline in Ireland at a moment when he had remarked unashamedly to Lady Melbourne that it was necessary to 'write all manner of absurdities to keep her quiet'. Yet this long letter which he wrote to her seems to evoke the very essence of romance. Reproduced in a miscellany of love letters of the world it could surely hold its own. Any romantically-minded girl, receiving a letter such as this, could not fail to be deeply moved by its sentiment and its seeming sincerity. It seems almost inconceivable that it was not written from the heart. It ran as follows:

'MY DEAREST CAROLINE,—If tears, which you know I am not apt to shed, if the agitation in which I parted from you, agitation which you must have perceived through the *whole* of this most *nervous* affair, did not commence until the moment of leaving you approached—if all I have said and done and am still but too ready to say and do, have not sufficiently proved what my real feelings are towards you, my Love, I have no other proof to offer. God knows I wish you happy, and when I quit you, or rather when you, from a sense of duty to your husband and your mother, quit me, you shall acknowledge the truth of what I again promise and vow, that no other, in word or deed, shall ever hold the place in my affection which is, and shall be, most sacred to you till I am nothing. I never knew till *that moment* the *madness* of my dearest and most beloved friend; I cannot express myself, this is no time for words, but I shall have a pride, a melancholy pleasure, in suffering what you yourself can scarcely conceive; for you do not know me. I am about to go out, with a heavy heart; because my appearing this evening will stop any absurd story which the event of to-day may give rise to. Do you now think me *cold* and *stern* and *artful*? Will even *others* think so? Will your mother even—that mother to whom we must indeed sacrifice much, more, much more than she shall ever know or imagine? Promise not to love you! Ah, Caroline, it is past promising. But I shall attribute all concessions to the proper motive, and never cease to feel all that you have already witnessed; and more than can ever be known but to my own heart—perhaps to yours. May God protect,

136

forgive and bless you. Ever and ever, more than ever,

Your most attached,
BYRON.'

The effect of such a letter on a girl already hoplessly in love could scarcely be more calculated to rekindle hope and to sustain blind adoration.

It surely cannot have been written with tongue in cheek. Yet at this time Byron was in the midst of a sexual association with Lady Oxford and was simultaneously making tentative plans in his mind for a proposal of marriage to Annabella Milbanke. All that one can think is that, at the moment when he wrote to Caroline, he was plunged in a mood of nostalgia for the past.

She was out of sight but not yet out of mind. He remembered her gentler qualities, the warmth of her affection, her sweetness in tranquillity, her elfin charm. For a time, a very short time, he saw her through a golden haze of romantic time remembered.

Then a flood of letters, some childish and some hysterical descended upon him and brought him back to reality—and to the memory of Caroline in her moments of frenzy. And love died.

More and more the question of marriage occupied Byron's mind. Lady Oxford was proving delightfully acquiescent, but the winter was coming on, and Newstead remained unsold. His first task was to make a final break with Caroline. His second was to spy out the land in so far as Annabella Milbanke was concerned. He had no intention whatever of playing the obsequious suitor. Someone would have to sound her out first, and who better than his confidante and Annabella's aunt, the ever-sympathetic Lady Melbourne? And if anything should come of it, why then Lady Melbourne would be to all intents his aunt as well. The fancy tickled him immensely.

But first Caroline.

He wrote to Lady Melbourne, 'You will not regret to hear that I wish this to end, and it certainly shall not be renewed on my part. It is not that I love another, but loving at all is quite out of my way; I am tired of being a fool...'

In a subsequent letter he had to correct this statement somewhat, because he wished Lady Melbourne to act as his emissary with his proposal of marriage. He *did* love another—or rather he was in the process of convincing himself that he might be falling in love with another.

'...there was, and is one whom I wished to marry, had not this

137

affair intervened...' Lady Melbourne's eyes must have widened when she read this statement, and widened still further when she read on. 'The woman I mean is Miss Milbanke...I know little of her and have not the most distant reason to suppose that I am at all favourite in that quarter. But I never saw a woman whom I *esteemed* so much.'

How did one equate such a statement with his many cynical observations about women and about marriage? Had he not commented that the older a wife the better, so that she might be helped towards heaven? Had he not declared that in the end he would be forced either to marry some golden dolly, or else commit suicide? And now he was seriously planning marriage to someone who was young—and whom he *esteemed*.

Lady Melbourne was surprised, to say the least; but her surprise was tempered by relief. If Byron was seriously contemplating marriage with Annabella, then that would be the end of the Caroline affair. For Annabella was *not* the type of young woman who would permit philandering after the marriage; nor one who would condone an indiscreet association with Caroline before it. Indeed Annabella was probably more capable of dealing with both Byron *and* Caroline than anyone else who knew them both. She was a very determined young woman.

Even so, Lady Melbourne was nonplussed. Was Byron really serious?

He replied to her query by stating that he admired Annabella because 'she is a clever woman, an amiable woman, and of high blood, for I have still a few Norman and Scotch inherited prejudices on the last score, were I to marry. As to *love,* that is done in a week (provided the lady has a reasonable share); besides, marriage goes on better with esteem and confidence than romance, and she is quite pretty enough to be loved by her husband without being so glaringly beautiful as to attract too many rivals.'

And earlier he had remarked, 'I never risk *rivalry* in anything.'

Childe Harold, it seemed, was dead. His place had been taken by a materialistic suitor who was none too sure of himself.

He could not rid his mind of the memories of Caroline, and what he was saying—or what Lady Melbourne suspected that he was trying to say—was that the best way out of his predicament was to marry someone whom he quite liked, whom he found quite physically attractive, and who was rich.

He was not sure of himself, however, and he was none too sure of Annabella. His tactics therefore were to persuade Lady Melbourne to approach Annabella on his behalf; and to safeguard any possible loss of face by pretending that he did not really mind if her answer were 'no'. The whole thing could then be laughed at in retrospect. He would like to marry Annabella, he told Lady Melbourne 'if only for the pleasure of calling you *aunt!*'

To prove his disinterest, he withdrew to Cheltenham and entered upon an affair with an Italian songstress who had black eyes, a not very white skin and was fond of her husband, which made the seduction of her more exciting than if she had been unattached. But his heart was never really in the contest, and his old fastidiousness revealed itself in his criticism of her personal habits.

'I only wish she did not swallow so much supper,' he complained to Lady Melbourne, who was kept informed of this new affair just to ensure that she realized that he was still happily playing the part of Casanova. 'A woman should never be seen eating or drinking, unless it be *lobster salad* and *champagne*, the only truly feminine and becoming viands.'

Annabella seemed really to be little more than an afterthought— an amusing whim. 'If your niece is obtainable, I should prefer her; if not, the very first woman who does not look as if she would spit in my face...'

Lady Melbourne approached the matter somewhat deviously. First of all she asked Annabella how she saw her ideal husband. Annabella's description of this paragon did not compare with Byron on a single point.

'He must have consistent principles of Duty,' she wrote, 'I require a freedom from suspicion, and from *habitual* ill-humour—also an equal tenor of affection towards me, not that violent attachment which is susceptible of sudden increase or diminution from trifles...'

Somewhat discouraged, Lady Melbourne tried again. How would her niece view a proposal of marriage from Lord Byron?

Annabella took several days to answer. Her ruling, when given, was that of a judge in the High Court giving a prisoner a suspended sentence. Firstly, she chided Byron for his precipitous action.

'He is inclined to open his heart unreservedly to those whom he believes *good*, even without the preparation of much acquaintance. He is extremely humble towards persons whose character he respects, and to them he would probably confess his errors.'

Annabella had a curious gift for summing up Byron more accurately than any other of his acquaintance.

Her conclusion, when giving judgement, was that his offer must be rejected. But she added that she yet had no wish to withdraw 'from an acquaintance that does me honour and is capable of imparting so much rational pleasure'.

Thus her reply was couched in the terms of a politician planning to make a deal with a difficult opponent. The answer was 'no', but the door was left open for further negotiation.

The news was passed on to Byron, who found himself quite out of his depth. He prided himself on being a sophisticated man of the world and he was being outmanoeuvred by a woman of transparent unworldliness. His vanity was seriously wounded, but in order to save face he had to resort once again to his jocular air of complete indifference. And he wrote to Lady Melbourne a casual little note in which he referred patronizingly to Annabella as 'the amiable *Mathematician*' and added, 'I thank you again for your efforts with my Princess of *Parallelograms,* who has puzzled you more than the Hypotenuse...Her proceedings are quite rectangular, or rather we are two parallel lines prolonged to infinity side by side, but never to meet.'

This concluded the first round in their contest, and there could be little doubt as to who had won it.

It was necessary for him to revive his self-esteem, and the best place to do so was at Eywood, with Lady Oxford. Here he was able to resume his role of the irresistible lover, and to convince himself that he was doing a kindness to a middle-aged matron.

Byron's delight in tossing off worldly epigrams was particularly applied to women, and his summary of the Lady Oxford affair was, 'A woman is only grateful for her *first* and *last* conquests. The first of poor dear Lady Oxford's was achieved before I entered on this world of care; but the last, I do flatter myself, was reserved for me, and a *bonne bouche* it was.'

Now that he had been rejected by Annabella, Byron was in a mood to revenge himself both upon Caroline and her mother. He had always resented Henrietta. She had made a fool of him at the outset when she had told him that he had no chance with Caroline because she was in love with someone else, and so had aroused his interest. Now Henrietta and Caroline must be punished. They must be made to look foolish when the news reached them that he was planning to get married.

He had no intention of telling Caroline the news himself. His devious mind preferred to 'leak' the information through a third party; and once again he decided to make use of Lady Melbourne.

Caroline was in Ireland. He was determined to make the final break before she returned to England. His aim was to end the whole affair so abruptly—and if necessary so brutally—that she would never pester him again.

On the subject of mother and daughter he wrote to Lady Melbourne with feminine malice. 'It is an odd thing to say, but I am sure Lady B. will be a little provoked if I am the first to change...and doubtless will expect her daughter to be adored (like an Irish lease) for a term of 99 years. I say it again, that happy as she must and will be to have it broken off *anyhow,* she will hate me if I don't break my heart; now is it not so? Laugh—but answer me truly.'

Lady Melbourne no doubt laughed and answered him truly.

Later on he wrote, 'I mean (*entre nous,* dear Machiavel) to play off Lady Oxford against her, who would have no objection *perchance,* but she dreads scenes, and has asked me not to mention that we have met, to C. or that I am going to Eywood.'

His tactics demanded that Caroline should learn of his affair with Lady Oxford without knowing that he was at Eywood, where she was quite capable of bombarding him with letters or even of appearing quite suddenly and uninvited. 'You can make as much use of the incident of our acquaintance as you like with C. only do not say I am *there,* because she will possibly write, or do some absurd thing in that quarter, which will spoil everything.'

Lady Melbourne was happy to play her part in this intrigue, but she was wiser than Byron realized. She knew that he was protesting about Caroline too much, and did not trust him. He swore to her that he was having nothing more to do with Caroline and never communicated with her. 'I have not written these two months but twice...you were never more *groundlessly* alarmed.'

Needless to say he was still corresponding quite regularly with Caroline, who was mishandling the affair with her usual lack of tact. Sometimes she assured him that she was enjoying herself immensely in Ireland. At other times she declared that she was dying of a broken heart.

His letters to her ceased, however, soon after he had established himself at Eywood in October. This was all part of the plot, for he knew that if Caroline knew he was there, and then received no further letters from him, she would at once suspect what was going on.

It was not surprising that she reacted violently. Caroline was intensely loyal to her friends, and it came as a shock to her to discover that her friends were not loyal to her. William had warned her in the past against Lady Oxford and she had ignored these warnings. Now the truth was being brought home to her.

She was tormented by jealousy and wrote violent and semi-incoherent letters to both of them, either abusing them or else boasting of her indifference to the whole affair as she had now so many lovers of her own. And sometimes she was coy and playful.

'My dearest Aspasia,' she wrote to Lady Oxford (Aspasia having been a noted beauty in ancient Athens, who had been the mistress of Pericles), 'Only think, Byron is angry with me! He is tired of me, I see it by his letter. I will write no more—never tease him—never intrude upon him, only do you obtain his forgiveness.'

She was surprised and wounded when her letters to both parties remained unanswered. In her overwrought state she never realized that they might be laughing at her. Byron, left to himself, might well have been moved to pity by the unhappiness which Caroline's letters so clearly revealed, but Lady Oxford had no patience for such weakness, and he was happy to adopt her derisive attitude.

Meanwhile he kept Lady Melbourne informed of what was happening. 'Caroline threatens to revenge herself upon herself; this is her concern...The abhorrence I feel at part of her conduct, I will not trust myself to express. That feeling has come part of my nature; it has poisoned my future existence. I know not whom I may love, but to the latest hour of my life I shall hate that woman. Now you know my sentiments; they will be the same on my death-bed...I beg to be spared from meeting her until we be chained together in Dante's *Inferno*.'

This was the woman to whom he had written only a few short weeks before to beg that she would acknowledge 'the truth of what I again promise and vow, that no other, in word or deed, shall ever hold the place in my affection which is, and shall be, most sacred to you till I am nothing.'

Caroline continued to behave so irrationally that she forfeited the pity of those who were still her friends. Her madness continued to take the form of brazen provocation towards men, whilst she tried to convince herself, as well as others, that she was indeed a woman of irresistible allure. This was combined with a mounting obsession to revenge herself upon Byron, and she offered herself as the prize to any stalwart young man of her acquaintance who would challenge him to a duel.

142

Her letters reflected her alternating moods of madness and misery. Lady Melbourne wrote to Byron to tell him that she had received two letters from Caroline in one day, the first full of high spirits and idle chatter about parties and dances, the second telling of her broken heart.

With two such formidable opponents as Lady Oxford and Lady Melbourne in the Byron camp, Caroline had little hope of victory. The depths of cruelty to which Byron—under their influence—was now prepared to sink were revealed when she begged him to send her a lock of his hair. He sent one of Lady Oxford's instead, in a letter bearing Lady Oxford's crest, and then dined out on the story of how clever he had been.

It seemed now as if all his pent-up bitterness against women was being concentrated on Caroline. Memories of the young women whom he had loved in his boyhood and who had not loved him in return were still festering in his mind, and to him Caroline now typified them all.

'Do you think I could care anything for that lame boy?' Mary Chaworth had asked scornfully, and in his hearing. Now Caroline was being made to pay for that rejection.

On 9 November Lady Oxford received a letter from Caroline in which she demanded to know what was the situation in regard to Byron. He took it upon himself to furnish her with the answer: 'Lady Caroline—our affections are not in our power—mine are engaged. I love another...my opinion of you is entirely alter'd, and if I had wanted anything to confirm me, your Levities, your caprices and the mean subterfuges you have lately made use of while madly gay—of writing to me as if otherwise, would entirely have open'd my eyes. I am no longer yr. lover...'

It was a schoolboy's letter and revealed how immature he still remained. He could behave badly, but she was forbidden to do so. But if his aim was to wound her, it succeeded. Caroline and her mother were at this time staying at the Dolphin Hotel in Dublin, preparing for the crossing back to England. Caroline received the letter at the hotel and when she read it she seized a razor and made as if to cut her throat with it. Henrietta succeeded in grasping the razor by its blade, Caroline realized that she would cut her mother's hand if she continued to struggle, and she was forced to give in.

It may have been no more than one of her melodramatic gestures, but her declaration that she was dying of a broken heart and had no further wish to live was at least confirmed by her frail and wretched appearance. She was by now a walking skeleton, thin and haggard, with her eyes starting out of her head. On arrival in England she was forced to go to bed for a fortnight. It was remarkable that she had remained on her feet for so long.

Yet in all her desperation and moments of near madness, she retained one coherent desire. This was that she must see Byron once again. Pathetically she clung to the belief that she might yet win him back.

A further catastrophe was now looming up for her had she had the eyes to see it. Her husband, William Lamb, who had loved her so devotedly, who had always remained so loyal to her, and who had comforted her when she could not rest or sleep, was finding that the strain was becoming too great for him. His family had for long been advising him to separate from his neurotic and unstable wife, and he was now beginning to realize that he must do so.

He knew that he could not go on as he had done in the past. He was no longer a member of Parliament and his public career seemed at an end. He certainly could not hope to pick up the threads again whilst his private life was so chaotic. Yet he still hesitated to take the final step and enforce a separation from his wife. In desperation he took Caroline to Brocket, in the hope that the peace of the country-side there might have a quietening effect and help to restore her health.

Caroline now showed evidence of her astonishing stamina. Although still weak, she began riding wildly up the dangerous surface of the turnpike road and sent a message to Byron that this was to be her method of self-destruction. 'You have told me how foreign women revenge; I will show you how an Englishwoman can.'

Next she began to pester him for the return of her letters and then of her presents, having conceived the idea that he had probably given the latter to Lady Oxford. But when he asked her, in return, to send back his own letters, she refused.

Byron left Eywood at the end of November and returned to London, where he took rooms in Batt's Hotel, in Dover Street. The news which reached him now was sufficient to make him almost forget Caroline. His financial affairs were in a critical state. The down-payment on the sale of Newstead had still not been forthcoming and he was heavily in debt to both tradesmen and his friends. He became so depressed that he stayed in London for only a short time, during which he was engaged in the traditional Byron pastime of dodging creditors, and then went back to Eywood for Christmas.

It was here that he received an account of a Caroline extravaganza. Brocket was not far from the Hertfordshire village of Welwyn, and Caroline had always been most friendly with the villagers. She was kind to them and interested in their welfare. They, for their part, did not attach much importance to the gossip and scandal about her that filtered through to them from 'below stairs' at Brocket Hall.

They considered that Lady Caroline was a little weak in the head, but certainly did not hold this against her. The aristocracy were anyway notoriously eccentric.

There was a village band which played at local festivals and also in Brocket Park, together with a number of young village girls who danced and sang. These were rustic performers of limited talent, but eager to give of their best. Caroline organized them from time to time for local celebrations and Christmas activities.

Now she decided to co-opt them as part of her campagn to vilify her unfaithful lover, Lord Byron. Acting as author, producer, choirmistress, choreographer and costume designer, she decided to stage a remarkable one-night performance of execration, the purpose of which was to denounce his infamy to the world and to proclaim that her love for him was now irrevocably dead.

The highlight of the performance was to be the burning of her god in effigy, accompanied by the solemn ritual of casting all the sacred Byronic relics into the flames.

She composed a special incantation for the occasion, which was to be recited by one of her pages, whilst her chorus of village maidens, dressed in white and probably representing—in theory at least—the theme of spotless virginity, were to dance round the flames and join in the singing.

There is no evidence of what William thought of this extraordinary production, or what the simple villagers of Welwyn made of it. They certainly would not have been surprised to learn that she was planning to cast herself into the flames at the height of the ceremony. Nothing that Caroline did at Brocket surprised anyone.

This solemn ceremony of the renunciation of Lord Byron and all his evil works was duly staged on a December evening in Brocket Park, and carried off without a hitch. The bonfire was lit, the maidens danced, the shadows flickered and the villagers stared in wonderment at all that was going on.

It was all highly melodramatic, very childish, and rather pathetic.

Caroline lacked that sense of the absurd which was always one of Byron's more endearing qualities; and the fact that this performance of hers in the winter darkness enveloping Brocket Park was nearer farce than tragedy altogether escaped her. At the back of her mind was the thought that the news of it would soon reach Byron, and the belief that he would be deeply mortified to learn of it.

To this end her small page recited the following incantation on her behalf:

Is this Guy Fawkes you burn in effigy?
Why bring the traitor here? What is Guy Fawkes to me?
Guy Fawkes betrayed his country and his laws,
England revenged the wrong: his was a public cause.
But I have private cause to raise this flame,
Burn also these, and be their fate the same,
Rouge, feathers, flowers, and all those tawdry things,
Beside those pictures, letters, chains, and rings,
All made to lure the mind and please the eye,
And fill the heart with pride and vanity.
Burn, fire, burn, these glittering toys destroy,
While thus we hail the blaze with throats of joy.
Burn, fire, burn, while wondering boys exclaim,
And gold and trinkets glitter in the flame.
Ah, look not thus on me, so grave, so sad,
Shake not your heads, nor say the lady's mad.
Judge not of others, for there is but one
To whom the heart and feelings can be known.
Upon my youthful faults few censures cast,
Look to my future and forgive the past.
London, farewell; vain world, vain life, adieu!
Take the last tears I e'er shall shed for you.
Young tho' I seem, I leave the world for ever,
Never to enter it again; no, never, never!

Caroline sent a description of the performance to Byron, who passed it on to Lady Melbourne with the comment, 'Long account of a bonfire, full of yeomanry, pages, gold chains, baskets of flowers, herself, and all other folleries.'

As for the line 'Shake not your heads, nor say the lady's mad', his own belief was that Caroline was now possessed of 'the foul fiend

146

Flibbertigibbet, who presides over mopping and mowing'. He rightly assumed that the verse would find its way into the local newspaper, and he forecast that collectors of 'extraordinaries' would seize upon it as a choice item.

He was not displeased by the whole affair, however, because it was one in which he occupied the centre of the stage—even if only in effigy—and he was delighted to learn later that the letters of his which she had consigned so dramatically to the flames had in fact been only copies, as she had never had any intention of destroying the originals. He therefore surmised that she was as infatuated with him as she had ever been.

Her anti-Byron campaign was later taken a step further when she had the buttons on the livery of her pages inscribed with the legend *Ne crede Biron*—an amplification of his ancient family motto *Crede Biron*—trust in Byron.

Such acts were no more than minor pinpricks by which she tried to score off him. But there was a feeling developing in Society that Byron really had treated her very shabbily. It was not a view that was shared by Lady Melbourne or Lady Oxford, but by this Christmas of 1812 the Byronic cult in Mayfair was beginning to lose its appeal. There were those who were finding his ever-increasing vanity offensive, and the younger women began to resent the manner in which he fawned upon their elders but did not take very much notice of themselves. The reign of any literary lion tends anyway to be short.

Byron was quick to sense this growing hostility towards himself. He took note of the 'compassionate countesses' who were beginning to take the side of Caroline; and he observed that 'Lady W' thought him the greatest barbarian since the days of Bacchus.

'All who hate Lady Oxford—consisting of one half of the world, and all who abominate me—that is the other half—will tear the last rag of my tattered reputation into threads, filaments and atoms', was his comment to Lady Melbourne.

But although he enjoyed being thought wicked, he did not enjoy being unpopular, and his resentment against Caroline continued to increase. Yet even at this late stage in the affair, he could not quite rid himself of certain memories of her. He was still half in love with her.

Ten

Byron - The Ultimate Sin

January 1813 found Byron re-established at Eywood with Lady Oxford, enjoying the many amenities made available to him there and troubled only by doubts as to what mischief Caroline might be planning against him.

Caroline was in fact gainfully employed in the gentle art of forgery. She was a talented young woman who could sketch as well as write, and now she was devoting her attention to forging Byron's handwriting. This presented few problems. His letters to her were such treasured possessions, and had been read so often, that she knew every trick of his style as well as every flourish of his pen.

John Murray, Byron's publisher, had at this time a portrait of the poet which Caroline greatly coveted. In the first place it was an excellent likeness. In the second, she knew that Lady Oxford also admired the portrait and was hoping to be given it. Caroline therefore wrote a letter to Murray in Byron's handwriting, instructing him to hand over the portrait to her. This he did.

Byron was furious when he learned of this, and so was Lady Oxford. He wrote to Caroline demanding the return of the picture. He also sought the assistance of Lady Melbourne.

Caroline then resorted to blackmail. She was prepared to restore the picture, she told him, if he was prepared to meet her in return. Byron countered by saying that he was willing to see her, but only in the presence of Lady Oxford. Caroline had no intention of complying with such terms, and there the matter rested. She continued to write to him, but he ignored her letters.

By now he was quite infatuated with Lady Oxford and her practised skill at making love. One day Lady Oxford turned to him and said 'Have we not passed our last month like the gods of Lucretius?' And when he entered this in his journal he added the comment 'And so we had'. He commissioned a portrait of Lady Oxford for a sum of one hundred guineas, which he certainly could not afford and had little intention of paying.

Nothing came to mar this tranquil scene until Lady Oxford carried him off to London at the end of January. She felt the urge for high society and was anxious to renew several acquaintances. Byron was none too happy to go, and settled himself down in far less congenial surroundings at Bennet Street, just off his old haunt of St James'. His natural vanity made him reject the idea that Lady Oxford might be getting a little tired of him, but his innate suspicion of women made him wonder whether she might not be playing a double game.

He retaliated by making amorous advances to Lady Oxford's schoolgirl daughter, Lady Charlotte Harley. Lady Oxford was outraged, although there was little reason to suppose that her daughter had been. Their relationship began to deteriorate.

However he was back at Eywood in March, believing himself fully restored to his former place in her affections. At this point she made use of a gambit much favoured by Caroline when seeking to extricate herself from an awkward situation. Lady Oxford hinted to her lover that she was pregnant, but with no certain evidence as to who might be responsible.

Meanwhile Caroline continued to pester him with letters and gifts. When she sent him a ring with her deepest love, he promptly gave it to Lady Charlotte, on whom his eye still rested and about whom he noted that he could love her for ever, 'if she could always be only eleven years old, and whom I shall probably marry when she is old enough, and bad enough to be made into a modern wife.'

By now he was growing bored and discontented. He had lost all interest in his political career and had written to Augusta to tell her that he had 'no intention to "strut another hour" on that stage'. He had lost interest in the plight of the weavers of Nottingham.

Money remained his constant problem. Funds had to be conjured up from somewhere, and he found himself thinking once again of Annabella. Not only because she was rich. There was still something that intrigued him about her. A few months previously he had congratulated both himself and her 'on our mutual escape' and had tartly remarked of their marriage that it would have been 'but a *cold collation*, and I prefer hot suppers'.

Meanwhile Caroline kept demanding an interview and now Henrietta took up the cudgels on her daughter's behalf. Byron met and discussed the matter with her and played his aloof but not unreasonable man-of-the-world role: but he still refused to see Caroline.

William was now quite out of his depth in all that was going on,

F

and came to the conclusion that it was Byron who was being obtuse and not Caroline. 'Now this is really laughable,' he said angrily, 'If I speak to her, he is insulted; if I don't speak to her, she is insulted.'

By mid-summer an ominous calm had descended upon Caroline, who was clearly working up to another scene. Byron, meanwhile, suffered a considerable blow to his self-esteem when Lady Oxford and her husband announced that they were going abroad—and proceeded to do so without even bidding him a final farewell. He was hurt, and wrote to Lady Melbourne that he felt 'more *Carolinish* about her than I expected'—a curious observation under the circumstances.

It was at this moment that his half-sister, Augusta, re-appeared on the scene. He had invited her to visit him in London after the Oxfords had sailed, and they came together at the end of June. He felt depressed and in need of comfort. She also felt depressed, because of her dreary life at Newmarket, her wayward husband, her noisy children and her mounting debts. He had always been her 'Baby Byron' and now she felt more affectionate to him than she had ever done before. She sensed at once his mood of disillusion.

It was typical of him that he should have ignored her until things had begun to go badly for him, but once they met his old charm re-asserted itself and captivated her once more. She looked upon him with love and pride.

He looked upon her with new interest. She was now twenty-nine, and a typical Byron in her looks. She had the large eyes, the fine nose and the full and sensuous mouth. She had dark brown hair which clustered in curls around her temples, and her figure was full and rounded. But she was quite unconscious of her physical charms, and remained shy and reserved in all company except that of her 'Baby Brother'. When they were together they were as children— laughing, teasing each other and sharing each other's enthusiasms and prejudices. Byron's greatest need throughout his life had always been for affection. But his intimacy with women in the past had only been the cause of jealousies and frustrations. With Augusta everything was different.

Augusta was wholly without artifice or malice. She was simple, immature—and very sweet. She had much of Caroline's lack of worldliness, but had none of her instability and excitability. She knew nothing of the ways of men. In the years to come her naïvety was to prove her undoing.

Now she and Byron entered happily upon a period of intimate

friendship. He escorted her to dances and assemblies and took her to the theatre; but they were happiest when they were alone together, and it was no longer necessary for him to play a part.

He shortened her name to 'Gus', and then turned this into 'Goose' because she chattered away so much, often losing the thread of her conversation.

It was a period of tranquillity before the storm. The principal characters in the Byron drama were now moving towards a crisis, but they remained unaware of it. Augusta stayed happy and affectionate, enjoying the season and the rest which her stay in London afforded her. Annabella was calm and reticent, awaiting Byron's next move and quietly confident of what it would be. Caroline was lying low. But she was determined that sooner or later she would confront her lover and then win him back. She had regained a little weight and her energy remained seemingly inexhaustible. She was waiting to pounce.

Byron still wanted the return of his picture but was not prepared to pay the price which Caroline was asking for it—an intimate reunion in his room. His stipulation that Lady Oxford must be present at any such meeting was now no longer possible as she had left the country. In a letter to Lady Melbourne he wrote that he was happy to return to Caroline whatever letters and trinkets she might demand from him, declaring that she had finally worn out his wish to please her or displease her.

His patience was quite exhausted. 'The detestation, the utter abhorence I feel at part of her conduct I will neither shock you with nor trust myself express. That feeling has become part of my nature; it has poisoned my future existence. I know not whom I may love, but to the latest hour of my life I shall hate that woman.'

He had suggested that Lady Melbourne should take the place of Lady Oxford at any meeting that might be arranged between himself and Caroline, but finally agreed to see her alone, if this was what she wanted.

At this critical moment Caroline fell ill, possibly because she was consciously or subconsciously seeking to awaken his pity before he saw her.

This she succeeded in doing. Caroline ill or in tears had always aroused a feeling of compassion in him, just as it had always aroused compassion in William, for no one could look more lost and forlorn than she.

As a result of her illness Henrietta and Lady Melbourne brought

151

her up from Brocket for a short interview. Caroline's account of this meeting differed from that later given by Byron's friend, Thomas Medwin, in his *Conversation*.

'He asked me to forgive him,' she recorded. 'He looked sorry for me; he cried; I adored him still, but I felt as passionless as the dead may feel. Would I had died then! I should have died pitied and still loved by him; and with the sympathy of all.'

Dramatic death-scenes always played a prominent part in the many fantasies in which Caroline and Byron loved to indulge.

Having achieved little by this meeting, and having failed to expire either during it or immediately afterwards, Caroline determined that the situation called for an even more dramatic encounter. The threat of suicide must be pursued, and the stage set for a truly heart-rending performance that would focus Society's attention upon herself and cast Byron in the role of heartless villain. Her heated imagination toyed with numerous melodramatic incidents, but when she finally came to perform her act of hara-kiri, things did not work out quite as she had intended.

It took place at Lady Heathcote's ball on the night of 5 July. It was a small and select gathering, and amongst those present were Lady Melbourne, Lord Grey, Lady Rancliffe, Lady Ossulstone, Lady Westmoreland, Sheridan and other leading members of London Society. Byron was there, but unaccompanied by Augusta on this occasion. According to Caroline the spark which ignited the flame was the long-established rule between them that Caroline should never waltz in his presence.

Byron arrived late, his limp more in evidence than usual, and his habitual pallor more than usually accentuated. Caroline was already present, looking thin and haggard. Silence fell upon the room as the guests parted to allow them to come face to face.

At this moment the band began to play a waltz, and Lady Heathcote, sensing the tension in the air, hurried forward to Caroline and said, 'Come, Lady Caroline, you must begin.' Caroline replied angrily, 'Oh, yes, I am in a merry humour!'

She joined her partner and as she passed Byron she whispered, 'I conclude I may waltz *now*.'

'With everybody in turn,' he answered sourly. 'You always did it better than anyone. I shall have pleasure in seeing you.'

Caroline then took the floor and danced the waltz, but soon felt ill and had to stop. She then asked to be escorted into the supper room, where she could sit down.

Up to this point their two accounts more or less agree. Caroline maintained that Byron was sarcastic when she asked if she could dance. He declared that all he said was that it would be best for her to dance because she danced so well; and he would only be blamed if she refused to dance.

The climax was reached in the supper room. According to Caroline, Byron entered the room soon afterwards with Lady Rancliffe and said sarcastically, 'I have been admiring your dexterity.' Caroline then seized a knife from the table and made a pretence of stabbing herself.

'Do, my dear,' said Byron. 'But if you mean to act a Roman's part, mind which way you strike with your knife—be it at your own heart, not mine—you have struck there already.'

Whereat, according to Caroline, she burst into tears and started to run out of the room. But Lady Rancliffe screamed out that Caroline was about to kill herself, and so several guests crowded round her and tried to wrest the knife from her grasp. In doing so she was cut, and blood stained her gown.

Byron's account played down the whole incident. He said that he remained at Lady Heathcote's until five in the morning without realizing that anything untoward had occurred. He had spoken to Caroline just before supper, when she had seized hold of his hand as he passed her in the doorway and pressed some sharp instrument into it, saying 'I mean to use this.' To which he had replied, 'Against me, I presume?' and had then passed on with Lady Rancliffe on his arm, and 'trembling lest Lord Y. or Lady R. should overhear.'

He denied any responsibility for the scene and argued that he was escorting Lady Rancliffe whom he could not have left with any politeness 'to drown herself in wine and water, or be suffocated in a jelly dish, without a spoon or a hand to help her'.

He dismissed the whole incident as a storm in a teacup—or a knife in a jelly dish.

Lady Westmoreland subsequently attacked him and told him that he must have done something, adding, 'you know between people in your situation, a word or a look goes a great way.' This was certainly true enough in the case of Caroline.

Byron's final comment on the matter was that if he was to be plagued by hysterics wherever he went, it was he who should be pitied and not Caroline.

Caroline was taken back to Melbourne House and handed over to William, who did his best to comfort her and then put her to bed.

Dr Thorn, the family physician, was summoned—it was then long after midnight—and shown the patient. He was accustomed to such scenes and the method of dealing with them. He administered a sedative and went home.

The next day Caroline lay prostrate on her bed, seemingly too ill to correspond with anyone. Lady Melbourne therefore sent a report to Byron, informing him that the patient was now calm. It then transpired that Caroline had already written to him herself, although she had at first denied this. She now began to complain because she had not received an answer.

Lady Melbourne was convinced that Caroline had gone to the ball for the sole purpose of creating a scene, and that she had danced the waltz in front of Byron simply to annoy him. Caroline, she told Byron, had been working up to one of her tantrums for some time past.

'She is now like a Barrel of Gunpowder,' wrote Lady Melbourne, 'and takes fire with the most trifling spark.'

Napoleon had left Paris in April, had won the battle of Lutzen in May, and forced the allies to retreat into Silesia after Bautzen. By mid-summer he had 400,000 men assembled on the Elbe. The allies were preparing to oppose him with three armies and half a million men. The conflict in Europe was moving towards a grand climax.

But in London Society the talk was all of the events at Lady Heathcote's ball and the scandal which followed it. Lurid and contradictory reports were in circulation of the near-fatal stabbing. Some said that Caroline had broken a glass and cut herself with it. Others maintained that the wound was caused by a pair of scissors that she was carrying in her hand.

Lady Melbourne, who was viewing the whole incident with an understandably jaundiced outlook, blamed the general hysteria on the hostess, Lady Heathcote. Her screams, said Lady Melbourne, were due to her desire 'to display her fine feelings'.

Soon the whole affair became hopelessly distorted by gossip. The Duchess of Beaufort, isolated from first-hand news in the depths of the country, wrote anxiously to Lady Holland asking for the latest intelligence and declaring, 'These tales of horror strike me, I assure you, with aggravated terror...' It was almost as if the violence of the French Revolution were spreading to London, and the tumbrils were beginning to roll.

The press seized upon the story with glee, but some writers took Byron's side rather than that of Caroline. *The Satirist* wrote a spirited and inaccurate story of the wounding under the heading 'Scandalum Magnatum' and concluded with the observation it was the husband of Lady C. L**b who was to be pitied, because her attempted suicide had proved unsuccessful.

Outwardly Caroline remained impenitent. She was always quick to realize when she had gone too far, and despite the support of her 'compassionate countesses' she now felt that she had made a fool of herself.

The surprising result of this whole affair was that despite their avowals of bitter resentment and eternal hatred, the parties now began to correspond with each other once again, and with some warmth.

This was their custom. Indeed at the very height of all their quarrels, when Byron was loudly proclaiming that he never wished to see or hear from Caroline again, he was quite liable to be answering her letters and even permitting himself a few endearments.

Soon after the incident he was able to write to Lady Melbourne, 'C. has been a perfect lake, a mirror of quiet, and I have answered her last two letters,' and when the question of seeing Caroline once more was raised, he replied, 'See C.! *if* I should see C.! I hope not, though I am not sure a visit would be so disagreeable as it ought to be.'

Yet these moods of tolerance and even of affection could quickly evaporate in the face of one of Caroline's more outrageous acts. He was now living in rooms in the Albany and she called upon him one day when he was out. Having been admitted by his valet, Fletcher, over whom she had always been able to exert her powers of persuasion, she began her usual inquisitive inspection, and came upon a copy of *Vathek*, a romantic story which had been sent to him by his publisher.

Having glanced through this, she boldly scrawled across the flyleaf, 'Remember me,' and then left.

On his return Byron found the book and the inscription and promptly lost his temper. He sat down and wrote beneath it as savage an indictment of her as he had ever penned:

> Remember thee: remember thee!
> Till Lethe quench life's burning streams
> Remorse and shame shall cling to thee
> And haunt thee like a feverish dream.
> Remember thee! Ay, doubt it not,
> Thy husband too shall think of thee,

> By neither shalt thou be forgot,
> Thou *false* to him, thou *fiend* to me!

By the mid-summer of 1813 Byron was bored with Society and planning to go abroad, but he was held back by three commitments which were in sharp contrast to each other.

Firstly, he was attracted to the wife of his old friend, Wedderburn Webster. Lady Frances Webster was simple in some ways, worldly in others. Her husband thought her a paragon of virtue. Byron looked at her and wondered. Was she really so innocent? She was pretty and her air of chastity intrigued him. It was just the type of affair that appealed to him.

Secondly, he found himself falling ever more under the spell of his half-sister, Augusta. They understood each other so well, were so happy together, and had no secrets from each other. At times they were more like man and wife than brother and sister.

And thirdly, there was the inscrutable Annabella, who was still biding her time. She was still distant and withdrawn, still tantalizing in her detachment. The conquest of Lady Frances Webster did not seem to present any major obstacles, but the conquest of Annabella bristled with them. Annabella remained the one woman in his life whom he could never fathom. Her emotions were hidden from him by the iron curtain of chastity.

On 22 August she wrote him a long letter which came as a surprise to him. 'It is my nature to feel long, deeply and secretly,' she told him, 'and the strongest affections of my heart are without hope.' This, he felt, could only be interpreted as meaning that he now had a rival.

The Princess of Parallelograms could be as devious in her ways as he was himself and he could not decide what to make of all this. 'No longer suffer yourself to be the slave of the moment,' she warned him, 'nor trust your noble impulses to the chances of Life.'

It was rather as though she were reading his horoscope. Her belief in the nobility of his soul continued to confuse him. She refused to accept him as the wicked Lord Byron.

She made a further request in her letter. He was not to discuss its contents with Lady Melbourne.

Byron now adopted his standard gambit for dealing with a girl seeking to hold him at arm's length. Friendship alone would never satisfy him, he warned her. And he made dark references to the fact that he could no longer continue to trust himself in her presence.

He was handicapped in the whole affair by not being able to hurry round to Lady Melbourne to ask for her advice. Annabella clearly distrusted her. And now Augusta was beginning to behave in a similar manner. He had already suggested that Augusta should go abroad with him for a holiday. She had been willing to consider the suggestion, but had scribbled to him that 'This must not go to Ly. Me.'

Inevitably he found himself quite unable to keep such exciting secrets to himself. And so he wrote to Lady Melbourne and told her that he had exciting secrets, but that he must keep them to himself.

Then gradually the tenor of his letters to Lady Melbourne began to alter. He grew more evasive and less boastful. It seemed to her that he now had a secret which he did not wish to mention—and that he was anxious to hide. It was almost as if he had suddenly developed a conscience.

Lady Melbourne knew all about the Webster affair, which she rightly assessed as no more than a routine seduction. She also surmised that Annabella had probably decided to marry Byron, and that being a very determined young woman she would almost certainly attain her objective. But there were other problems on which her judgement was less astute. The problem of Augusta was quite outside her experience.

In the middle of August he wrote to tell her that he was a very weak person. This she knew, but it was unlike him to say so. He added that he had something which he wished to tell her, but found himself unable to do. He said that he had written her three letters and torn each one up. This was very unlike him, and very disturbing.

He spoke of Lady Oxford's departure abroad, which had left him without a companion with whom he could stay. He needed companionship, he said, and he felt that he would like to go abroad himself, and so he was proposing to take Augusta with him. She would prove far more of a companion to him than Lady Oxford, but he complained because she was anxious to take her children with her and this he did not want. It would spoil everything.

Lady Melbourne was both alarmed and perplexed. She was permissive in her own attitude to life and she was tolerant of sexual extravagance in others. And yet, like Henrietta and Georgiana, she was quite inexperienced in certain fields of sexual abnormality. None of her lovers had been homosexuals, nor did she know anything about homosexuality. And now Byron was hinting at something infinitely worse. He was implying that he was about to indulge—

157

or had already indulged—in an incestuous relationship with his sister. What she did not know was that towards the end of August he had written a letter to his intimate friend, Thomas Moore, in which he said that he was in 'a far more serious and entirely new scrape than any of the last twelve months'.

Incest! It was a sin that could send a chill down the spine of even the loosest woman in London Society. Immorality was one thing but this same Society was careful to preserve certain sacred taboos. Such taboos were even reflected in the laws of the land. As for the Church ...

Homosexuality was still at this time punishable by death. Other acts of perversion, such as sodomy, were considered so terrible as to be quite unmentionable. And incest was held to be almost the worst sin of all, because of the universal superstition that a child born of an incestuous relationship must inevitably be a moron or a monster.

The important point was that Byron himself believed incest to be a sinful act. His ancestors had been guilty of incest for generations. He himself was steeped in ancient myths and superstitions and in the orgies that he had staged at Newstead during his Cambridge days he had even practised a little satanism. When he worshipped Satan, he half expected the devil to appear. Thus he secretly believed that if ever he practised the dreadful act of incest, he might produce a monster child as evidence of his sinful act.

It can neither be proved nor disproved that his relationship with his half-sister, Augusta, was an incestuous one. Byron strongly hinted that it was, but he was such a liar that it may not have been. Later he was to state, 'As for A., my feelings towards her are a mixture of good and diabolical.'

The relationship between Byron and Augusta was always close and always intimate. They loved each other, and their embraces were warm and spontaneous. But of the two, only Byron was conscious of the danger that existed in such intimacy, and only he was aware that it might develop, in the eyes of the world, into something obscene and wicked.

One fact remains, and the evidence is clear. Byron believed he was involved in an act that was sinful. But Augusta was not aware of this. Her demeanour at the time was that of a person who had no sense of guilt. In the years to come, when she was being accused of having indulged in unnatural behaviour, she remained in ignorance of what it was that she was supposed to have done. She may never have realized that the intimacies which she permitted to her beloved brother went further than acts of sisterly love.

The important point is that Byron was fascinated by wickedness, and could even glory in it. He was therefore capable of magnifying the wickedness of his behaviour. Augusta had no desire to fulfil the fearful traditions of her Byron ancestors. She was always herself. Unlike her brother, she never played a part, and she had no love of melodrama.

Byron's biographers have pondered on when the incestuous relationship began—if at all. If it did develop, it was probably in this high summer of 1813, whilst Caroline was driving him distracted by her antics and after Lady Oxford had deserted him and London Society had begun to turn against him.

If he *did* have an incestuous relationship with his much-loved half-sister, then he should never have mentioned it to anyone. If he did *not* have any such relationship, then he should never have implied that he did. His behaviour in either case was deplorable. He revealed once again the worst side to his character, which was that he could not resist boasting about his sexual conquests. There was no harm in his advertising to the world that Lady Oxford was his mistress. It pleased his vanity to do so, and it pleased her vanity that her name should be coupled with his. But to imply, as he did, that his relationship with Augusta was a sinful one only served to blacken the character of the one woman whom he really loved.

He told Lady Melbourne about it, because it was his habit to confide in her all his notorious escapades, and it was her habit to encourage him to make these confessions. He told Caroline about it because he wished to shock her, and to humiliate her. His aim was to arouse her jealousy and anguish.

All that can be said in extenuation of his conduct at this time is that he was by now undermining his constitution—and, worse still, his character—by drinking excessively, and by adopting a policy of semi-starvation allied to overdoses of laxatives and indigestion remedies which together began to destroy his mental equilibrium. In company with so many of the rakes in history, and certainly with such as Rochester, he was deliberately adopting a policy of self-destruction. Already he was beginning to fear that the madness which had overtaken so many of his line now had him in its grasp.

Summer passed, autumn came, and in a short and hectic spell of writing in October he produced *The Bride of Abydos*, with its theme of incest. He clearly had Augusta in mind when he wrote this, and in his first draft Selim and Zuleika were brother and sister, although prudence made him alter this to cousins in the completed work.

In November he began writing a journal, and confiding his thoughts to it. He was twenty-five and already growing disenchanted with life and none too satisfied with his work. 'I by no means rank poetry or poets high in the scale of intellect,' he told Augusta; and added that he preferred the talents of action, and notably of war. A great poet, he yet remained throughout his life a frustrated actor and a frustrated soldier.

A further factor came to influence his life at this time and to deepen his disillusion. In October 1813 his idol Napoleon was defeated by the allies at Leipzig. During the winter that followed Wellington drove northward from the Peninsula towards France, and it was evident that an allied attack on Paris must soon be launched. Time was running out for the Man of Destiny.

Byron's romantic attitude to war, his love of all its panopy and dramas, and his hero-worship of great military leaders, had led him into an obsessional admiration of Napoleon. The effect of Napoleon's gradual decline and fall was to arouse in Byron a sense of impending doom. If this hero could be defeated, then all heroes could be defeated. He was astonished that Napoleon did not commit suicide when his cause seemed lost. Byron shut himself up in his room for four days in the spring of 1814 and wrote an Ode denouncing Napoleon.

One of the effects of this mounting disillusion was to strengthen his determination to marry. It was almost as if he were declaring that he himself was now ready to submit to the enemy, which in his case was the female sex.

During the winter of 1813/1814, Byron saw little of Caroline. After the debacle at Lady Heathcote's ball, she had entered upon one of her periods of relative calm. She was biding her time, conscious of the fact that Byron was seemingly pre-occupied with his writing and with trivial social affairs.

William Lamb was grateful for the respite, but his hatred of Byron continued to grow. He had become resentful at the manner in which his mother continued to correspond with the poet, and to tolerate his bad behaviour. William's loyalty to his wife demanded that those who were wounding her should be despised. But Lady Melbourne treated Byron almost as if he were her son, and condoned his numerous indiscretions.

The effect of this disloyalty in his family was to increase his own determination to stand by Caroline no matter what might happen. The Whig cause was in abeyance and his own political career seemed ended. He lived in a vacuum, listless and bored.

He tried to help Caroline in every way he could, but her moods were so variable, and her health so poor, that he was at a loss to know how he could make life easier for her. He engaged a companion for her—a Miss Webb—who suggested that Caroline should learn to play the harp, as this would help to soothe her. Caroline remained uncooperative, however. She refused to play the harp, and—contrariwise as ever—decided instead to learn how to play the organ.

Caroline never did anything by halves, and so she played the organ all day and until far into the night. She was by now suffering from insomnia and often refused to go to bed. Instead she wandered aimlessly about the passages at night, like some forlorn little ghost.

She ate very little and continued to grow thinner and look ever more emaciated. Yet her stamina remained seemingly unimpaired, and in her moods of vivacity she could display the highest spirits and talk with unflagging eloquence. But these moods of sudden cheerfulness were always brittle and without genuine gaiety. She drove herself on unflaggingly, and always towards the goal of greater self-advertisement.

The story current about her in Society that she had once been carried naked into the dining room concealed under a vast silver platter was never authenticated, but this was the sort of act in which she revelled.

She continued to think only of Byron, but she also tried to conceal the fact by behaving with brazen immodesty and by making advances towards the men whom she met. Her behaviour was increasingly suggestive of nymphomania, which is usually indicative of a state of extreme frustration rather than of unbridled sensuality.

She and Byron met occasionally, but formally, at social functions. There were many of these during this spring of 1814, when the menace of Napoleon was being banished from men's minds, and 'the summer of the sovereigns' began. Even Byron could not fail to respond in part to the mood of gaiety. 'Do you recollect,' he wrote to Moore many years later, 'in the year of revelry of 1814, the pleasantest parties and balls all over London?' He was writing then in exile in Italy, but there was a genuine nostalgia in the recollection.

He threw himself into the social whirl in order to forget his mounting problems, and he tried to ignore the cause of all the revelry—the defeat of Napoleon.

161

Caroline reacted to this general mood in the way which William had grown to dread. She attended every party that she could, and sought always to command attention by her unflagging zest and brittle gaiety. Her laughter rang out with a near-hysterical note, she talked incessantly, and she discarded all sense of modesty in her dress and conversation. The pursuit of pleasure seemed her only aim.

Yet still she stalked her prey, convinced that sooner or later she would re-capture Byron and re-awaken his love. 'I am haunted by a skeleton,' he wrote to Lady Melbourne, and indeed Caroline now looked so thin that she seemed little more.

Lady Melbourne was alarmed by Caroline's persistence and warned Byron to avoid her at all costs. He assured her, in reply, that 'all that bolts, bars, and silence can do to keep her away are done daily and hourly.' They were not always successful.

England's hero, and Caroline's also, was the Duke of Wellington —who much enjoyed the fuss which the ladies were making over him. 'It's a fine thing to be a great man, is it not?' he said to one of his young admirers.

The highlight of the summer was the masked ball which was held in his honour at Burlington House on the night of 1 July. Byron, for some devious reason, elected to go as a monk. This sombre apparel may well have reflected his mood, for Wellington had defeated his hero and he saw no reason for celebrating the event.

William, looking somewhat embarrassed in fancy dress, escorted Caroline, who had chosen to appear once again as a boy. She was masked and wore a cloak over her green pantaloons. But as Byron sourly observed, the mask was worn in such a way as to ensure that everyone recognized her instantly. She was *not* a person who enjoyed dancing *incognita*.

Caroline was on her worst behaviour—coquettish, loquacious and full of exaggerated animation. Byron considered that she was making a fool of herself and told her so. As he commented later, 'I scolded her like her grandfather upon these very uncalled for and unnecessary gesticulations.'

One might have supposed that having separated from her for ever, he would not have troubled to take any further notice of her behaviour, but in fact he observed her keenly. He was shocked by her talk and by her green pantaloons. When in one of his critical moods he could become quite an old woman in his outlook.

She continued to behave badly, however—and all the more so when she knew that his disapproving eye was fixed upon her. She became a little drunk and persuaded a Guards officer to take off his scarlet uniform for her benefit. Byron glared across the room at her.

He returned at dawn to his rooms in the Albany, off Piccadilly, feeling too disgruntled to go to bed. He settled down to compose a poem before trying to sleep. It was called *Lara,* and in it he described himself:

> There was in him a vital scorn of all:
> As if the worst had fall'n which could befall,
> He stood a stranger in this breathing world,
> An erring spirit from another hurl'd ...

It was soon after this that he must have seen Caroline for the last time. She described this last meeting years later in a letter she wrote to his friend, Medwin, 'As he pressed his lips on mine (it was at the Albany) he said, "Poor Caro, if everyone hates me, you, I see will never change..." and I said, "Yes, I *am* changed, and shall come near you no more." For then he showed me letters, and told me things I cannot repeat, and all my attachment went. This was our last parting scene.'

What were the unrepeatable things that he told her? Perhaps accounts of his homosexual loves and his incestuous relationship with Augusta. Yet he must have realized, as he told her these stories, that her love of gossip and scandal could only result in her repeating them to others. He knew, better than anyone, that Caroline could not be trusted to keep a secret, any more than he could be trusted to keep one himself. Later he was to declare his hatred for her because she had betrayed his confidences. But he never blamed himself for his own lack of discretion. It was almost as if he wanted these stories repeated, so that his shame could be broadcast to the world. This did not prevent him from castigating Caroline for what she was doing to him.

'She may hunt me down—it is the power of any mad or bad woman to do so by any man...torment me she may; how am I to bar myself from her! I am already almost a prisoner; she has no shame, no feeling, no one estimable or redeemable quality...I would lose a hundred souls rather than be bound to C. ...'

Yet there was no suggestion that he need ever be bound to C., or to anyone else, if he did not wish it. But in his heart there existed this overpowering urge to attach himself to *someone*. And as he hated the thought of being tied to Caroline and felt that he could no longer be bound to Augusta, whom alone he really loved, then some alternative would have to be found. In order to escape from the prison of his loneliness he might yet be forced to retreat into the prison of matrimony.

His mind was in turmoil. The Calvinism of his childhood and his love-hate relationship with acts of wickedness and his basic homosexuality, had so complicated his attitude to sex that he could no longer analyse his own desires. And now he was, by his own estimate, in the worst scrape of all. He was in love, both spiritually and physically, with his half-sister.

Byron was happy to condemn Society for its narrow-mindedness. But, on the other hand, he had little use for free-thinkers who thought differently from himself. Had he been told at this time that incest was but a minor indiscretion, and that it could in no way be described as wicked, he would have been both shocked and indignant. The whole structure of his immature philosophy would have collapsed had his beliefs in wickedness been seriously challenged.

On 15 April, 1814, Augusta had given birth to a daughter, who she named Medora. To many, this seemed an act of unbelievable folly, for Medora had been the heroine of his poem, *The Corsair*. This suggested to some that Byron was the father of the child; his close association with Augusta had begun just nine months previously, in the mid-summer of 1813.

The child *might* have been his. And a gentleman, seeking to protect the good name of the mother and of the infant, as well as his own, would have been at pains to deny all such rumours. But Byron, true to form, did much to aggravate them. Adopting his usual note of schoolboy flippancy, he wrote to Lady Melbourne that she need have no fears lest the child might have been born abnormal, '... it is *not* an *Ape*, and if it is that must be my fault; however I will positively reform.'

His devotion to Augusta remained as strong as ever, and although he took no particular interest in this little girl, who in later life always believed herself to be his daughter, he sent Augusta a present of £3,000. He was never ungenerous; but he did have a tendency to give away money that he did not possess. His creditors were the sufferers in the long run.

He spent August with Augusta and her children at the seaside at Hastings. When they separated, she wrote him frequent letters in her

Caroline's sketch of herself being attended by Dr Warren.
'Sure means to make the mind and body part,
A burning fever and a broken heart'

Caroline's sketch of Cupid drowning in a merciless sea.
'*Craignez mes enfants cette mer orageuse. L'amour y a fait naufrâge*'

Opposite top and middle The
flowers that fade: Caroline's
mood of melancholy reflected in
two sketches of a child in a basket
of flowers — 'Everything blooms —
but everything dies'

Opposite bottom Caroline at the
time of her marriage. Attributed
to John Hoppner

Above Byron — the perfect profile
and the 'under look'. After
R. Westall

Above Byron's half-sister, Augusta Leigh – the only woman he ever really loved. From a sketch by G. Hayter

Below Byron's wife, Annabella Milbanke, 'The Princess of Parallelograms'. After a miniature of 1812 by G. Hayter

Above Caroline tired and dispirited. From a painting by Miss E. Trotter

Below Caroline wearing her favourite décolletage style. From an engraving by Henry Meyer

Opposite Byron in Albanian dress —painted in 1813 soon after his tour of the Mediterranean. By Thomas Phillips

Below Brocket Hall in Hertfordshire —the Melbourne country seat. From an engraving after Paul Sandby

Opposite below Byron in exile at Pisa in 1822. After W. E. West

William Lamb as Lord
Melbourne, Queen Victoria's
Prime Minister

childish hand, with crosses at the foot of the page to represent kisses. She could be very Carolinish in her ways.

He was getting nowhere in life, and so marriage seemed a rational objective. He discussed the problem with Augusta, who told him that he must find a wife for the sake of each of them. Her love for him was untainted by feelings of jealousy. All that she asked of life was that her 'Baby Byron' should be married and should settle down happily. Annabella she knew to be a good woman, who would love him and do her utmost to reform him.

Throughout the summer—and throughout his many love affairs—Byron had been corresponding regularly with Annabella. And he had received 'prim and pretty letters' from her in return. They were almost hypnotic in their effect. They drew him on towards his destiny. The wicked Lord Byron had to be sacrificed on the altar of purity and reform.

'I am not in love with her,' he wrote to Lady Melbourne, but added, 'seriously, I do admire her as a very superior woman, a little encumbered with Virtue...'

On 9 September he wrote to Annabella a half-hearted proposal—'I neither wish you to promise or pledge yourself to anything; but merely to learn a *possibility* which would not leave you the less a free agent.' Were there, he wished to know, any insuperable objections to her becoming his wife?

He sent the letter, and having done so, regretted that he had. But he felt reasonably sure that she would refuse—or would at most continue to prevaricate. But at the back of his mind was the frightening suspicion that she might accept him. He dismissed it and made plans to winter abroad.

Her reply—forwarded on to him from the Albany—reached him as he and Augusta were sitting down to dinner at Newstead. He looked at the envelope and turned so pale that Augusta feared he was about to faint.

'It never rains but it pours,' he said, and opened the letter.

Eleven

Byron - The Treacle-Moon

Annabella wrote frequently to Byron after her acceptance of his proposal. She viewed their forthcoming marriage with serene confidence, and read him solemn little lectures on the purpose of life, the existence of an Infinite Being, and the sacredness of the marriage ties.

'Feel benevolence and you will inspire it,' she wrote, and added with conviction, 'You will do good.'

Lady Melbourne asked Annabella to compile a list of the qualities which she required in a husband, and Annabella gravely complied.

'He must have consistent principles of Duty governing strong and generous feelings, and reducing them under the command of Reason.

'Genius is not in my opinion *necessary*, though desirable, if *united* with what I have just mentioned.

'I require a freedom from suspicion, and from *habitual* ill-humour—also an equal tenor of affection towards me, not that violent attachment which is susceptible of sudden increase or diminution from trifles.

'I wish to be considered by my husband as a *reasonable adviser*, not as a guide on whom he could implicitly depend...

'Rank is indifferent to me. *Good connections* I think are an important advantage.

'I do not regard *beauty,* but am influenced by the *manners of a gentleman,* without which I scarcely think that anyone could attract me.

'I would not enter into a family where there was a strong tendency to insanity.'

Lady Melbourne was quite put out. On reading through this formidable list a second time, she could not find a single quality which applied to Byron.

On receipt of Annabella's formal acceptance Byron sadly kissed Augusta goodbye and left for Annabella's home at Seaham, a gloomy place, haunted by family traditions of sober living and pious thought.

On arrival there he greeted Sir Ralph and Lady Milbanke with suitable gravity, and found his bride-to-be looking flustered and nervous and also surprisingly silent. The flow of talk about virtue and rectitude seemed suddenly to have dried up. Her silence and her seeming frigidity intrigued Byron and he set out to discover if this chaste young woman was quite as passionless as she appeared.

His caresses became less platonic and more explorative. The results surprised him. And he wrote to Lady Melbourne, 'For my part, I have lately had recourse to the eloquence of *action* (which Demosthenes calls the first part of oratory) and find it succeeds very well, and makes her very quiet; which gives me some hopes of the efficacy of the "calming process", so renowned in "our philosophy." In fact, and *entre nous,* it is really amusing; she is like a child in that respect, and quite caressable into kindness...'

Later it became necessary for Byron to leave the house, because Annabella expressed alarm at what was happening and hinted that she might be unable to control herself for very much longer.

The next problem was how to tell Caroline. It is possible that he was genuinely a little concerned about the distress that it might cause her, but his chief problem was to prevent her from staging a major scene.

At first his fears seemed to be realized. He announced his betrothal and almost at once a contradiction of it was printed in *The Morning Chronicle.* This savoured very much of Caroline, for as he remarked, 'No one else had the motive or the malignity to be so *petty.*' But in fact it was not Caroline, and he felt almost guilty that he had suspected her.

Should he write to her, he asked Lady Melbourne. But before he could do so, she wrote to him and congratulated him warmly.

He was slightly piqued. No scene? No tears? No tantrums? It was a little galling. But Caroline was all sweetness and generosity. She wished him every good future and assured him that the union with Annabella would prove a happy one.

'I do hope C. will continue in this mood,' he wrote to Lady Melbourne, 'It becomes her; and it is so provoking to see her throwing away her own happiness by the handfuls...'

Caroline's sweetness continued until the marriage. She realized well enough that Annabella did not like her, but she was nevertheless anxious to send a wedding present. She asked Lady Melbourne

167

whether this would prove acceptable, and Byron—when approached
—replied, 'I wonder C. should think it necessary to make such a
preface; *we* are very well disposed towards her, and can't see why
there should not be peace with her as well as with America.'

It was rather a chilling reply, and yet—in an earlier part of the
letter—he had referred to her not as 'C.' but had used the pet name
which she loved—Caro.

It seemed that whatever he was planning, and no matter whom
he was courting, he could never quite get Caro out of his system.

The marriage took place on 2 January, 1815, and was a disaster from
the start. Seldom can a bridegroom have come more unwillingly to
the altar (he made repeated efforts to postpone the ceremony) and
seldom can one have behaved worse on his honeymoon.

There had for long been evidence that his heart was not in this
union. During their engagement he had talked constantly of Augusta
and described her endearing little ways with such enthusiasm that
Annabella had tried to imitate them, but without success. He frequently lapsed into moods of sombre foreboding, and she finally
offered to break off the engagement, whereat he 'fainted entirely
away'.

The more he looked at his future bride, the less glamorous he
found her. 'Miss Milbanke is rather dowdy-looking,' he noted, 'and
wears a long and high dress, though her feet and ankles are excellent.'

He sulked before the wedding and during it. He did not give his
bride any sort of present and there was no reception. The couple had
been lent Halnaby Hall, in Yorkshire, for their honeymoon. It was
some forty miles distant, and he quarrelled with Annabella throughout the journey. On arrival at the Hall, he stepped out of the
carriage in front of his wife and strode up the steps and into the
house, leaving her to greet the servants who had assembled to
meet them.

It was late, and dinner was shortly to be served. The entry he
made in his *Memoirs* was brief. '*Had* Lady B. on the sofa before
dinner...'

Later that evening he asked her whether she intended to share
the same bed with him, as he had an aversion to sleeping with any
woman, but added that she could do as she pleased.

She chose to sleep with him. It was bitterly cold outside, but the
room was cosy and warm, with a roaring fire. There was a four-
poster bed, surrounded by a crimson curtain. He was in no mood

for love-making, but he was conscious that he had a long family tradition of lust and rapaciousness to fulfil.

The girl who lay by his side was innocent, but she was well aware that he had a reputation for uninhibited love-making. She was also well aware that he had enjoyed numerous women in the past, who had given themselves to him willingly and passionately. Now that she had married him it was necessary for her to give herself as willingly and to prove her love by accepting whatever method of intercourse he might choose. Moreover he had frequently accused her of being frigid. It was therefore also necessary for her to prove to him that she was not frigid; and also to prove it to herself.

She was later to allege—by strong implication—that on this first night of their marriage he sodomized her; and that he did so again when she became pregnant and was no longer able to satisfy him in the normal way.

It may have been so. Her innocence had always irritated him, as had her piety. Moreover the Byrons had indulged for centuries in the act of defloration. Women had to be overcome by violence, and then humiliated by acts of grossness. He had already deprived her of her virginity. It therefore behoved him to take her sexual education a step further. She must learn exactly what it was to sleep with a man of depravity and wickedness before she attempted to reform him.

Years later Annabella was to say of her husband that he was a victim of a classical education. It was one of those surprising flashes of insight which were characteristic of her. The comment, in the context of her first night of marriage, might well have been perceptive.

Both homosexuality and sodomy were widely practised amongst the ancients. It was not uncommon for a young bride to be sodomized on her wedding night, when it was felt that her natural fear of pregnancy could be allayed by a sexual act that was unproductive. She could thus be initiated into the pleasures of sexual intercourse without even losing her virginity.

A chaste but passionate young girl might well derive satisfaction from this act, for in some people the act of sodomy can arouse a stronger reaction than is attained by normal entry.

The *Don Leon* poems, which were published many years later, and which, although they almost certainly were not written by Byron were yet the work of someone who knew him well, imply that this act of sodomy took place.

The argument has frequently been put forward that even with

the most compliant of wives, sodomy is not easily achieved, and that with an unco-operative one it is almost impossible. This is true.

The argument has also been put forward that devout and innocent young girls do not indulge in extremes of sexual behaviour on their wedding night. But human sexual behaviour is often unpredictable.

There are two points that must be considered. Did Annabella in fact submit to this act? And secondly, if she did, was her submission a willing one? Did she, in fact, enjoy it?

The relevant lines in *Don Leon* are those which state:

> 'Tis true, that from her lips some murmurs fell—
> In joy or anger, 'tis too late to tell;
> But this I swear, that not a single sign
> Proved that her pleasure did not equal mine.

What Byron failed to realize at the time—assuming that this act did take place—was that he was giving hostages to his wife. Thereafter, if ever she wished to leave him, she was possessed of the strongest possible reasons for doing so, and could damn him for ever in the eyes of posterity. Or, as *Don Leon* remarks:

> Thence sprung the source of her undying hate.
> Fiends from her breast the sacred secret wrung,
> Then called me monster; and, with evil tongue,
> Mysterious tales of false Satanic art
> Devised, and forced us evermore to part.

To all of which one question remains to be answered. If he did behave in this way on his wedding night, and she was utterly revolted by his conduct, why did she not leave him immediately? The separation did not take place for over a year.

The answer was that in spite of his churlish behaviour and sexual deviations, the 'treacle-moon', as he chose to call it, was not without warmth and gaiety. When Caroline was excitable he found her impossible to live with; when Annabella was smug and humourless (and alas she was quite without a sense of humour), he found her boring and exasperating. All he had ever asked of women was companionship and affection. When Annabella forgot to play her role of the reformer and became his companion, he enjoyed her company and she enjoyed his. There were moments when they were genuinely happy together.

170

It was a great period for nicknames and he began to call her 'Pip-pin' because of her round and rosy face, and she called him 'Dear Duck'—perhaps in an attempt to copy Augusta's nickname which was 'Goose'. He wrote to Lady Melbourne, 'Bell and I go on extremely well so far, without any other company than our own selves...I have great hopes this match will turn out well.'

There were moments, too, when she could bring him comfort; and moments when her love for him touched his heart. She was greatly distressed by his restlessness at night, and his habit of keeping a loaded pistol and a dagger by his bedside. And when he suffered from fearful nightmares, cried out in agony and roamed the corridors in his distress, her mother instincts were aroused and she realized that he was in truth no more than an unhappy little boy.

One night, when her heart was filled with pity for him, she laid her head on his breast to try and comfort him. And he said to her, 'You should have a softer pillow than my heart.'

But unfortunately there was a malicious streak in his character, as Caroline had already discovered. He was fascinated by innocence and yet he resented it. It amused him to shock his wife.

Annabella was easy to shock. Her piety was genuine and her desire to reform her husband was inspired by the highest motives. She was a tiresome woman, but she was also a devout Christian.

He not only ridiculed her moral outlook but he attacked her religious outlook as well. A cynic himself, he was able to launch a blistering attack on her faith. Yet she remained convinced that there was good in him and that he, too, believed in God and Christianity. And in this she was right.

'The worst of it is I *do* believe,' he once confessed to her in a moment of truth.

'Three great men were ruined in one year,' said Byron when considering the events of 1815, 'Brummell, myself and Napoleon.'

Of Byron and Napoleon it can be argued that their ruin was brought about by a combination of ill-health and the inability to face facts. In the case of Byron the breakdown of his health and marriage was accentuated by the collapse of his finances. Tension and depression held him in their grip. The laudanum bottle was always by his bedside, together with the pistol and the dagger. He suffered from fearful dreams, and moods of extreme irritability. And he resorted more and more to alcohol.

Nothing, however, could diminish his inquisitiveness and his love

171

of gossip. Nor was he able to forget Caroline, although he continued to maintain an air of indifference about her when writing to Lady Melbourne. At the beginning of the year, when his own marriage already seemed to be drifting towards its inevitable breakdown, he wrote to Lady Melbourne and asked her whether there was 'any foundation for the rumour that has reached me, that *Les Agneaux* are about to separate? If it is so, I hope that this time it is only on account of incompatibility of temper, and that no more serious scenes have occurred...'

He remained oblivious of the fact that the only cause of any such breakdown would be himself.

Lady Melbourne wrote back, scotching the rumour and declaring, 'They are in the country, to all appearance like two turtle Doves.' But she felt constrained to add that although Caroline was behaving better than in the past, she remained 'troublesome in private and a great bore to Society'. And she added, 'I hope someday to see you undergo a dinner when she wishes to show off.'

Caroline's exhibitionism was more than ever in evidence during this year of victory and its resultant celebrations. On 18 June, 1815, Napoleon was defeated at Waterloo and it was not long before the English tourists were flocking back to Paris, with the Lambs well in the van.

The Lambs had good reason to go there, for Caroline's brother, Colonel Frederick Ponsonby, had been seriously wounded during the battle. He had been ridden over by a troop of Prussian cavalry, suffered severe wounds and had then lain out on the field all night; but his life had been saved, in his opinion, by 'excessive bleeding'. He had fought with distinction throughout the Peninsular campaign, and had proved himself a brave and accomplished soldier.

Caroline and William travelled to Paris via the Low Countries, and Henrietta came up from the South of France to join them in Brussels, where Frederick was in hospital.

Caroline was in her element. She had a particular fancy for showing off in front of foreigners—and especially those who were easily shocked. Fanny Burney, who was in Brussels with her husband, described a large, pleasant party *chez* Mme de la Tour du Pin at which she just missed meeting: 'the famous Lady C—L—, who had been there at dinner, and whom I saw, however, crossing the Place Royale, from Mme de Tour du Pin's to the Grand Hotel; dressed, or rather *not* dressed, so as to excite universal attention, and authorize every boldness in staring, from the General to the lowest soldier among the military groups constantly parading La Place, for she had one shoulder, half her back and all her throat and neck displayed, as if at the call of some statuary for modelling a heathen goddess. A slight scarf hung over the shoulder and the rest of the attire was of accordant lightness.'

Caroline was still writing regularly to Byron, and he was writing to her, usually adopting his playful and rather arch mood, which had the effect of encouraging her still further. He expressed the hope that she was enjoying herself as much with the army as he was with his wife. It was a barbed comment, to say the least.

Having assured themselves that Frederick Ponsonby was on the road to recovery, the Lambs withdrew to Paris, where a number of the Devonshire House set were already assembled. Bess was there, noting with approval that the manners of the citizens were better than they had been when she encountered them during the Peace of Amiens in 1802. Hary-O was also there, still making waspish remarks at Caroline's expense. 'Nothing is *agissant* but Caroline William, in a purple riding habit, tormenting every one. Poor William hides in one small room, while she assembles lovers and tradespeople in the other. He looks worn to the bone. She arrived dying by her own account, having had French apothecaries in most of the towns through which she passed. She sent them immediately for a doctor, but by mistake they went for the Duke of Wellington.'

The most important person in Paris was the Duke of Wellington, and Caroline, who had always admired him, now set out to capture him.

The Duke had not much enjoyed the Battle of Waterloo. He had found it an unsatisfactory contest in almost every respect, apart from the outcome, and one that had been badly bungled by the majority of those involved. It had rained, too, which had annoyed him. But now he was happy to enjoy the fruits of victory in Paris, where it was sunny and dry and he could stride through the streets in his blue frock-coat, the cynosure of every feminine eye.

Amongst his most ardent admirers in Paris was the novelist Walter Scott, who arranged a select little dinner party for the Duke at which the only guests were two ladies, one of whom was Caroline. The dinner was a great success, but was interrupted from time to time by Caroline emitting a sudden scream, though for what reason was never apparent. In the years to come the Duke was to describe her as being 'as mad as a March Hare', and perhaps it was the occasional screams at this dinner which first put the idea into his head.

But on the whole Caroline was behaving herself reasonably well, although the mention of Byron could still trigger off a sudden outburst. William was thankful that Byron was in England, but the inevitable scene was in due course provoked by the rumour that he was about to visit Paris.

It occurred at a dinner given by Lord Holland, which William and Caroline attended. William was asked when he and his wife proposed to leave France for home, and he replied that they were leaving the next day.

Then, quite by chance, one of the guests mentioned that Byron was soon expected to arrive in Paris. Caroline at once turned to William and told him that on no account would she leave the next day. A scene between husband and wife was clearly brewing, and the guests were suitably embarrassed—and intrigued.

William and Caroline were staying at Meurices' Hotel, and when the pair arrived that evening, it was raining heavily and puddles had formed on the footpaths. Interested observers noted that William not only helped his wife to alight, but also carried her gallantly across the wet stones to the entrance.

The same interested observers could also see what happened when the Lambs reached their apartments, as the curtains were not drawn.

William came into the room and sat down on the sofa. Caroline then sat on the end of it, put her arms round her husband's neck and started to caress him, as though trying to coax him. She then slipped to the floor and nestled at his feet, looking up at him and talking earnestly to him.

Then suddenly the mood changed. Caroline lost her temper and jumped to her feet. In a few seconds she seemed to go mad and ran round the room, seizing cups, saucers, plates and ornaments, and dashing them to the ground. She then turned her attention to the furniture and the fittings and vented her wrath upon vases, candlesticks and anything else on which she could lay her hands.

William was doing his utmost to soothe her, but this only seemed to aggravate her mood. Unfortunately for the watchers, fascinated by this demonstration of Caroline's hysteria, the curtains were closed before the scene ended. But they were left in little doubt as to the cause of it.

It was surprising that Byron should have contemplated a visit to Paris. The city was still full of memories of Napoleon and all his past glories. He had travelled down to Plymouth to see the arrival of *Bellerophon*. The little boats, filled with sightseers, had clustered round the vessel and had fallen silent in awe at the sight of its prisoner; but Byron had resented the whole inglorious display. His god had shown himself to have feet of clay.

In fact Byron never arrived in Paris. Rumours that he was in the city did circulate, however, and John Mitford, a parson with literary inclinations and a nose for gossip, wrote in his book, *Fashionable Follies, Frailties and Debaucheries*, a highly melodramatic account of how Caroline and Byron went rowing on the lake in the Bois and then eloped to Switzerland, with William in hot pursuit. The incident can never have taken place, although the melodramatic ingredients were very much in keeping with the character of each.

If Byron's marriage was in danger of breaking-up, so also was Caroline's. William was by now under constant pressure from his brothers and sisters, and also—less openly—from his mother, Lady Melbourne. They had good reason to coerce him towards a step which they felt could only relieve him of much unhappiness and enable him to take up once again the threads of his political career.

Yet he still loved her and she still loved him after her fashion.

Once, when they were in Paris together, Caroline had turned to her neighbour at a dinner-party and had asked him brightly, 'Whom do you imagine I consider the most distinguished man I ever met?' When he had made the obvious reply that it was Lord Byron, she had answered, 'No, my own husband, William Lamb.'

He still remained her haven, and it is doubtful if she contemplated life without him. Byron remained a romantic dream, always to be pursued, but William was like a faithful dog, whose loyalty to her was beyond question. And although she was making life ever more difficult for him, so that his grey hairs were multiplying (he was only thirty-six and was doing his best to pull them out as they appeared); and although he had quite given up the pretence of defending her character to his relations; and although he had even gone so far as to initiate steps for a separation two years previously, he still could not bring himself to effect the final break. She could still wring his heart with her soft and gentle caresses and still arouse his compassion when she looked broken and ill.

At this time there seemed hopes that he might resume his political life. His friends had for long been trying to persuade him to do so, and Lord Holland had offered him a seat. He had declined for two reasons—firstly because he had no desire to be a Holland House man, and secondly because he was still finding peace and comfort in the solitude of the library at Brocket. He had always been an avid reader

175

and a detached observer of the habits of mankind. He had an objective outlook to life which was rare amongst the extrovert company in which he spent so much of his time at Melbourne House.

Yet he was still little more than an amateur philosopher, too idle to tackle the many problems of life. He was tolerant and impartial and had little enough use for bigoted views. Like so many of his set, he was alarmed by thoughts of a revolution, which could only lead to the destruction of his own comfortable way of life. He feared the mob—and had been given good reason to do so, after contemplating the terrible savagery of the French Revolution.

When he and his wife arrived back from Paris, Caroline at once took to her bed with a bad cold. Her health always tended to collapse after moments of stress, but her return to health was achieved by the advent of a new excitement. This was a rumour of the breakdown in Byron's marriage.

There was no duplicity about Caroline. Unlike her lover, her motives were always straightforward, although misguided. She was meddlesome, of course, and deeply inquisitive about his affairs, but she would never have stooped to sabotaging the marriage.

There had been little enough love lost between her and Annabella, but the coldness had been more on Annabella's side than on Caroline's. Byron had insisted that they should meet at his new home at 13, Piccadilly Terrace, soon after the marriage, although Caroline had been reluctant to visit them.

The meeting had been a failure. It was difficult to understand what Byron had hoped to achieve by it. Perhaps he had wished to convince Caroline, as well as himself, that his marriage was proving successful. In fact he proved that the reverse was the case. Annabella was cold and suspicious. Byron was plainly agitated and he looked tired and ill.

Both Caroline and Annabella were well aware that the cause of the breakdown was primarily his affair with Augusta. So at least they were able to share a mutual sense of horror and shock. Annabella had by now been forced to face up to something which at first she had tried to ignore. Byron had spoken frequently of Augusta during the honeymoon, always to the effect that Augusta understood him better than his wife, that Augusta was more sympathetic and more understanding, and finally that Augusta was more passionate and uninhibited.

But it was not until Augusta came to stay with them that Annabella's eyes were finally opened. He devoted his whole attention to

176

Augusta, displayed his affection for her in numberless ways, and discussed her constantly with his wife. He spoke Augusta's name in his sleep, and it was clear that his dreams were filled with the image of her. Sometimes, on wakening, he would brandish his pistol or his dagger and declare that he was about to kill Annabella and himself.

He had other far more cruel ways of undermining his wife's love. He would read out Augusta's letters, lingering gloatingly over any expressions of love, and when the three of them were together he would be at pains to exclude his wife from the conversation. He would make intimate little references to secrets which he shared with Augusta; and he would slyly compare the underclothes which they wore. In the evenings he would send his wife to bed early, making it clear to her that he wished to be alone with Augusta. Always there was the implication that *she* could satisfy him but that Annabella could not.

Sometimes he went even further. Annabella made notes of his behaviour, which she wrote in a kind of shorthand. She noted that there were occasions when they were staying with Augusta at Six Mile Bottom when he ceased to have intercourse with her because he implied that Augusta was satisfying all his needs; and on one occasion, when he did make love to Annabella, he implied that he was forced to do this because Augusta was menstruating.

Astonishingly, Augusta herself seemed to remain unaware of the trouble that she was causing, and made only tentative efforts to discourage her brother's displays of affection towards her. She tried to explain to Annabella how Byron should be laughed out of his sulks and tantrums, but Annabella, alas, had no aptitude for laughing anyone out of anything. Yet she was conscious of the wisdom of the advice, and of Augusta's very real desire to help her. 'She seemed to have no other view but that of mitigating his cruelty to me,' she was later to remark.

Soon both women began to irritate him by their behaviour. He became annoyed with Augusta because she refused to play up to him when he was tormenting Annabella; and he was irked by Annabella's martyred air of noble resignation.

Probably the last thing that Byron had expected was that the two women would ever combine against him, but this feminine alliance now began to be forged between them. It was destined to bring him down in the end.

Annabella, as befitted a mathematician with a practical mind, had at first concluded that her husband was only suffering from some

177

physical disorder which a doctor could cure. It was not an unreasonable assumption, for he was clearly a sick man. She watched him as he ground his teeth subconsciously, tossed from side to side in bed, groaned and writhed at night and dosed himself with laxatives. He complained of pain in his loins and liver.

The principal cause of his anguish, she decided, was indigestion. At one moment he starved himself; at the next he would devour his food with an insatiable appetite. He drank excessively and had now taken to brandy. He frequently resorted to laudanum either as a sedative or a pain-killer.

But as the first year of their marriage passed by and his condition grew worse, she came to other and more ominous conclusions. A copy of the *Edinburgh Medical Journal* for October 1815 chanced to fall into her hands and in this she read an account of the disease known as hydrocephalus, a disease of the brain. In fact her diagnosis was quite wrong, but she had good reasons for believing that her husband was going a little mad.

In some ways Byron was showing the same symptoms as those displayed by Caroline—outbursts of childish temper and periods of excitability followed by periods of intense depression. On one occasion he dashed a clock on to the floor and smashed it with a poker—a very Carolean gesture. On another occasion he threw a parrot in its cage out of the window.

His moods of frustration were not only due to the hopeless complexity of his sex life and the breakdown of his marriage. His financial affairs were also a constant source of worry. He had always been sensitive to the suggestion that he had married for money, and he did not like to discuss his debts with his wife. It had come as a shock to him to discover that Annabella was not as well off as he had believed. She certainly had 'expectations', but now he realized that it might be a long time before they materialized.

'The Baronet is eternal,' he wrote to Hobhouse, 'The Viscount immortal, and my lady (senior) without end. They grow more healthy every day, and I verily believe Sir and Lady Milbanke and Lord Wentworth are at this moment cutting a fresh set of teeth...'

His debts amounted to £30,000. Newstead was still unsold. There seemed really very little future for him, other than flight to the Continent. In England his problems were piling up day by day and his unpopularity increasing week by week as the scandal about him and Augusta was bandied about from mouth to mouth.

It was extraordinary that he should have been surprised by the extent of this gossip, for, after all, he had himself been at pains to promote it. He now convinced himself that it was Caroline who had been the chief promulgator of all these rumours, and his bitterness towards her increased.

She certainly had been indiscreet—as indiscreet as he would have been over any scandal involving herself—but she was by nature a gossip, as well he knew.

Caroline was still obsessed by him, but she was now confused and embittered. She could understand his former affairs, with eager young admirers or notorious women such as Lady Oxford, but the rumours about him which were now spreading round London, and which she herself was so busily helping to spread, concerned vices that she did not really understand. In a way he was betraying her, because he was involved with deeds which were degrading as well as shocking, and so her resentment of him increased. She still loved him, but now she began to hate him as well. And so she became a vessel of wrath.

Annabella's love was also beginning to turn to hate. And once it had done so, she began to welcome as her allies those who also hated him and were prepared to discuss his sins with her. She had never liked Caroline, and had always remained aloof in her presence, believing her to be a spoilt little minx who had made Byron's life miserable. But now she began to look upon Caroline as an ally, if not as a friend. They could meet on common ground, because they shared one thing in common. Each believed that she had given her love to a man who had now placed himself beyond the pale by his outrageous behaviour. But whereas Caroline only knew that he was being branded as a homosexual and a man guilty of incest, Annabella knew that his perversions included other crimes as well. She had no intention of revealing how he had misused her in the marriage bed, but she was willing to make ominous allusions and to drop dark hints about 'nameless crimes'.

Formidable forces were now being arraigned against Byron—the forces of women who had been betrayed by him and were eager for vengeance.

But to Annabella there was still one event which might yet alter the whole situation, and might even achieve the complete reformation of the husband whom she still believed to be noble at heart. He had made her pregnant early in the March of 1815, some two months after their marriage, and this evidence of her fertility had delighted him. He was determined that the child should be a boy, and that this boy should carry on the traditions of the Byron family. Annabella was also determined that it should be a boy. His nickname for her was 'Pip-pin'. Now she began to refer to her unborn child as 'young Pip'. But as the year had progressed, and his temper grew worse, he lost interest in the child. When asked how the pregnancy was developing, he replied that it was a subject 'upon which I am not particularly anxious'.

As the day of his child's delivery approached, his behaviour towards his wife became even worse. By December he was drinking heavily and was half-mad. When Annabella's labour pains began, he told her that he hoped she would die in child-birth and that the child would perish as well. If it lived he would curse it. At one o'clock in the afternoon of 10 December, the baby was born. It was a girl.

For a short time he seemed proud enough of his little daughter, and looked upon her with pleasure, but the bitterness soon returned. He insisted that the infant be called Augusta Ada, and referred to her as being a child 'born in bitterness, and nurtured in convulsion'.

After the birth, his moods of violence and bitterness increased. He and Annabella were now living in a house in Piccadilly Terrace, and Augusta was staying with them when the child was born. She sat up late with him on the night before the birth, trying to calm him. As Christmas approached, his madness became worse. He cursed his own marriage, and denounced that of Augusta, condemning her husband and her family. In one of his senseless rages he smashed to pieces a watch that he had treasured all his life.

His friend, Hobhouse, called round one day to see him at Piccadilly Terrace and found him morose and sullen. That same evening Hobhouse dined at Holland House, where he encountered Caroline. He mentioned that he had seen Byron.

Caroline feigned indifference. She was in excellent spirits—better than she had been for a long time. She chattered inconsequentially throughout the meal and commanded attention by her gaiety and wit. It was on this occasion that she gave her celebrated definition of truth as 'what one thinks at the moment'.

Twelve

Byron - The Unholy Alliance

Of the events of 1816, it can be said that they brought discredit on all the persons involved—the women for the manner in which they combined in an unholy alliance to bring about Byron's destruction; and Byron for the manner in which he allowed himself to be driven into exile and decadence.

Others who were equally discredited were the members of London Society, because of the pious and condemnatory attitude which they adopted. Their own behaviour was loose enough in all conscience, and they were in no position to condemn. Yet Society now branded Byron as a monster of depravity, and young girls drew away their skirts from ground over which he had walked.

It was their behaviour which prompted Macaulay to remark that he knew of no spectacle so ridiculous as the British public in one of its periodical fits of morality.

Byron had married Annabella on 2 January, 1815. His daughter, Augusta Ada, was born on 10 December of the same year. By the new year his mental health had broken down completely. On 3 January he told Annabella that he was bringing an actress to live with them. On 6 January he ordered his wife from the house. Annabella's mother had invited them all to visit her at her new home, Kirkby Mallory, in Leicestershire, and he sent a curt note to Annabella telling her to go, and to take the child with her. On the following day she replied, 'I shall obey your wishes and fix the earliest day that circumstances will admit for leaving London.'

She arranged to leave London for the North on 15 January. Byron disliked sentimental farewells. Now he became more boorish than ever. When she was told that her carriage was at the door she walked down the stairs past his room, with her baby in her arms. He knew that she was going, but made no effort to show himself.

As she recorded later, she paused outside his room, undecided

G

as to whether to go in and say goodbye to him. On the floor was a mat on which his Newfoundland dog used to lie. 'For a moment I was tempted to throw myself on it,' she wrote, 'and wait at all hazards, but it was only a moment—and I passed on. That was our parting.'

On the night before she had been prostrate with grief, having lost 'the self-command I could in general assume.' And it was on this last night, when she was with him and Augusta, that he turned to her and said to her with deep significance:

'When shall we three meet again?'
'In heaven I hope,' was her answer.
Perhaps they did. They never met again on earth.

And yet her love was still not completely dead. She wrote to him on her journey north, telling him that all was well with her and the baby, and reminding him to take his medicine. And she sent love from both of them. On arrival at her destination, she wrote again, beginning her letter 'Dearest Duck' and ending it, 'Love to the good goose, and everybody's love to you both from hence. Ever thy most loving Pippin...Pip—ip.'

What were her feelings towards him at this moment? It is difficult to say. On the same night as she wrote to him with all her old endearments she also wrote to an intimate friend, Selina Doyle, telling her that in view of her husband's mental condition a separation seemed inevitable, for as she declared in her old, pompous style, 'I must still undertake the responsibility of that Measure, which Duty, not Timidity, now determines me to postpone for a short time.'

Thus she was having it both ways. She continued to write to Byron with all her old affection whilst at the same time preparing herself for the final break. In fact, she had taken a leaf from out of her husband's book. It had been his habit to write loving letters to Caroline while at the same time abusing her to his friends. Now she wrote loving letters to him and began to revile him to her parents.

By now the unholy alliance was being formed. Augusta's allegiance to her brother was being slowly undermined by the growing intimacy between herself and Annabella. Augusta could not yet convince herself that her brother was cruel and vicious; therefore she was skilfully won over to the enemy camp by the suggestion, repeatedly propounded by Annabella, that what they referred to as Byron's 'malady', his insanity, was the cause of his infamous behaviour.

It was not long before Annabella was forced to play another card in her determination to persecute her husband. In one of her letters to Selina she had referred, in her usual evasive way, to the 'outrages' that she had suffered at his hands. She had not yet mentioned these to her parents. They were still anxious that Byron should join them at Kirkby, so that he might recover from his 'malady' and become reconciled to his loving wife. It may be that one of these letters fell into the hands of one or other parent. Annabella was at once cross-questioned on the meaning of the 'outrages' which she had suffered.

Annabella's growing resentment—and her burning self-righteousness—made her betray him. She defined the word 'outrage' and blackened his character in the eyes of her parents. They became convinced that their beloved daughter had married a monster and were determined that she should never return to him.

Yet Annabella never suggested at this stage that 'outrage' might mean anything more than infidelity, drunkenness and debauchery. She never mentioned the word 'incest' and she certainly never referred to sodomy.

The Princess of Parallelograms had been presented with a problem that she could not solve. Should she attempt to retain the love of her husband by renouncing her allegations of his wicked behaviour? Or should she revenge herself upon him for his heartless treatment by speaking out and denouncing him still further?

'There were moments,' she wrote, 'when resignation yielded to frenzy—and I would have forgotten myself, my child, my principles, to devote myself to that being who had cast me off.'

This was a letter such as Caroline might write. Each had been scorned, betrayed and shamefully ill-used, and neither could shake off the hold that he had upon them.

There was one great difference between them. Caroline's resentment varied with her changing moods, but Annabella was resolute and consistent in her condemnation, and the strategy of attack which she now developed was reasoned and practical.

Her first aim was to form an alliance between herself, Caroline and Augusta. Caroline presented no difficulties, for she was now in a mood to revenge herself upon Byron. But Augusta's loyalty to her half-brother could not easily be undermined. Caroline could be persuaded and flattered. Sterner methods were necessary with Augusta. She had to be dominated. The domination had to be prosecuted with some ruthlessness, but there was no doubt that it would finally be achieved.

Both Augusta and Caroline were far too simple to realize what was happening. Caroline was greatly enjoying the drama of it all, and the excitement of this breakdown of the marriage. However, she still saw herself in the role of a loyal friend and high-minded adviser to them both, whose aim must be to bring the unhappy pair together once again.

When the possibility of a separation first became public knowledge, Caroline sat down to her writing-desk to compose lengthy epistles filled with benevolent advice.

'I scarcely dare hope that I shall not offend, however I care not,' she wrote in one of her letters to Byron. She begged him to swallow his pride and to work towards a reconciliation.

'Go to her,' she implored, 'whatever the cause, little or great—it must be made up...If you knew what odious reports people circulate when men part from their wives, you would act in this instance prudently...I have disbelieved all the reports till now: but I trust they are of far less consequence than some pretend.'

Her further comment, to the effect that her husband was to be included amongst those who were 'most warmly, most whole-heartedly' supporting him did not ring quite true. William was no scandalmonger but it was hard to picture him rallying now to the Byronic cause.

In subsequent letters to Byron Caroline became a little more specific, and her hints became broader. She told him that if he found himself accused of anything of consequence he should 'deny it calmly and to all; do not fancy because every appearance is against you, that it is known. See your wife, and she cannot have the heart to betray you—if she has, she is a devil—and in mercy, be calm.'

All of which was tantamount to declaring that she knew full well that he had behaved outrageously and that his only hope lay in Annabella's refusal to expose him.

Finally there came from Caroline a dramatic appeal that he should make every effort to save himself.

'Lord Byron, hear me, and for God's sake pause before you rashly believe any report others may make. If letter or report or aught else has been malignantly placed in the hands of your wife to ruin you, I am ready to swear that I did it, for the purpose of deceiving her. There is nothing, however base it may appear, that I would not do to save you and yours...'

It was a typically melodramatic offer, but it may have been

184

written with some sincerity. Byron, perhaps unwisely, chose to see it as just another example of Caroline's willingness to keep the crisis on the boil, and he ignored it.

It was because he continued to ignore her that Caroline now allowed herself to be drawn into the enemy camp. She entered upon a correspondence with Annabella.

Annabella was busily collecting scurrilous information that she could use against Byron, and Caroline—as she well knew—was in possession of such information. Annabella had never liked Caroline but she was ready enough now to accept Caroline's friendship in order to achieve her purpose.

Caroline was invited to talk. She was happy to do so. She wrote asking for an interview:

'*I will tell you that which if you merely menace him with the knowledge shall make him tremble*...Above all intimate to *him* that you have the knowledge and proof of some secret which nothing but despair shall force you to utter.'

The meeting between Caroline and Annabella took place at the house of Mrs George Lamb on 27 March, 1816. Caroline was nervous and unsure of herself. Annabella was calm and authoritative. She took careful notes of all that was said.

Caroline opened the interview by saying that she considered herself to be bound by the solemn promise that she had made to Byron that she would never reveal his guilty secrets. But her conscience was now troubled by the fact that she had not warned Annabella of his sins before the marriage. If Annabella wished it, she would remain silent still. Her only desire was to do her duty.

Annabella expressed her admiration of these noble sentiments. Confidences such as these were, of course, sacred. But in this case she considered that since Byron had promised Caroline that he would never again resort to such sins, and then had done so, he had, by his betrayal of these vows, released her from those which she had made to him.

Annabella emphasized that there was also another vital factor to be considered. This was the well-being of the child, Ada. A rumour had been circulating in London that Byron was planning to leave the country, taking his daughter with him. The notes which Annabella was so industriously taking concluded with the pious observation that she could assure Caroline 'that neither on Earth, nor in Heaven, would she, in my opinion, have cause to repent so disinterested an action.'

Caroline then made a detailed statement, which was recorded by Annabella.

'She then confessed as follows, with an unfeigned degree of agitation—That from the time that Mrs L.—came to Bennet St in the year 1813—Lord B.—had given her various intimations of a criminal intercourse between them—but that for some time he spoke of it in a manner which did not enable her to fix it on Mrs L.—thus—"Oh I never knew what it was to love before—there is a woman I love so passionately—she is with child by me, and if a daughter it shall be called *Medora*"—that his avowals of this incestuous intercourse became bolder—till at last she said to him one day, "I could believe it of *you*—but not of *her*"—on this his vanity appeared piqued to rage and he said, "Would *she* not?"—assured Ly C.L.—that the seduction had not given him much trouble—that it was soon accomplished...since *that* avowal—Ly C.L.—never suffered any intimacy with Ld B.—though she had been prevailed upon to forgive "other and worse crimes".'

These other and worse crimes were then described. Byron had confessed to Caroline 'that from boyhood he had been in the practice of unnatural crime—that Rushton [his page] was one of those whom he had corrupted...He mentioned three schoolfellows whom he had thus perverted...Ly C.L.—did not believe that he had committed this crime since his return to England, though he had practised it unrestrictably in Turkey.'

Finally Caroline assured her listener that thereafter at the very recollection of these loathsome practices Byron 'several times turned quite faint and sick in alluding to the subject'.

Annabella returned triumphantly to her hotel after this interview to edit her notes and to add them to the dossier of her husband's crimes which she was about to place before her legal advisers. And she was able to note, for their benefit, that the interview had now transformed her previous suspicions 'into *absolute* conviction'.

A further outcome of this interview was that Annabella felt constrained to adopt an attitude of coolness—if not of actual hostility—towards Augusta. Augusta had already provided all the information she could, and there was always the danger that she might yet recant. Annabella therefore decided that she could no longer meet Augusta. She informed her of this decision through an intermediary—a Mrs Wilmot—who was instructed to pass on the message that Annabella was in weak health as the result of all her tribulations and that she no longer required of Augusta 'a Sacrifice which I should regret to ask'.

This action caused Byron's friend, Hobhouse, to declare, 'This has terminated, I believe, all correspondence between *My dearest Augusta* and *My dearest Annabella*! Such are female friendships.'

Had he understood Annabella, he would have realized that the correspondence was by no means ended. Annabella was but measuring out her fences one by one. The first which had to be surmounted was the need for obtaining a separation from her husband without any publicity. A public hearing had at all costs to be avoided. Thereafter she could devote her attention to Augusta whose painful reformation, she felt, had yet to be enforced.

Annabella's parents had placed her case in the hands of a leading solicitor, Sir Samuel Romilly, and he had called in the eminent barrister, Dr Stephen Lushington, as an adviser. Annabella had little difficulty in convincing them of the strength of her case. As they gazed upon her and saw before them a young woman of such obvious rectitude and godliness; and as they listened to her tragic stories of ill-treatment, their deepest indignation was aroused. Now these learned men allowed themselves to become a party to preparing a case full of loopholes and omissions; and full also of vague and unspecified charges against someone who was never to be given a proper opportunity to refute them.

Was the separation which they were now proposing to initiate based on charges of incest? Dr Lushington was later to state specifically that it was not.

Was it based on charges of homosexuality? It was not. The allegations of homosexuality rested largely on hearsay, and there was no evidence to show that Byron had engaged in such practices after his marriage.

What, then, was the charge against Byron? It was that he acted in a 'most foul and gross' manner upon the person of his wife. What exactly did this charge entail? No one ever knew.

When Annabella first laid her case before Dr Lushington, he advised her to reconsider the whole matter and to seek a reconciliation with her husband. Why, then, did he later change his mind? It was because she begged him to grant her a secret interview to that she might acquaint him with the full facts. To this he agreed.

The interview took place at the end of February; and before it began she made him swear a most solemn oath that he would never divulge anything that passed between them. After the interview, he agreed to do everything he could to help her achieve the separation

187

and to ensure that there would be no public hearing. What did she tell him?

No one knows. No one has ever known or will ever know. There was never any question of her allegations being challenged, or refuted. The only evidence that might have shed light on her allegations was contained in Byron's *Memoirs,* which Annabella insisted on being destroyed after his death.

Yet still the basic question remained. *Why,* if after being so monstrously ill-used, did she not leave his house at once, never to return? *Why* did she continue to live with her husband for a year and throughout this time write letters to him, when they were parted, which were couched in the most affectionate terms? *Why,* if the sexual advances which he made upon her were so degrading and repulsive, did she continue to share his bed until *he*—and not she— decided that they must part? And *why* was this extraordinary veil of secrecy thrown over the whole affair. *Why* was there always the suggestion that Annabella was doing her utmost to cover up something which was shameful in her own conduct, as well as in his?

But Dr Lushington was won over completely. He believed what Annabella told him, and thundered his denunciation. Yet at the same time he took every step to ensure that the case did not come to court, and the good name of his client was protected at all times. He was satisfied that Byron had no good name to protect.

Byron realized that his case was hopeless, and resigned himself to defeat. On the afternoon of Sunday, 21 April, 1816, he signed the deeds of separation and prepared to go into exile. The detestation which the public now felt for him, and the fact that he was bankrupt, made such a course inevitable. And in truth he was ready enough to turn his back on the country which had at first given him so much praise and had then reviled him.

A week before the signing of the deeds Byron bade what he knew must be his last goodbye to Augusta. It was Easter Sunday and she came to see him at his house in Piccadilly Terrace. They spent the day together, sadly and almost in silence. They had come to the end of the road.

He had always been selfish and self-centred, and it was only in these last few days in England that he began to realize that in destroying himself he had also destroyed her.

He could escape from the calumny. He could go into exile and live in the warmth of the Italian sun, far from his tormentors. But Augusta could not. It was her destiny to stay behind in England

and to try and live down her past. She was in the last stages of pregnancy and was shortly to give birth to the fifth of her seven children. Her husband was a rake, her health was wretched and she was persecuted and broken-hearted. She was already being ostracized by Society, and had even been 'cut' in public by Caro-George— Mrs George Lamb. There could be no future happiness for Augusta Leigh.

When the moment of parting came, she broke down and wept. So also did he. She gave him as her farewell gift a Bible. No one else would have dared to have done such a thing, for he had always scoffed at religion. But he took it gravely and treasured it for the rest of his life. It was by his bedside when he died.

After she had left him, he sat down to write a letter to Annabella: 'I have just parted from Augusta—almost the last being you had left me to part with—and the only unshattered tie of my existence— wherever I may go—and I am going far—you and I can never meet again in this world—or the next—let this content or atone. If any accident occurs to me, be kind to her—if she is then nothing—to her Children.'

During his last few days in England he found an outlet for his misery by composing a poem which he entitled *Stanzas to Augusta*. It included the lines:

> When fortunes changed—and love fled far,
> And hatred's shafts flew thick and fast,
> Thou wert the solitary star
> Which rose and set not to the last.

Only one further act remained to him. The grand exit, preceding the final curtain. The master of melodrama had to leave the stage with suitable flamboyance, even though he had long since lost his public's devotion and the stalls were emptying fast. But Londoners have always had a taste for a free show, and now they were to witness the passing of the town's most notorious aristocrat.

Byron was well known for his dislike of early rising, but it was shrewdly assumed by the cognoscenti that he would be required to make an 'early morning flit' if he were to dodge the bailiffs who made a daily descent upon him in the interests of his numerous creditors. And in fact he chose the hour just after dawn, when fashionable London was still asleep (or had only just gone to bed) to stage his exit from Mayfair.

Outside his house there stood waiting for him one of his most ridiculous possessions—a vast and cumbersome carriage which a coachmaker of Long Acre had expertly fashioned as an exact replica of Napoleon's coach. It would have cost an immense sum had it ever been paid for (the coachmaker was not present to witness the departure of his masterpiece and its owner), and now it stood, painted in blue, with a gold border and the imperial arms on the sides, loaded with luggage and looking absurdly out of place. Two bottles of champagne, a large cake and some Jewish pastries were placed inside to fortify the occupants on their journey to the coast, but when Byron finally descended the steps it was without his large assortment of pills, potions, herbs and tonics, which were left behind as items of interest when the house and its contents were later put up for sale.

The coachman whipped up his horses, the coach lumbered off down Piccadilly and the watchers raised a feeble cheer. Inside the face of Byron, pale as ever and wearing its habitual expression of sardonic disdain, was glimpsed for a moment before it disappeared.

His destination was Dover and the road led through Kent, where the buds were frothing into life on the trees and in the hedgerows, and the heady scent of spring was in the air.

The commotion caused in Dover by his arrival was considerable. And Dr Lushington, who was at pains to acquaint himself with all the facts concerning the departure, was able to report later to Annabella, 'the curiosity to see him was so great that many ladies accoutred themselves as chambermaids for the purpose of obtaining under that disguise a nearer inspection whilst he continued at the inn...'

Finally, on the morning of 25 April, he limped down the quay on Hobhouse's arm and went aboard the vessel that was to transport him to Ostend.

Having arrived safely on the Continent, he decided to break his journey south to visit Brussels and to take a look at the field of Waterloo. It was a form of pilgrimage.

The spring flowers were already in bloom and the land was under the plough. He hobbled about in search of bones, but there were none, and in the end he had to content himself with a few military buttons of doubtful authenticity which were sold to him as souvenirs by some ragged small boys.

Then for a while he sat in meditation in the warm sunshine, pondering on the mutability of human affairs.

Vanity of vanities; all is vanity.

He was twenty-eight, and his life seemed ended.

Thirteen

Caroline - The Edge of The Precipice

Byron's marriage had broken up at the beginning of 1816 and Caroline had been in part responsible for its failure and for his exile.

One can only guess at her feelings. A certain sense of triumph— of revenge achieved and of retribution visited upon the unrighteous —may well have been offset by a sense of loss. Perhaps there was also a sense of relief. He had gone into exile, and now at least the fatal passion would not constantly be rekindled by the sight of him. She realized well enough that it was unlikely that she and Annabella would ever see him again. He would die in exile and only his body would return.

But if her mind dwelt upon thoughts of retribution, she had now to face up to retribution herself. As the year of 1816 progressed it became increasingly evident that the collapse of her own marriage was now imminent.

William's patience had at last become exhausted. He had suffered her tempers and tantrums for nearly eleven years. Now he was quite worn out. Life with Caroline had become unbearable.

He realized that the departure of Byron would never solve her problems, for by now her problems were insoluble. The twin demons of tension and depression had her in their grip. She was racketting herself to pieces and placing herself under a nervous strain which neither her mind nor her body could continue to withstand. And now he was beginning to suffer from a similar strain.

It was a curious coincidence that the preparations which were being made for Annabella's separation from Byron were carried on at much the same time as were William's for his separation from Caroline.

Perhaps it was not coincidental. Just as Byron saw Napoleon's downfall as a forerunner of his own, so may Caroline have seen her downfall as a reflection of his. She was sleeping badly, roaming the house at night like a forlorn ghost and drinking heavily—of brandy,

191

in imitation of her lost lover. She was seeking to escape from herself.

This growing restlessness was accentuated, at the time of Byron's departure, by William's decision to take up once again the threads of his political career. Caroline may well have resented this decision. He was the one to whom she always turned for comfort when her problems overwhelmed her, and he had no right to give his attention to other things.

Stories of her eccentric behaviour continued to circulate in Society. After the Heathcote affair she had made no major scene in London, but strange tales were told of her antics whilst at Brocket. One that gained currency at this moment concerned her attack upon one of her small army of pages. It was whispered that in a fit of rage she had severely injured one of these defenceless little boys.

There was some truth in the story, but the attack was not as bad as it was made out to be and the page in question was in need of correction.

It was his custom to play practical jokes on the household and he had a particular leaning towards fireworks. These he was in the habit of throwing into the fire, where they would explode and cause much consternation. One of the chief sufferers was Lord Melbourne who was no longer young. He was still in search of the quiet life which had always been denied him in his home, and was finding an ever-increasing consolation in the bottle.

Caroline remonstrated with the child and lectured him on this dangerous habit. One day in April, when she was playing ball with him in the drawing room, he produced yet another squib and threw it in the fire. It exploded with a loud bang. Caroline lost her temper and flung the ball at him. It hit his forehead and caused a small gash which at once began to bleed.

At the sight of the blood both Caroline and the small boy went into hysterics.

'Oh, my Lady!' he cried out. 'You have killed me!'

Caroline was convinced that she had murdered one of her pages. For days afterwards she remained in the same hysterical condition, even after it had been explained to her that the boy was not seriously hurt.

The story was spread abroad and gave support to the growing belief that Caroline was going mad—and was likely to get madder now that Byron was about to leave the country.

William had to suffer this hysterical outbreak at a time when he was trying to devote his whole attention to politics. He felt that he could not go on in this way and his family were still urging him to make the break. He now realized that his future happiness and the success of his political career could only be ensured if he obtained a judicial separation from his wife.

But still he held back. He was only too well aware of the problems that were now facing Annabella. She was trying to obtain a separation whilst avoiding all the gossip and scandal that would attend a public hearing. He had no desire to see his own dirty linen washed in public, for he would become a laughing stock at just the moment when he was seeking to be accepted as a serious and high-minded politician.

The pattern of Caroline's drinking now followed the usual course of those on the way to chronic alcoholism. Admittedly the evidence of this drinking came chiefly from the disclosures made by her French maid, Thérèse, some time after she had left Caroline's service, but Caroline's behaviour at this time was nevertheless consistent with what the maid had to tell.

Thérèse was a gossip and it was also her habit to spy on her mistress. It was known to the household that Caroline had adopted the habit of running every now and then into her bedroom in order to *dédommager* herself—to revive herself with a glass of cognac. The story that Thérèse was later to tell was that this habit persisted throughout the night and that in this drunken state she would sometimes waken her husband and demand entry into his bed.

At this time they were sleeping in different rooms and Thérèse told of how she had once heard Caroline screaming at William late at night, demanding to know why she was being forced to sleep alone. When she refused to leave him, he shouted at her, 'Get along, you drunken little bitch.'

Thérèse had further gossip to spread which may have been true. One of her stories concerned the good-looking young doctor whom Caroline saw fit to employ when she was worried about the health of her sickly child, Augustus.

Thérèse reported that it was her mistress's habit to visit this young man when he was in bed, ostensibly because the boy was ill. It was certainly true that the servants did once report the discovery of one of Caroline's stockings at the bottom of his bed.

And yet Thérèse was not wholly antagonistic to her mistress. Of William she said that she found him 'at all times proud, severe and altogether disagreeable'.

He had good reason to be.

At this critical time in her married life, when William was under strong pressure from his family to get rid of her, and was already showing signs of weakening, Caroline sought an outlet from her problems in writing. Her remarkable aptitude for committing major blunders at the most inopportune moments now asserted itself.

She produced a novel which she called *Glenarvon*.

It seemed at this time that Caroline was heading for a complete nervous breakdown. Yet one of the most remarkable things about her was her extraordinary stamina and her reversion to periods of complete lucidity at moments when she seemed to be mentally deranged.

She had always been of an artistic bent. She could sketch, paint, compose quite passable verse—and she could write. She now chose to write a novel.

Her reasons for doing this were mixed. She resented her husband's pre-occupation with his political career and decided to prove to him that she, too, could start out on a new career. Byron had written, and she decided to emulate him. And finally she decided that the best way of getting the spleen out of her system; of ridding herself of all her pent-up frustration; and of expressing her deep resentment against Society would be to follow the example of her ancestor, Sarah Jennings, Duchess of Marlborough, by proving that the pen could be more hurtful than the sword. She forgot about the enemies which Sarah had made for herself as a result.

Society at this time offered a rewarding field for the novelist who sought to criticise it. In the years to come Disraeli was to use the novel as a splendidly informative mirror of the social and political world of the Victorian age.

Caroline was not prepared to approach her subject in quite the same scholastic way. True to her life-long dedication to escapism, her novel had to be a fantasy. It had to have Gothic overtones, sinister undertones and be charged with gloom and despair. It had to be peopled by heroes and heroines who were far larger than life. It had to be filled with sensational incidents, dire happenings and violent deaths.

It had also to display Byron in all his infamy. He had to be the unmistakable hero-villain of the piece. He was Glenarvon.

Authors have their own conceits about the manner in which they work. Some like to describe the long and weary hours which they spend in their search for perfection. Others like to suggest that their masterpieces have been tossed off lightly over a period of a few days or weeks. Byron himself had declared that two of his most popular works—*The Bride of Abydos* and *The Corsair*—were written in four and ten days respectively.

Now Caroline, not to be outdone, declared that her novel, *Glenarvon,* which she produced almost casually, like a conjuror producing a rabbit out of a hat, was written in a month and always at night. She was unable to sleep and so decided to spend the night hours producing a best-seller. This she most certainly did. Not even *The Corsair* was so successful.

Glenarvon was written in the early part of 1816. It was written in long-hand—in Caroline's scribbled handwriting—and it was necessary for her to employ a professional copier when it was completed.

The scene which she staged when the time came for this professional copier to collect the manuscript from her at Melbourne House was pure Caroline, and her description of it must surely be accepted as factual. According to her own description of it, given later to her friend, Lady Morgan, she placed her companion, a governess named Miss Welsh, at the harp, and seated herself at her writing table. She was dressed in her page's livery and looked 'a boy of fourteen'.

On his arrival, the copier, an elderly scribe named Mr Woodhead, looked in bewilderment at this incongruous pair, and being required to guess at which was the more likely to have summoned him with such urgency to Melbourne House—an elegant lady strumming on a harp or a diminutive page-boy sitting at a desk—he plumped for the harpist and addressed her as Lady Caroline.

The page-boy then rose from the desk, handed him the manuscript and told him that it had been written in secret and was the work of a Mr William Ormonde. However, on his second visit, Mr Woodhead was informed that William Ormonde had unfortunately died and that it would therefore be necessary to publish the novel anonymously, this being the last sad wish of the deceased.

The novel was sent to John Murray and rejected. It was then sent to Henry Colburn, a publisher of light fiction and an astute judge of public taste (Bulwer Lytton, Lady Morgan, Captain Marryat, Harrison Ainsworth and Disraeli were later to be numbered amongst his authors). Having read it, he decided that he had a best seller on his hands and that his only problem was just how many copies he should print.

Glenarvon was published on 9 May, 1816, exactly a fortnight after Byron's departure from Dover. The presentation was handsome. The novel was published in three slim volumes, in a rich gilt and leather binding. The title page bore a picture of Love contemplating a burning heart and the inscription *L'on a trop chéri.*

Since it was obviously written by someone with an intimate knowledge of Society; and since the background was clearly that of Devonshire House and Holland House; and since the central character, Glenarvon, was unmistakably Byron, there could be little doubt as to the identity of the author.

Any doubt at all on this score was at once settled by the acidity with which the writer had expressed herself. Only Caroline could have harboured quite such bitter feelings towards her central characters. And only Caroline could have dressed up her plot with such preposterous trappings. Society was held up to ridicule, and no one felt this public humiliation more than Caroline's husband, William Lamb.

He was condemned for his insensitivity and—worse still—for the manner in which he had corrupted the innocence of his young bride. His social circle was condemned and London Society was presented as an oligarchy run by ambitious and unprincipled women who led their husbands by the nose. In essence it was an attack on Byron, but much of the venom was reserved for Holland House, Melbourne House and Devonshire House.

It was an outrageous work in many respects and badly written; but it was yet sharply observant of the foibles of those whom it ridiculed. It was the creation of an immature mind, with its Gothic absurdities, its extravagant passages of purest melodrama and its penny-dreadful plot. But despite all this it was compulsive reading for both upper and middle classes alike. The gossip papers serenaded it. The public devoured it.

After Byron, the principal target of the work was Lady Holland. Caroline had not previously revealed any outstanding animosity for this very forthright and ambitious hostess, but now she received the full force of Caroline's invective, as did all the hangers-on and sycophants with whom Lady Holland was so fond of surrounding herself.

Lady Holland appeared as the Princess of Madagascar who resided at Barbary House, 'three miles beyond the turnpike', which was just about the distance between Holland House in Kensington and the turnpike at the western extremity of Piccadilly.

The poet of 'an emaciated and sallow complexion' who stood

behind the Princess, who was outwardly of 'the kindest and most engaging manner' but who at all times said 'that which was most unpleasant to the person whom he appeared to praise' was Samuel Rogers, of whom Caroline was to note, 'This yellow hyena had however a noble heart, magnanimous and generous, and even his friends, could they but escape from his smile and tongue, had no reason to complain.'

Caroline herself appeared as Calantha, the sugar-sweet heroine of impressive nobility and simple innocence, who was enchanting to know but was handicapped in her life by her impulsive nature. Calantha noticed that all the critics and reviewers who surrounded the Princess wore chains and collars, which were the badge of their servitude, and without which they would not have gained admittance.

It was all hard hitting, well below the belt, and calculated to turn those whom she ridiculed into Caroline's enemies for life.

Lady Holland, writing to Mrs Creevey on 21 May, described the novel as Caroline's defence against her husband, 'accusing him of having overset her religious and moral! principles by teaching her doctrines of impiety etc...Lady Melbourne is represented as bigoted and vulgar.'

As for her own portrait, she wrote: 'The *bonne-bouche* I have reserved for the last—myself. Where every ridicule, folly and infirmity (my not being able from malady to move about much) is portrayed. The charge against more essential qualities is, I trust, and believe, a fiction; at least an uninterrupted friendship and intimacy of 25 years with herself and her family might induce me to suppose it. The work is a strange farrago, and only curious from containing some of Lord Byron's genuine letters...The work has a prodigious sale, as all libellous matters have.'

Lady Melbourne, though only referred to as 'bigoted and vulgar' was deeply humiliated by the contents of *Glenarvon*. She had always criticised Caroline to William and had advised him to get rid of this tiresome creature. Yet she had at the same time been happy to act as an intimate confidante to Byron when he was seeking to make Caroline his mistress. So it could be argued that Lady Melbourne was treated more lightly than she deserved. Therefore when Caroline was attacked for the manner in which she had dealt with her mother-in-law in *Glenarvon,* she had ammunition in plenty to fire back. In a letter which she wrote at this time to Lord Granville she described how Lady Melbourne and her daughter, Emily, now Lady Cowper, had consistently supported Byron, even to the indigna-

197

tion of her son, William, who had never understood his mother's treachery in this respect.

It was during the writing of this novel that Lady Melbourne's campaign against Caroline was reaching its height. Caroline was therefore able to declare with some justice that 'wrongs, crimes, follies, even the least, were raked up from the days of infancy and brought forth to view without mercy. *To write this novel was then my sole comfort.*'

But the person who was most vilified by the novel—namely Byron—was the only one who treated the publication with humorous resignation and was never put out by it.

Caroline was seeking revenge on her tormentors, but her timing could not have been worse. The publication of *Glenarvon* occurred at the very moment when matters were coming to a head between herself and her husband. It did not require much at this stage to convince him that his wife's behaviour had become impossible to endure, and that he must part from her.

Glenarvon was Caroline's attempt to justify her conduct towards him. In it she sought to prove that her downfall had been brought about by her husband's insensitive treatment of her after her marriage. What she was trying to say was that heroines of either fact or fiction should be looked upon as ethereal creatures of beauty and innocence who should never be required to submit to the indignities of sexual intercourse.

Byron's friends reacted more strongly to *Glenarvon* than he did himself. Hobhouse was so incensed that he wrote, 'The hero is a monster and meant for B.' His first reaction was to go round to Melbourne House and tell Caroline what he thought of her. 'I called on the bitch,' he said, 'and was asked whether any harm had been done by her book...she showed me half bawdy pictures of hers of B.'

A defiant Caroline was in no mood to be bullied. She had reproduced one of Byron's letters, and when Hobhouse expressed his disgust at this and threatened to publish some of her own letters, she tossed her head and answered that she would then be forced to publish *all* Byron's letters, as well as the journal which she had kept of the whole affair.

Hobhouse retired, defeated. Caroline in militant mood was not a person with whom one could argue.

The picture of Byron which she had painted in *Glenarvon* was admittedly a lurid one, but he was not portrayed as a monster. He was, after all, the heroine's lover and he had to be endowed with his full measure of glamour. Many of her descriptions of him were accurate; and when she exaggerated his appearance and character, it was only to make him even more beautiful and irresistible than he was in real life, although certainly far more wicked.

Her aim in writing her book was ostensibly to revenge herself upon him and upon Society, but only Society was portrayed with a pen dipped in vitriol. She made a gesture towards crucifying her lover, and the hero, Glenarvon, was made to commit murder and to indulge in kidnapping, rape and all the other traditional sins committed by the Byron males over the centuries, but this could be seen as a novelist's licence. But Caroline went that one step further than the Victorian novelists by fusing her hero and her villain into one. It is a formula which is rarely unsuccessful.

If *Glenarvon* proved one thing more than anything else, it was that Caroline was still infatuated with Byron. She hated him but she still worshipped him. What Caroline was saying in *Glenarvon* was that this man, with all his faults and sinfulness, was her conception of what a hero should be.

Byron, adrift in Europe, was sent a copy by Mme de Staël and professed himself bored by it and indifferent to its success. In fact he may well have been secretly quite flattered by it. But a comment suitable for repetition in England had to be made and so he wrote to Moore: 'It seems to me, that if the authoress had written the *truth*, and nothing but the truth—the whole truth—the romance would not only have been more *romantic*, but more entertaining. As for the likeness, the picture can't be good—I did not sit long enough.'

The comment was widely quoted and it was generally felt that it had put Caroline in her place. Few remarked that no one had less appreciation of the truth than Byron, whose love life had been built upon a succession of lies.

What, one may well ask, *was* the truth in this affair? Certainly the two central characters were quite incapable of distinguishing between fact and fiction in their romance; and now even Annabella, that one-time pillar of rectitude, was busily engaged in distorting the truth to suit her purpose of vindication of herself and vilification of her husband.

The truth in *Glenarvon* lay more than was generally realized in the portrait of Caroline herself. The heroine, Calantha, marries Lord Avondale when she is very young and innocent. He loves her but is a worldly and cynical man who laughs at her inexperience. Of her

199

introduction to sexual love, Caroline wrote of her heroine: 'Love, like other arts, requires experience, and the terror and ignorance on its first approach prevents our feeling it as strongly as at a later period. Passion mingles not with a sensation so pure, so refined, as that which Calantha then conceived, and the excess of a lover's attachment testified and overpowered the feelings of a child.'

It is a study of an over-romantic young virgin in the arms of a virile, though not insensitive husband on her wedding night, and it has about it the sad ring of truth.

Later in the book she was to observe that, 'When we love, if that which we love is noble and superior, we contract a resemblance to the object of our passion' and was then to add, 'Woe be to those who have ever loved Glenarvon.'

Glenarvon enjoyed an immediate success. Leaders of Society bought it to read about each other. The middle classes bought it to read about the permissive way of life enjoyed by their betters.

Three editions were sold within the first few weeks. An Italian edition was brought out within the year.

The success of *Glenarvon* and the adverse publicity it brought down upon the heads of all those mentioned in it, especially the Lamb family and William in particular, seemed now to make the break-up of the marriage inevitable.

Even William's loyalty, which had in the past been strengthened by any persecution of his wife, was unable to withstand this final act of disloyalty.

Caroline's only course was to try and bluff herself out of her predicament, and this she did by maintaining that William had read the book before publication and had thoroughly enjoyed it.

This was a lie. He had known nothing of the book, and its appearance and contents were a great blow to him. *Glenarvon* shocked him deeply. In it the public could read of all the secrets of his married life, with its quarrels and intimacies. He saw it as an act of gross betrayal and he was further depressed by the knowledge that many of his dearest friends, as well as his family, had been wounded almost as greatly as himself. He felt that he could not face them. He longed to sink into oblivion.

'I wish I were dead,' he muttered. 'I wish I were dead.'

Caroline was startled by his reaction. She had never imagined that he would take her book so much to heart. Now she realized that she had gone too far.

After he had received the book and read it, he visited her in her room and told her that if she did not withdraw it he would never wish to see her again. She knew that he was speaking the truth, but there was nothing that she could do. The book was already being circulated.

As a result he told his family that he now accepted that a separation from his wife was inevitable. The necessary steps should at once be taken.

As with Annabella, so now with him. The lawyers were summoned to Melbourne House, and a Deed of Separation was drawn up. And as with Annabella, every effort had to be made to keep the plans a secret from the Society gossips. A public scandal at this moment would ruin his political career.

The Lamb family made no effort to conceal their delight. Now that Caroline was no longer able to shelter behind William, they condemned her openly. Even Henrietta was included in their attack.

Caroline became a hunted hare. She was banished to Brocket whilst the Deed was being prepared, and told that no one wished to see her face at Melbourne House until it was ready for signature. The Lamb family did not trust her—and they did not trust William. They realized that his resolution might yet fail him if he were subjected to Caroline in one of her little-girl moods of pathos and tears. They realized that he was still in love with her.

William himself was well aware of the danger, but on the evening before the Deed was to be signed, he went down to Brocket for the night. It was mid-summer and the countryside was quiet and serene. He went wearily to bed, but was astonished to hear a strange sound coming from outside the door, as though a dog were scratching to get in. When he opened the door, he found his wife curled up on the doormat.

What she said to him is unknown, but he came to London the next day with his mind made up. The lawyers assembled in Lord Melbourne's study on the ground floor of the house, and members of the family, including William's brother, George, were there to witness the final act of separation. A query arose over a clause that involved the child, Augustus, and William went upstairs to see Caroline, who had returned to London for the signing and had been banished to the upper regions.

The minutes passed and he did not return. The lawyers drummed their fingers on the table and gazed at the ceiling. Finally George left the room to find out what was happening.

He found William sitting in a chair with Caroline on his knee. She was laughing with him and caressing him, and feeding him with tiny scraps of bread-and-butter.

The old magic had triumphed again. The elfin charm had melted his heart as it had melted it so often in the past.

The lawyers withdrew, shrugging their shoulders resignedly, and the Lamb family were left in disarray. Caroline had beaten them once again. It was a remarkable victory.

William had already proclaimed that one of the reasons why he had to separate from his wife after the publication of *Glenarvon* was that Society would otherwise assume that he had condoned the writing of it. Now he was remaining with her and Society were left to think as they pleased. All his old loyalty returned.

'Caroline,' he said to her, 'We will stand or fall together.'

Yet his heart was heavy. There was little enough hope for Caroline now. This was why he stood by her. Laudanum, pills, brandy— and a broken heart. It was a mixture that must destroy her in the end.

Fourteen

Caroline - The Summer of a Dormouse

'How much remains of downright existence?' Byron asked himself as he grew fat and disillusioned in exile. Existence to him had become no more than a weary round of 'sleeping, eating, swilling—of buttoning and unbuttoning. The summer of a dormouse.'

In 1821 he wrote:

> Through life's road so dim and dirty,
> I have dragged to three-and-thirty.
> What have these years left to me?
> Nothing—except thirty-three.

Three years later, on his thirty-sixth birthday, he wrote his last love-lyric:

> My days are in the yellow leaf;
>   The flowers and fruits of Love are gone;
> The worm, the canker and the grief
>   Are mine alone!

Byron was destined to make his exit from the stage with a final flourish, but it was Caroline's fate to fade away in sad seclusion after the flowers and fruits of love had died; if indeed they had ever really blossomed for her. They shared the same mood of melancholy and disillusion.

Caroline never showed the slightest sign of shame at having written *Glenarvon*, she even adopted the attitude that her family should be proud of having a literary genius in their midst. She invited Hary-O to visit her soon after its publication, and greeted her effusively but without any suggestion of guilt. Hary-O was highly indignant.

'And this is the guilty broken-hearted Calantha who could only expiate her crimes with her death!' she said angrily. She had never had much sympathy for Caroline, although there had been moments when she had been sorry for her.

203

Having written one best-seller, Caroline determined to write another. Authorship gave her an outlet for her inhibitions as well as for her quite considerable creative talent, but she failed to realize that *Glenarvon* had been written out of the fire of bitterness and that it was based on an easily recognizable hero. In *Glenarvon* she was writing her autobiography, even though the plot was wrapped up with many Gothic extravagances, and she was writing it from the heart. No future work was likely to have the same driving force behind it, or the same truth of feeling.

In 1820 she wrote her second novel, *Graham Hamilton*, which was more mature and certainly less melodramatic. Those who write bestsellers at their first attempt are often made to suffer when their second work fails to achieve the same success. This happened to Caroline.

Not that she was ever confident of its success. She delayed publication of *Graham Hamilton* for two years and then published it anonymously. She had made the mistake of listening to the advice of the successful Italian author, Ugo Foscolo, who told her to 'write a book which will offend nobody—women cannot afford to shock'.

Caroline could not afford *not* to shock. It was expected of her. *Graham Hamilton* did not shock; but it also did not sell. This may, of course, have been due to the fact that with Byron in exile in Italy, and with her own withdrawal from Society, she had lost the stimulus for writing which she had previously enjoyed. In essence it was a book of memories and was a recollection of her much-loved aunt, Georgiana, Duchess of Devonshire, who had died in 1806.

The health of the two sisters had never been good, and in November 1821, Caroline's mother, Henrietta, died in Florence, at the age of sixty-one. Her last days had been spent in Parma, where she had gone to help nurse her little grandson, who was dying of an incurable illness. Hers had been in many ways a tragic life. She had been devoted to Caro, but there had only been one grand passion in her life, and that was for her lover, Lord Granville, who had married her own niece, Hary-O.

Caroline missed her mother greatly. She was still unsure of William's continuing affection, and still uncertain of her future. Her father offered her no sense of security. He had never suffered from ill-health, or from the worries that had beset her.

The death of her mother-in-law, Lady Melbourne, three years earlier, in the spring of 1818, had caused Caroline no distress. They had never liked each other. Her death, however, had been a sad affair. It seemed that she, too, was made to suffer the curse of the

Byrons, for her health had begun to deteriorate in the same year as his departure into exile. Thereafter she had gone rapidly down hill and had grown lethargic, coarse and repellent.

William mourned his mother, but Caroline did not. She hoped that her relations with Melbourne House would improve after this, but in fact William's sister, Emily, the youngest of the family, at once took on her mother's mantle as defender of the family honour and the scourge of Caroline.

Emily had married the 5th Earl of Cowper a few weeks after Caroline had married William. Lord Cowper was very rich, but heavy and stupid. Emily was a lovely girl, warm-hearted and gay, but she and Caroline had never got on together. Emily adored William, and with the death of Lady Melbourne she felt it her duty to protect him from Caroline's tantrums. After a dinner-party which she gave for Lord and Lady Holland, William and Caroline in the summer of 1822, she noted that William seemed in better spirits than he had been in the past, but added that Caroline 'is odious and ill, always raging or fainting, and Augustus is in a state worse than ever; he was in fits all yesterday and they called in the doctors. The critical time is coming on and very awkwardly too. She is frightened about it...'

Both Emily and William were worried by the growing intemperance of their father. Lord Melbourne, who was now in his seventies, had become an alcoholic. He took no exercise, but drank steadily throughout the day, became drunk by dinner time, then slept until midnight and then began drinking again. And this chiefly on sherry. But fortunately a lethargic temperament allied to the constitution of an ox had enabled him to survive in relative peace of mind. Only Caroline's tantrums, and the antics of her tiresome regiment of pages, served to inject some moments of passing indignation into an otherwise uneventful existence.

Caroline spent much of her time at Brocket, where she was left to her own devices and made herself an intolerable nuisance to the staff. By now she was being generally ostracized by Society, and so she turned again to writing as an outlet. In 1823 she completed her third novel, *Ada Reis,* which was also inspired by the advice and guidance given by Ugo Foscolo. It was a better work than *Graham Hamilton,* and was equally unsuccessful.

The hero, Ada Reis, had more than a touch of Byron about him, being a man of outstanding good looks, with curly auburn hair, who becomes a pirate and goes marauding in the Mediterranean after plunging a knife into his mistress's heart in a fit of jealousy. He then carries off her young daughter, Fiormonda, who travels with him, and is later brought up in oriental splendour with a hideous and half-mad Egyptian governess.

There was something to be learnt of Caroline's past from all this. By now her memories of her own childhood in Naples, in the care of a governess who did not understand her, had been distorted in order to explain the wilfulness which she had developed as a child. The theme of the book is that the child would have developed normally had the wicked governess never been placed in control of her.

But if Caroline saw her governess in a false light, she presented a fairly accurate picture of herself, for Fiormonda is a girl of violent temper. And although she is described as 'a lovely, gentle child' she nevertheless smashes priceless vases in a state apartment, tears an exquisite veil into shreds and gives one of her slaves a 'terrible bump over the right eye'.

There was no question of these two later novels being written without the knowledge of William. He was called in to advise upon them, and although conscious of their faults, he was much impressed by the power and imagination in the writing.

At the same time as she was writing her novels Caroline was also producing some passable verse. At moments she could fall into bathos, as when she produced a poem in praise of her husband which opened with the couplet:

> Oh, I adore thee, William Lamb,
> But hate to hear thee say God damn.

But although her poems never did anything more than show the child-like simplicity of her mind, she yet could strike a nostalgic note, as when she wrote:

> Little birds in yonder grove,
> Making nests and making love,
> Come, sing upon your favourite tree
> Once more your sweetest songs to me.

This is the beginning of a poem which she wrote when she had finally to leave Brocket Hall. There is no doubt that by the time she had reached her thirties she had lost her love of London, and of the gay life in Society. At Brocket she found peace, and here she could be with her son, whose health she so firmly convinced herself was getting ever better, whereas in fact it was getting ever worse.

Sometimes she was stimulated by a flash of the old gaiety and exuberance of spirit, but for the most part she lay in bed, almost too weary to speak. For hours she would fix her gaze on a chair that was in the bow window. This was the chair in which Byron had sat for his portrait by Sanderson.

'The loss of what one adores affects the mind and heart,' she had once written, and although the fact that William Lamb had accepted her back, and seemed once more to love her as before, it was only of Byron that she thought as she lay in her bed, 'wrapped in fine muslins' and gazing out of the window with eyes that so often filled with tears.

At the time of George Lamb's assault upon the electors of Westminster she had struck up a friendship with the young author, William Godwin, and she wrote to him several times from Brocket to explain to him why she stayed in the country and did not come to London. In one of her letters she said:

> You would not say if you were here that nature had not done her best for us. Everything is looking beautiful, everything in bloom. It is impossible for me to come just yet to London, but I will if I live in June. Yet do not fancy that I am here in rude health, walking about and being notable and bountiful. I am like the wreck of a little boat, for I never come up to the sublime and beautiful—merely a little gay, merry boat, which perhaps stranded itself at Vauxhall or London Bridge; or wounded without killing itself as a butterfly does in a tallow candle. There is nothing marked sentimental or interesting in my career; all I know is that I was happy, well, rich, and surrounded by friends. I have now one faithful kind friend in William Lamb, two more in my father and brother, but health, spirits and all else is gone—gone how? O assuredly not by the visitation of God, but slowly, gradually, by my own fault. You said you would like to see me and speak to me. I shall, if possible, be in town a few days. When I come I will let you know. The last time I was in town, I was on my bed three days, rode out, and came off here on the fourth. God preserve you.

> Yours C.L.

Sadly William watched the slow process of degeneration in his wife. He saw the frail image of his beloved Ariel fading away for ever. Often she looked like a little old woman, hunched up in bed with her draperies around her and gazing with her unseeing eyes past the chair in the bow window and out into the Park.

By now their son, Augustus, was full grown, tall and handsome like his father. But mentally he was still a child. The doctors who looked after him believed that he should be kept very quiet, given very little to eat and constantly bled. As a result the fine head was covered with the marks of leeches. He suffered from frequent fits.

Yet he remained exuberant and childishly playful, chasing the maidservants and throwing them down. Sometimes this horseplay became excessively rough and he tried to kiss them and fondle them. Many left once they had been subjected to this treatment.

Emily went to the theatre to see a play about Frankenstein and noted how the horrible, lumbering creature reminded them all of Augustus. Yet Caroline refused to see that there was anything abnormal about the boy. And always she was convinced that he was responding to his medical treatment. She would send reassuring reports about him to the family, declaring herself so happy to know that he was now almost cured, and able to go for ten weeks or more without having a fit.

William was less optimistic, but he still clung to the hope that his son might one day be normal. The sense of compassion, and the great pity that he felt for all those whom Nature had misused, now made him devote himself to the boy as he had once devoted himself to Caroline.

He could still feel a deep sympathy for Caroline when she was quiet and depressed, but it was her moods of almost hysterical animation that caused him embarrassment and distress.

If anything, her exhibitionism had increased with the onset of middle age. She still loved to display herself and she still invited—and indeed demanded—the sexual attentions of the young men whom she met. Many were alarmed by her complete lack of restraint, but others were flattered by her attentions. She was, after all, both highly born and a celebrity. She had been mistress of the great Lord Byron, reputedly one of the most virile and handsome lovers of the century, and here she was, inviting them to take his place in her bed.

But when the moment came for them to prove themselves—and for Caroline to prove herself as well—they often discovered, as Sir Godfrey Webster had discovered in the past, that she made but a poor partner in the sexual act, being prone to floods of tears. She could satisfy neither herself nor them.

It was rumoured that the doctors whom she introduced into the house to look after her son were chosen for their youth and good looks; and that they were required to attend more to her needs than to those of the boy. Emily, writing of a concert-party which she attended at Hatfield House, spoke of the way in which Caroline behaved with a Dr Walker whom she had brought along with her. Sometimes Augustus would be sent to stay in London, and the doctor of the moment taken down to Brocket.

Dr Walker was a Scot, and Emily remarked, 'It's such a low-lived thing to take a Scotch doctor for a lover, and William looks so like a fool, arriving with them and looking as pleased as punch.'

Perhaps William realized what his sister failed to appreciate—that Caroline could only be calmed by pretending to herself that she was still attractive to men. She had failed to attract Byron physically and this failure had been one of the causes of her frustration and ultimate breakdown.

The accolade which she awarded her lovers was the privilege of wearing a ring given to her by Byron. With this singular honour went the implication that the wearer of it might be imbued, as a result, with the same inexhaustible virility as the donor. But of course the lucky recipient was required to return the ring as soon as he was displaced by a rival.

The last of her great loves was Bulwer Lytton, third and youngest son of William Earle Bulwer and his wife, the former Elizabeth Barbara Lytton, whose country seat at Knebworth House was situated only a few miles from Brocket.

Young Bulwer had been born in 1803 and was already aspiring to become a writer. He had been a brilliant schoolboy whose imagination had been stimulated by his tuition under the eccentric Dr Hooker, the smuggler-parson of the little Sussex village of Rottingdean, and he was at his most impressionable age when he witnessed an incident involving Caroline that stirred his adolescent imagination. This caused him to sit down and describe it in verse, with an explanatory title and dedication—'To Lady C. L., who at the Private Races given by Lord D., set a noble example of humanity and feeling, when a poor man being much hurt, she had him conveyed to her carriage and interested herself most anxiously in his recovery.'

Several years later, when Bulwer was in his third year at Cambridge, he encountered Caroline again and she invited him to spend a week at Brocket with her. He was by then a charming and handsome young man, still very impressionable. He was recovering from a disastrous love affair with a girl whose father had forbidden her to have anything more to do with him.

The affair which followed between Caroline and Bulwer, who was at this time half her age, was looked upon as the shameless seduction of an inexperienced youth by a designing woman.

Bulwer asked her to write to him at Cambridge and she sent him long and intimate letters in her usual, breathless style of writing. In return he sent her copies of his poems, and she made intelligent and helpful criticism of them. This was at a time when he was receiving little encouragement from other sources.

He soon became infatuated with her. In a letter he wrote to his mother after the romance was over, he explained this infatuation to her: 'When I first went to Brocket Lady Caroline, after two or three days of constant conversation, not merely upon common topics but those more sentimental ones which knit people together in a few hours more closely than a whole age of talk upon commonplace, attracted me more than it is easy to imagine. But I did not make what is called "love" to her till I saw how acceptable it would be. In short, she appeared to feel for me even more than I felt for her. It is but justice to her to say that we had every opportunity of acting ill; though I was young and almost in love, though everything conspired to tempt her, I believe she resisted what few women would have done.

When I left her in London to go to Cambridge, she wept bitterly and there was not a day during my stay there which I did not receive letters alternately full of passion and sentiment. All this was very flattering to me as you may suppose. I believe my love to her has as much its origin in gratified vanity as anything else. On both sides I think it had little to do with the heart but a great deal with the imagination.'

The affair caused another Caroline scandal, and Frederick Lamb wrote in high indignation to Emily to tell her that Caroline was behaving abominably as usual and 'putting herself in the power of foolish boys'.

A September affair? It certainly seemed so. And those who did not actually scoff at it viewed the association as but another example of Caroline's extravagant emotionalism. The cynics contented themselves with the observation that if she wanted a young and virile bedfellow in place of her husband, the least that she could do was to keep the matter to herself.

Yet there was evidence that this was a genuine emotion—a momentary union of two unhappy people who were widely separated by age but who shared a common sorrow. Both had suffered the pangs of a frustrated love. Both were impulsive and immature. Both were vulnerable.

It was an affair that could not possibly last, but sadly it ended on a note of recrimination. And as always, Caroline emerged as her own worst enemy.

Towards the end of the summer, she fell ill and believed herself to be dying. In the years to come she was to be accused of staging one of her notorious death-bed scenes in order to retain Bulwer's affection, but although this may have been so, Bulwer himself always denied it.

'When she thought herself dying,' he wrote, 'she sent for me and there was nothing theatrical in this; the doctors told me there was everything to apprehend. I sat by her bedside for hours. When I left she wrote me a few words, though expressly forbidden by the doctors to do so.'

Caroline was undoubtedly seriously ill, although she may have dramatized the situation. However she soon recovered some of her strength and was able to return to the social scene once more.

But now she behaved in a way that was typical of Caroline at her worst. That Christmas there was a party at Emily's home at Panshanger, and Bulwer, who was staying at Brocket, expected to travel over there in Caroline's carriage. But instead she invited young Lord John Russell, an illegitimate son of the Duke of Bedford, to travel with her. Bulwer was much distressed, and his jealousy was aroused when he noticed at the ball that Russell was wearing the famous ring which Byron had given to Caroline.

Bulwer had himself worn this ring often enough and had even been offered it as a gift, but had refused it because he believed that Caroline should never part with it.

That night, after they had returned to Brocket, he told Caroline that he was leaving early in the morning, but she at once became penitent and begged him to stay.

The next evening, however, she reverted to her old, rebellious self and not only attached herself to young Russell but also made pointed remarks about Bulwer's obvious distress.

It was the end of the affair. Caroline had acted on impulse, as she always did. But her change of heart was not the result of a casual flirtation. She had known Russell all her life, and her feelings towards him were much the same as her feelings towards Hart, who

211

had also loved her since he was a child. Russell, like Hart, had always been a rather forlorn young man, in need of protection. Of him Caroline had once written that she had nursed him as a little boy of three and had loved him ever since because 'he stood by me when no one else did'.

There was no reason why she should not have taken him to the party in her carriage. But there was every reason why she should not have snubbed her other young admirer and caused him to suffer in the way that she did. Caroline was not heartless, but she was thoughtless. Now her thoughtlessness robbed her of one to whom she had given much comfort, and who had given her affection and admiration in return.

The surprising thing about Caroline at this time was that she could still appear attractive and desirable at one moment, whilst looking raddled and dissipated at another. This was because her attraction lay in her mood rather than in her face or figure. When she was animated and her eyes were sparkling, she could still look young. But when she was alone and dispirited at Brocket, she could look dishevelled, ugly and old. Emily once scathingly observed that Caroline at Brocket often looked as if 'she had been rolled in the kennel'. It was a sad comment, for although Caroline had always been careless and haphazard about her appearance she had always looked dainty and clean.

Perhaps she was influenced subconsciously by the news that was filtering through to her of Byron's growing degradation in Venice; and the sordidness of his personal habits may have prompted her to imitate him. In Venice he no longer seemed to care how he looked or behaved. He was living in dirt and squalor, and associating, as Shelley complained, with 'wretches who seem almost to have lost the gait and physiognomy of man and who do not scruple to allow practices which are not only not named but, I believe, seldom even conceived in England...' Shelley had also found the smell—of animals, pimps and whores—to be overpowering.

Caroline's eccentricities in the home became more marked in middle age. Although she had never had any knowledge of how the lower classes lived, she yet liked—on occasions—to mix with them on familiar terms. In the days when she had courted Byron she had often spent the time whilst waiting for him to emerge from some dance or party in mixing with ostlers, coachmen and footmen—often to their embarrassment.

These habits still persisted. One afternoon, when setting out to

212

pay a call, she decided not to sit by herself in the carriage but clambered up onto the box beside the coachman. When she arrived at her destination and a surprised footman came forward to help her down, she cried out gaily, 'I'm going to jump—you must catch me,' and sprang into his arms.

On another occasion she went into the dining-room at Brocket when the butler, Hagard, was arranging the table for a dinner-party. She began at once to interfere, and told him that the decoration in the centre of the table required 'feature, expression and elevation'.

In order to demonstrate what she meant, she swept the existing decorations aside with her hands, jumped onto the table, struck an exaggerated pose and then ordered the unfortunate man to imitate it. He hurried from the room to find William, who came to see what was the matter.

'Caroline, Caroline,' he said gently and with infinite pity. Then he lifted her down and carried her out into the garden in his arms, soothing her as though she were an over-excited child.

Later, at the dinner party, she behaved quite normally and received her guests 'with a calm look and tone as in happier days'.

She made desperate but impractical attempts to economise in the running of Brocket, but if she saved a few shillings in one direction she only wasted many pounds in another. She had no business sense whatsoever, and when she economised it was the servants who, as often as not, were the victims. She failed to appreciate that economies in food in no way affected herself, for she had the appetite of a sparrow. But the servants, who were accustomed to good, old-fashioned English fare, not unnaturally felt aggrieved.

The butler, Hagard, was one of those who suffered most from her moods and tantrums, and yet he always remained loyal to her. He had known her for many years, and looked upon her more as a child than as an adult. A critic of Caroline's once described Hagard as a pearl thrown to swine. It was a harsh indictment and one to which Hagard himself would never have subscribed.

It was the younger members of the staff who most resented Caroline and who tended to give in their notice after only a few months service under her. As Emily once acidly observed, 'The servants at Brocket still continue to pass through, like figures in a magic lantern.'

When she was ill, Caroline was miserable and full of self-pity, but once her temperature dropped and her spirits rose, she could quickly revert to her old exuberant ways. She still found relief in riding at break-neck speed through the park, and on more than one occasion she was badly thrown. Her courage had never been in doubt, and when her black mare threw her and she had to be 'bathed, cupped and done everything to' she left her bed before she was fully recovered, rode the mare again and was back again in bed, bruised and shaken, within the hour.

In a letter which the family physician, Dr Goddard, wrote to William in the October of 1825, he reported:

'Lady Caroline has a predisposition to the high form of insanity which shows itself at certain times, and particularly so when exposed to any excitement, whether mental or physical. Such is my answer to your letter of enquiry which I had the honor to receive this morning. I have hesitated in forming my decision, but her conduct lately has been very inconsistent and certainly proclaims that many of her actions proceed from other causes than the mere impetuosity of passion. Positive coercion is seldom justifiable in any case; with reference to Ly Caroline it is by no means requisite—I consider that her Ladyship, with kind treatment and occasional restraint, might recover, or at any rate become calm and rational. But there are friends who *must* be removed from her; measures *must* be taken to make her take less wine, and some situation must be chosen for her where she can be governed with every appearance of favouring herself.

Lady Caroline is very suspicious and therefore I have only had time to write these few lines...'

Dr Goddard knew her whole case history, and he always gave the same advice—that coercion of any sort should be avoided and that she should be treated sympathetically and humoured as far as possible. But to Caroline's enemies, and certainly to the practical, down-to-earth members of the Lamb family, vigorous and even violent restraint was just what Caroline needed. They had little use for Dr Goddard's views.

William, with his more compassionate outlook, was willing to follow Goddard's suggestions, but unfortunately he was by now reaching a stage where his own nerves were beginning to fray under the strain.

Caroline made some pathetic attempts to entertain, but her eccentricities caused embarrassment to some of her guests who found that one visit was all they wished to experience. As a result she began to attract to herself a company of hangers-on and social upstarts who were prepared to put up with her antics in return for the social advancement which she could offer them.

214

For one of her parties at Brocket she went to great trouble to decorate the house and to illuminate it with countless candles. The supper tables were loaded with expensive food and drink, and a band of twenty-four musicians was in attendance. Eighty people were invited in all, but at the time appointed, only ten had arrived—and they were chiefly close friends or members of the family. In desperation she sent her carriage to fetch some other friends, who excused themselves because they said their own horses were out and they could not travel. Her carriage was sent back empty.

It was a cruel snub, both to Caroline and to William. And as Lady Morgan noted in her diary, William was 'all the time miserable, fretted to death, flying into passions continually and letting her have quite her own way'. Yet this was the man who, at the time of his marriage, was so dignified, calm and reserved.

At other times she made the mistake of mixing people of rank and title with simple, middle-class folk. It was not a democratic age, and such tactics only caused acute embarrassment to all concerned. Country people dressed differently, spoke differently and lived very different lives from the wealthy upper-classes who inhabited Mayfair.

Her literary activities had brought her into contact with a raffish set with a very different background from her own. Two of her principal friends in the literary world were Lady Morgan and a Miss Benger. Lady Morgan, before her marriage to the distinguished physician, Sir Charles Morgan, had lived in humble circumstances as the daughter of Robert Owenson, a grocer, of Shrewsbury, who had later moved to Dublin. Her marriage had placed her on the fringe of fashionable society in London, and her first novel, *The Wild Irish Girl,* had brought her quite near to the centre of the literary circle. It had been published under the pen-name of 'Sydney Owenson' and had caused a mild stir.

Miss Benger was a minor poet, a minor novelist and something of an historian. A friendly, cheerful woman, of delicate health and living in straitened circumstances, she gained the friendship of a number of writers, including Bulwer Lytton.

Caroline found real affection and sympathy in the company of this oddly assorted literary pair, both of whom she embarrassed by her failure to realize that they could in no way match her own style of living. She was astonished to discover one day that Lady Morgan had only a modest staff and said to her, 'My dear Creature, have you really not a groom of the chambers with you? Nothing but your footman? You must let me lend you something, you must indeed.

You will never get on here, you know, with only one servant—you must let me send you one of my pages.'

This conversation was noted by Lady Morgan in her diary, which was soon filled with descriptions of Caroline and the strange remarks that she made. Caroline, towards the end of her life, and especially after the death of her mother, confided more in Lady Morgan than in anyone else. Lady Morgan was of much the same age as Caroline, but knew far more about the world. She was able to offer Caroline almost a mother's guidance and comfort in her moods of melancholy.

Miss Benger, though equally kind-hearted, was less of a confidante. She, poor woman, not only had no groom of the chamber and no footman, but only a dingy room and occasional domestic help. She did her own washing, and was sadly embarrassed one day when Caroline arrived suddenly to see her, so that Miss Benger was forced to push a heap of dirty handkerchiefs and stockings under the bed. Here they were run to earth by Caroline's pet dog, who dragged them out into the centre of the room.

For a time Caroline gave them expensive presents, attended their literary gatherings and invited them to visit her at Melbourne House. On these occasions she would play the part of the famous novelist and former mistress of Lord Byron, and would drape herself on a couch, gaze upon the souvenirs of her immortal affair, sigh deeply and talk of her fatal passion. It savoured of Lady Oxford in *her* Byron period, and was pathetic, vulgar and rather unkind.

But at least the confidences which she gave to Lady Morgan enabled an independent witness to build up a reasonably accurate picture of how Caroline looked and behaved in these years of her ultimate decline.

An entry which Lady Morgan made in her diary at the time of Caroline's death sums up her character as accurately as anyone in her intimate circle was capable of doing. It ran as follows:

'She was tall and slight in her figure, her countenance was grave, her eyes dark, large and bright; her complexion fair; her voice soft, low, caressing that was at once a beauty and a charm, and worked much of that fascination that was peculiarly hers; it softened down her enemies the moment they listened to her. She was eloquent, most eloquent, full of ideas, and of graceful gracious expression; but her subject was always herself. She confounded her dearest friends and direst foes, for her feelings were all impulses, worked on by a powerful imagination; all elements of great eloquence, but not good for guidance; one of her great charms was the rapid transition of

216

manner which changed its theme. The chief cause of the odd things which she used to say and do, was that never having lived out of the habits of her own class, yet sometimes mixing with people of inferior rank, notable only by their genius, she constantly applied her own sumptuous habits to them.'

Here is an intelligent and observant commentary on an elusive personality. It contains two phrases, in particular, which explain so much of Caroline's character. 'Her subject was always herself' and 'Her feelings were all impulses'.

In England, Caroline was wasting the precious years that remained to her in senseless emotional extravagance and petty frustrations. In Italy, Byron was doing much the same. He had been blessed with a stronger body than Caroline, but a weaker digestion. Now he was destroying himself with indecent haste.

There was one noble and unselfish impulse left in him. He had always been a dedicated defender of freedom and liberty, with a passionate desire to free the Greek nation from the tyranny of the Turks. When the idea came to him that he might, even at this late stage, revive the glories of his family's past by leading a revolt against the Turks, it stimulated him like a potent drug and his spirit was re-kindled with fire. At last his life had purpose.

One final act of melodrama was called for in the Byron saga; or perhaps two, for if his one-man rebellion should end in glorious victory, a grateful Greek nation might decide to elect him as their King.

King Byron of Greece! That was a title which would establish him as the greatest and the most spectacular of all the Byrons!

He had grown tired of his young mistress, Teresa Guiccioli. She had succeeded for a while in re-awakening some of the lusts of his youth, but in the end she had wearied him. 'She is pretty, but has no tact,' he wrote to Hobhouse, 'She answers aloud when she should whisper.' He had really been happier living with his pimps and whores in carefree squalor.

She had re-awakened his vanity when first she had become obsessed by him; but there had been other things about her which had exerted a curious fascination. And he had written once to his friend, Douglas Kinnaird, describing her as 'a sort of Italian Caroline Lamb, except that she is much prettier, and not so savage. But she has the same red-hot head, the same noble disdain of public opinion...'

He could remember so little about so many of his conquests, but Caroline still remained vividly alive in his mind.

Now, as his end drew near, he found himself drawn again to the love of his own sex. At Cephalonia his expedition was joined by a dark-haired, dark-eyed Adonis of fifteen, named Loukas, whom he took as his page. And once again he was inspired by the contemplation of the very spirit of youth.

The women who had played so important a part in his life had only caused him to suffer. His mother had been even worse than Caroline in her alternating moods of adoration and violence. Mary Chaworth had ignored him. Lady Oxford had in the end deserted him, and his wife, Annabella, had set out to destroy him. Even Augusta, who had once understood him so well, had now fallen under the influence of Annabella.

He lavished presents upon Loukas; and he lavished on him his love. But Loukas remained indifferent. He gave back neither gratitude nor affection in return. He behaved as Mary Chaworth had behaved. He accepted the priceless gift of love and secretly mocked the giver.

The irony of the situation did not escape Byron. He had trifled with the affections of so many young women in his life, and now a young boy was trifling with his own.

And why not? There was no longer anything beautiful about his own body, as there once had been in the days of his glorious youth. Now his body was sordid and gross. And yet he brooded over the boy's ingratitude and his callous indifference. In what may well have been the last lines that he ever wrote, Byron mourned the tragedy of unrequited love:

> I watched thee on the breakers, when the rock
>> Received our prow and all was storm and fear,
> And bade thee cling to me through every shock;
>> This arm would be thy bark, or breast thy bier.
>
> I watched thee when the fever glazed thine eyes,
>> Yielding my couch and stretched me on the ground,
> When overworn with watching, ne'er to rise
>> From thence if thou an early grave hadst found.
>
> Thus much and more; and yet thou lov'st me not,
>> And never wilt! Love dwells not in our will.
> Nor can I blame thee, though it be my lot
>> To strongly, wrongly, vainly love thee still.

Perhaps his cynicism was sufficient for him to contemplate with resignation the fate which he encountered now. He died not gloriously in battle as befitted a Byron, but miserably and without even a touch of melodrama from a fever contracted when he insisted on riding in the rain. His doctors surrounded his bed, eager to apply the sovereign remedy of bleeding, but he refused their administrations. It was a token gesture, for he knew that they would do this to him the moment that he lost consciousness and could no longer keep them back.

A fortune-teller in Scotland had warned him as a boy that his thirty-seventh year would prove fatal to him. Now this prophecy weighed heavily upon him. His little charade was ending. Before he had set out for Greece he had designed for himself an absurd red and gold uniform and an equally absurd helmet to wear with it: and now the whole adventure was ending in absurdity. This was not the material of high tragedy; it was the material for an indifferent farce.

But Nature, at least, came to his rescue to deprive the scene of its bathos. At the moment of his death a tremendous storm struck the coast and raged over the mainland. The lightning was vivid and great claps of thunder echoed round the heavens. The rain poured down, and it seemed to the terrified peasants as if the furies were proclaiming the death of a favoured son.

'Let not my body be hacked, or be sent to England,' was one of his requests, and this, too, was absurd for he knew that these wishes would be ignored.

He died on 19 April 1824, and the surgeons at once descended upon the body to hack it up. They were able to report that his heart was enlarged and that his liver was badly damaged. Then turning their attention to the cranium, they sawed as well as hacked, and were able to note that the bone of the skull was very hard and without any traces of the sutures, so that it resembled that of a man of eighty.

In fact the probable cause of death was uremic poisoning, which had been gravely aggravated by frequent and excessive bleedings. But this at least enabled them to note that the body was much thinner than they had expected it to be. As for the Greek woman who laid out the body, she was able to report that it was 'white like the wing of a young chicken'.

The Greeks of Missolonghi would have liked their hero to have been buried amongst them. Failing this, they pleaded for some part of the body to remain with them. This wish was granted to them and they were given the lungs.

Nelson's body, nineteen years earlier, had been placed in a coffin filled with brandy, camphor and myrrh to preserve it for the long voyage home. Now Byron's corpse was parcelled into a chest of rough wood, with a lining of tin. The heart, brain and intestines were neatly packaged in separate containers and as a further precaution, the coffin was placed in a cask containing one hundred and eighty gallons of spirit, which was lowered into the hold of the *Florida*, at Zante.

The ship set sail on 24 May for England, and arrived in the Thames estuary on 29 June. The news of Byron's death had preceded it and in fact was known in London on 14 May.

For some months previously, Caroline had been troubled by dreams and premonitions of Byron's death. In March 1824, a month before he died, she had been very ill, and tormented by insomnia. A nurse and a friend, Mrs Russell Hunter, sat up with her to comfort her.

One night she awoke from sleep with a scream and implored them to save her from a vision which she had had of Byron. She described him as looking horrible, and grinding his teeth at her. 'He was fatter than when I knew him, and not near so handsome.'

At the time she believed that this apparition was an indication of the imminence of her own death, rather than of his, but she was so frightened by it that she subsequently avoided any enquiries about the day on which he died, lest it were the one on which she had had her dream.

He had never written to her since the publication of *Glenarvon*, several years before; and she declared that she had never previously dreamed of him since the day of their parting in the spring of 1816.

She was told the news of his death abruptly, and without warning, when she was laughing and gay at Brocket. It came in a letter from her husband, in which he said, 'Caroline, behave properly, I know it will shock you—Lord Byron is dead.'

She collapsed and was carried to her bed, suffering as she believed from some form of fever, but probably from shock. It was a shock from which she was never fully to recover, and by a cruel twist of fate it was later to be made much worse.

She remained in bed for two months, seemingly without the will to live, but by mid-July she was sufficiently recovered for her to get up and go for a short drive in an open carriage. William accompanied her on horseback and he rode on ahead along the road towards Welwyn.

At the turnpike on the road he met a funeral procession and asked whose it was. He was told that it was the coffin bearing Lord Byron on his way to Welwyn, and thence to Nottingham and the family vault in Hucknall Torkard Church, near Newstead.

The cortège passed on, and William rode back to the carriage. He did not tell Caroline what had happened, but she sensed that something had disturbed him.

She had not imagined for one moment that the procession might be that of her dead lover, because she had assumed that he would be buried in Westminster Abbey, as the newspapers were suggesting.

But the news could not be kept hidden from her for long and when she learned that she had so nearly passed his coffin, she collapsed once again.

Further shocks awaited her. In company with many other women who had loved him and had written him passionate and highly indiscreet letters, she now became alarmed about her own correspondence to him. Hobhouse, in whose possession they now were, refused to part with them unless she gave up Byron's letters to her in return, for he feared that she might be tempted to write another *Glenarvon*-type novel. She refused to part with his letters and therefore did not receive back her own.

She became obsessed with the desire to learn what his last words were and whether or not he had mentioned her name on his death-bed. She wrote to Murray, asking for any information which he could give and declaring, 'I am very sorry I ever said one unkind word against him.'

She also tried to cross-question his faithful valet, Fletcher, who was making the most of his notoriety as one who had tended the dying man in his final hours. But Fletcher's recollections were clouded by grief and were none too reliable. Annabella, also, sought out Fletcher to cross-question him on the poet's last words. So did Augusta. Each hoped that it would be of *her* that he was thinking as he lay dying. Had they learnt that during his last weeks he had been tormented by the indifference shown to him by a young boy with whom he had fallen deeply in love, they would have been shocked and bitterly resentful.

Yet in his last rambling sentences, he had indeed thought of Augusta, of his wife, and his daughter, Ada. Also of the fate of Greece, and of the faithful servants whom he was leaving behind him.

221

He never mentioned Caroline.

Fletcher would have made much of the fact that Byron had a Bible laid on his bed-side every day during his last illness, but Hobhouse was doubtful of the value of this incident. Byron, he well knew, was scornful of religion and the significance of the Bible lay in the fact that it had been given to him by Augusta. In his last moments he was thinking more about her than about his ultimate salvation.

The world mourned his passing and literary England was profoundly shocked by his death. Carlyle spoke of him as 'the noblest spirit in Europe'. The young Alfred Tennyson, a boy of fourteen, was desolate. But Society, mindful of the fact that Augusta was his nearest kin and would therefore be the chief mourner at the funeral, showed a marked disinclination to be present at the ceremony.

As always after the death of a celebrity, there was a rush by those who had known Byron to get their stories about him into print. Murray commissioned Moore to write the official biography and did his best to stem the stream of memoirs from Dallas, Medwin and others. But Medwin quickly published his *Recollections of Lord Byron,* which Caroline read eagerly, although in some apprehension over what the book might say about herself.

Many of the references to her came as a shock, for she had always believed the flattering comments he had made to her, and had written to her, and she had refused to believe the stories of the malicious comments he was alleged to have made.

It was in these *Recollections* of Medwin that she learnt for the first time of the cruel lines which he had written under her scribbled message 'Remember me' on the flyleaf of his copy of *Vathek,* which she had found in his rooms at the Albany.

There were other comments that were equally wounding. Now she could read a description of herself which was not only heartless but also unjust:

'She possessed an infinite vivacity, and an imagination heated by novel reading which made her fancy herself a heroine of romance, and led her into all sorts of eccentricities. She was married, but it was a match of *convenance* and no couple could be more fashionably indifferent to, or independent of, one another than she and her husband. She had never been in love, at least where the affections were concerned—and was perhaps made without a heart, as many of the sex are, but her head more than supplied the deficiency.'

Yet on the whole she reacted calmly to these exposures. She wrote

222

to Medwin, but it was a letter remarkable for its humbleness and lack of resentment. She told him that in his book he had left a bitter legacy to one who had always adored Byron. And although she accepted that the lines on the fly-leaf of *Vathek*—'thou false to him, thou fiend to me'—were genuine, she begged Medwin that she might be allowed to tell him the truth about her relationship with Byron. 'I have been very ill,' she wrote, 'and am not likely to trouble anyone much longer.' Then she spoke with deep emotion of the love which they had felt for each other when they first met, and denied Medwin's right to refer to her in the way that he had done.

'Byron never, never could say I had no heart. He never could say either that I had not loved my husband. In his letters to me he is perpetually telling me I love him the best of the two.'

This was certainly true. Byron, in the early days of their affair, had been very jealous of William, and had on occasions tried to force Caroline to swear that she loved him better than she loved William. Byron's vanity demanded that Caroline should consider that *he* was the only man in her life, and this she had refused to do.

In this letter to Medwin she refuted the suggestion that it was vanity which made her pursue Byron. 'I grew to love him better than virtue, Religion—all prospects here. He broke my heart and still I love him—Witness the agony I experienced at his death and the tears your book has cost me.'

In fairness to Medwin it must be recorded that in subsequent editions of his *Recollections* he deleted some of the passages which had caused Caroline such distress.

223

Fifteen

Caroline - The Final Curtain

Byron was dead, but memories of him remained. So also did his *Memoirs,* which he had written whilst in exile between 1818 and 1821.

What did these *Memoirs* contain? Who was mentioned in them and what reputations could they destroy?

There were several people connected with him who became alarmed at the thought of their publication. Above all, Annabella, his wife. She had been hinting for so long at the dark secrets of their marriage. Yet she had been married to him for a year, had borne him a child, and had often expressed her love for him. What, then, might these *Memoirs* reveal about their married life?

At least the danger of blackmail did not exist, which it would have done had these papers ever fallen into unscrupulous hands. In fact it was Byron's old friend, Thomas Moore, who held them. They had been close and intimate friends for many years, and Moore and Hobhouse had often done their best to keep Byron out of his endless succession of scrapes. Moore had published some sentimental and erotic verse which Byron had first read while he was still at Harrow, and they had always shared a common delight in sexual experiences. Moore was therefore no prude. He had not found the *Memoirs* unduly pornographic and he had realized from the outset that their publication would help to save Byron's reputation in the future. He also argued with some force that the destruction of the *Memoirs* would imply that they were disgraceful and obscene and would therefore 'be throwing a stigma upon the work, which it did not deserve.'

John Cam Hobhouse, another intimate and loyal friend of Byron's, strongly opposed this view. He had not read the *Memoirs,* but he feared that their publication could only serve to blacken Byron's name. This view was shared by Byron's publisher, John Murray, even though he had already paid Moore two thousand guineas for them. Byron had once described John Murray as the 'most timid of God's booksellers'. He now showed a remarkable hesitancy to publish a book which could have made him a fortune.

Moore had at first thought he might save the memoirs by giving them into Augusta's hands as a treasured souvenir of her dead half-brother. This manoeuvre might have been successful had Augusta been left to make her own choice, but both Hobhouse and Annabella impressed upon her the need for destruction. It was, they assured her, a sacred duty to the dead.

And what of Caroline? The furore which the fate of these *Memoirs* was arousing in literary circles provided just the kind of stimulation that she most enjoyed. To burn or not to burn—that was the question.

Caroline was in an advantageous position for she alone amongst the women concerned had read the *Memoirs,* and knew what revelations they contained. (She had in fact made a passing and highly critical reference to them in her novel, *Ada Reis*). Now she was faced with an internal conflict. If the *Memoirs* were burnt, time would inevitably soften the condemnation of Byron, and posterity might well adopt a tolerant attitude towards him, declaring him to have been a better man than his contemporaries believed. But if they *were* published, then posterity would be forced to face up to his sexual deviations.

She had therefore to decide what was her real attitude to Byron. Did she still love him so much that she would still do anything to save him? Or did she now hate him so much that she would do anything to expose him, even though he were dead?

Being Caroline, she made no serious attempt to resolve this mental conflict, and simply adopted both courses, alternately praising and reviling, according to her mood of the moment. Her attitude towards him had always been inconsistent, and for some years past she had been in the habit of writing letters about him that were wholly contradictory. There had been letters, for example, in which she had blamed herself alone for all that had occurred between them, and expressed her utter desolation over his departure.

'My heart's in torture and my soul the same—it is as if there was a sword run through me—or a fire burning in my brain—no ship that ever was lost on a strange sea without daring to anchor anywhere—or in immediate fear of being lost ever yet was so distressed as I am.' Caroline had always excelled herself when describing her own emotions. She continued, 'If this is what is called remorse how can people say there is no Hell? What burning flames can be worse? I shall die very soon and when I do—do you remember it and tell them that I suffered enough—tell it Byron—but I only accuse myself not him.'

In this mood she was willing for the *Memoirs* to be destroyed. But on another occasion, not long before his death, she had written of him:

'He has the curses of hearts that are broken of souls torn from virtue and peace on him by night after day, he is wicked, cruel— mean coldly cruel—and most barbarous.'

But as an afterthought to this outpouring she added the request:

'Do tell me why you say he is ill—after all I trust in God he is not ill.'

The only person who kept her head throughout all this excitement was Annabella. She was in no doubt whatever as to what the fate of the *Memoirs* should be. They *had* to be destroyed. She had played the part of the loving wife and saintly reformer, the purpose of whose marriage had been to wean her erring husband from acts of degrading sensuality and to save his immortal soul. Her lawyers, her parents, her intimate friends, had all accepted this picture of herself as a devout and chaste young woman who had been made to suffer the most monstrous ill-treatment.

What if the *Memoirs* should reveal that this was not an accurate picture of what had occurred? What if they revealed that she had been a willing partner in some of these acts of sexual abandon?

There was a simple solution to her problem. She could demand to see the *Memoirs* and could then judge for herself whether they should be suppressed. In fact they had already been offered to her by Byron, before he died, when he had written to her to warn her that they contained a long and detailed account of their marriage and separation. But he had stated that it was his earnest desire to tell the truth, and although he realized that his story might not coincide with hers, he was yet anxious that she should indicate any passages to which she might take exception. His letter went on to say, 'But I do not choose to give to another generation statements which we cannot arise from the dust to prove or disprove—without letting you see fairly and fully what I look upon you to have been—and what I depict you as being. If seeing this—you can detect what is false— or answer what is charged—do so—*your mark* shall not be erased.'

But Annabella refused to read the *Memoirs,* either then, or after Byron's death. It was an astonishing refusal. She could have questioned—and had erased—any passage which she deemed to be untruthful. Yet she chose not to exercise this privilege.

In her opinion, the *Memoirs* had to be destroyed. Once they had been destroyed, she could turn her attention to silencing those who had dangerous knowledge of what they might have revealed. Caroline would have to be coerced, and so would Augusta. The former was notoriously hysterical and mendacious, and it would not be difficult to discredit anything she might see fit to divulge. The latter was a weak and ineffectual character who would have to be convinced that she had sinned; and that only by drawing a veil over the past might she ever hope to win salvation.

On 17 May, 1824, the parties concerned met together in the parlour of John Murray's house in Albemarle Street in order to decide the fate of the *Memoirs*.

There were present Moore, Murray and Hobhouse, representing Byron's interests, even though they could not agree upon what his interests might be. There was a Colonel Doyle, who was representing Annabella, and a Mr Wilmot Horton representing those of Augusta. Also present was a Mr Luttrell, who was a friend of Moore's. It had previously been suggested that the meeting should be held at Augusta's house, when presumably she would herself have been present, but it was later decided to meet at Murray's home, which was also his office.

The purpose of the meeting was to discuss the advisability of destroying the manuscript; and if destruction were agreed upon, to burn it.

Moore, however, remained adamant. The *Memoirs* should be preserved at all costs. They could either be given into Augusta's custody or stored in the vaults of a bank.

Unfortunately Augusta disliked and distrusted Moore, and liked and trusted Murray. There was no question of Murray's being out of pocket on the deal, as Moore was prepared to repay the two thousand guineas.

Of those present, only Moore and Luttrell had read the *Memoirs* and were therefore in a position to express an opinion as to whether they were obscene or likely to be damaging to the dead man's reputation. Horton and Doyle were in favour of destruction, though not strongly so. Murray was most strongly in favour of their destruction.

A bitter argument went on between Moore and Murray, and Moore continued to protest even up to the moment when the only

227

copy of the *Memoirs* in existence was brought into the room, then torn into shreds by Wilmot Horton and Doyle and finally consigned to the flames. As these flames roared up the chimney, Colonel Doyle, with a magnanimous gesture, offered a bundle of the hand-written sheets to Hobhouse, so that he might partake in the cere-mony. But Hobhouse, who had always insisted that the *Memoirs* should be burnt, could not bring himself to accept.

Once the deed was done, however, Hobhouse regained his self-assurance and turning to Moore he told him that what had been done was in the best interests of everyone and that they would none of them ever live to regret their actions.

The company then left the room where the embers were glowing in the grate, still assuring each other that what had been done was in the best interests of everyone concerned and still trying to convince themselves that they would never have any reason to regret their actions.

Yet Professor de Sola Pinto, writing some hundred and forty years later, was to declare, 'The loss of Rochester's Memoirs and those of Byron are, perhaps, the two greatest disasters that English literature has sustained through the misplaced scruples of well-meaning people.'

Byron was dead, but memories of him remained, even though the *Memoirs* had been destroyed. It had been his belief that the curse of the Byrons would descend upon the women whom he had loved, or who had loved him, and now there seemed evidence that the curse did exist. Augusta was living in poverty and wretchedness, her health ruined and her looks gone. Mary Chaworth, his first true love, was living in misery, her health broken. Caroline was also in bad health, and her marriage was once again on the point of breaking up.

Only two of Byron's women remained healthy and seemingly happy. His young Italian mistress, the Countess Guiccioli, lived on in Italy, radiant and contented. Annabella was also in excellent health and outwardly happy. She devoted herself to good works, turned part of her house into a schoolroom and arranged for the education there of children of all classes. Thus she sublimated her daily existence to the exaltation of the spirit.

But Caroline was now rapidly declining. Byron was dead, and there was now little enough left for her to do but to follow him into eternity. The fatal passion still had her in its grip. She thought of him constantly, sometimes remembering him as her adored lover with whom she had spent so many happy hours, and sometimes brooding over his faithlessness and his many acts of cruelty towards her. But he remained the obsession which dominated her dreams as he dominated her waking hours. She knew that she could never forget him.

But her misery and her failing strength did not render her any the less aggressive and unpredictable; and the burden of caring for her and of controlling her continued to rest on the shoulders of her husband.

Finally it became a burden which he felt that he could no longer bear. Within a year of Byron's death he felt forced to resort once again to the Deed of Separation which he had planned and had then abandoned ten years previously. His domestic troubles were multiplying. It was now clear to him that his son, Augustus, was incurable, and that he was steadily deteriorating. Everything had been done for the boy and every expert had been consulted. A special tutor had been engaged for him, and William had mapped out a curriculum of studies, including logic and philosophy. It had all proved useless. The boy was mentally deficient.

Caroline still refused to acknowledge this. She convinced herself that he was growing better. This placed an additional burden on William. The tragedy of their son's health was not one that he could share with his wife. He had to face it alone.

Brocket, which he had once so loved, now became a place that he avoided, for there was so little peace to be encountered there. Life with Caroline frayed his nerves, and he found himself growing tense and apprehensive whenever he passed through the Park gates.

In the past he had always been noted for his even temper and quiet good humour, but now he was becoming as irritable as his wife. He dreaded her sudden outbursts, and when they occurred he lost his temper and shouted back. In the past he had only sought to calm her, but now he was hasty and unsympathetic. The old tolerance had left him. The final break, when it occurred, was therefore a sad affair, filled with animosity and without compassion.

The first Deed of Separation had been prepared without rancour, and had been generous in its terms. Now he resented the thought of paying out large sums which he could ill afford, for he was not a rich man by the standards of those with whom he mixed.

Nor could he summon up his courage to tell Caroline that he was preparing to rid himself of her for ever. So, for a time, he lived a life of pretence, and broke the news harshly, and by letter, in the same way as he had broken to her the news of Byron's death. He

I

then escaped to Brighton, and wrote to tell her that he would never return to her again.

It was all so unlike him. The William of old would never have shirked such a duty. But now he was tired and dispirited. He was bored with life and resentful of its injustices. As always, his family were constantly urging him to have done with Caroline, once and for all. They had no love for her—and never had. They thought her mad and said so openly. On one occasion she overhead the comment. She realized that it might be true.

Madness, after all, was in the air. Byron had always declared himself to be mad, and the whole country had known that the old king, George III, had been out of his senses for the last twenty years of his reign. No one knew anything about mental illnesses. People were believed to go mad as easily as they caught a chill. There was then no hope for them, and they were forcibly restrained and even put into strait-jackets. The well-to-do were sent into privately-run madhouses which were more interested in collecting fat fees for their patients than ever they were in curing them. Not that William had any such plan for constraining Caroline. All that he wanted was to rid himself of the intolerable burden of her presence.

Her chief enemies in the Lamb family were William's sister, Emily, and his brother, George. They had evidence enough to prove that Caroline was already half-mad; and that she was incapable of carrying out the duties of a wife and mother. And in truth Caroline, since the death of Byron, had made little effort to control herself or to organize her way of life. It was not madness that beset her, but an inability to meet the simplest problems of living. She could not sleep, and her eating habits were chaotic. Being no longer able to organize proper meals, and certainly having no desire to eat them, she had scraps of food placed about the house so that she could eat whenever and wherever the fancy took her. But she had the appetite of a sparrow and only nibbled at her food.

Her bedroom was a grotesque combination of a shrine and a slut's boudoir. There was an altar cloth on one wall, a portrait of Byron on another, and a crucifix on a third. Her clothes, which were largely tattered or in holes, were discarded haphazardly about the room, plates of food were scattered about on the furniture or even on the floor, and the whole atmosphere was one of slovenly disregard for tidiness or even for personal cleanliness.

On her dressing-table was the bottle of brandy which now played so important a part in her life, with a prayer-book on one side of it and a bottle of lavender-water on the other.

She was still liable to spend her days riding madly through the Park, and the servants were exasperated with her. Emily had been at pains to exaggerate the incidents concerning one of her pages, and warned them of the danger which they ran by serving their hysterical mistress, who was liable one day to kill one of them.

Now, as always throughout her life, Caroline forfeited sympathy for herself by behaving aggressively at a time when her only hope was to arouse pity for her plight. When the settlement that William was to make on her was discussed, she demanded an annuity of £3,000, which—as she well knew—was more than he could afford. He offered £2,000, which was certainly sufficient to keep her in comfort for the rest of her life.

Her reaction to this was to storm at his meanness. And now she began to copy Annabella, by inventing stories of her husband's past cruelties to her. William, she alleged, had frequently beaten her. But in truth one of the tragedies of their married life was that he had never beaten her at all, and scarcely even slapped her. Such treatment might have brought her to her senses.

Next she returned to her old grievance—that he had corrupted her when first they married. Then she blamed him for having over-indulged her. Next she resorted to melodrama, and piously announced that she still loved 'the hand upraised to shed my blood'. Finally, just like Annabella, she hurried to her family and poured out to them her stories of the monstrous treatment which she had received from her husband in the past.

Her brother, William Ponsonby, at once rallied to her side. He was a stupid man, much given to blustering. Now he took it upon himself to write to William, calling him a cad and threatening him as to the consequences if he persisted in his intentions. He even went so far as to suggest that William was a social climber who had only married Caroline in order to better himself.

This was more than Emily could stomach. She had already labelled William Ponsonby 'an ass and a jackanapes' and her anger was further stimulated by the knowledge that although her brother had married Caroline because he loved her, it was yet possible that Lady Melbourne might have encouraged the match for the very reasons which William Ponsonby was now suggesting. Emily's brother, George, shared her indignation, and together they set to work upon William to ensure that there would be no weakening in his attitude. He had been injudicious enough to visit Caroline once or twice before the storm broke over the monetary settlement, and she had succeeded in holding his attention and even making him laugh. She was able to savour the absurdity of the situation in which they found themselves. 'Like Mr and Mrs Bang reviling each other' was how she later described it.

In the end it was Emily who succeeded in forcing acceptance of the separation upon Caroline by a mixture of cajolery and threats. 'In a quiet way I have bullied the bully,' she wrote. 'She threatened and raged for the first half hour I was with her.' But later she noted with more sympathy that Caroline was in a strange state, 'always muddled either with Brandy or laudanum.'

Caroline behaved very badly at this interview and threatened that she would publish her journal and once again expose the whole Lamb family to ridicule. Emily replied that if Caroline adopted this attitude, William would take the matter to court, where 'many things might be said disagreeable on both sides'. She emphasized that he was quite ready to accept this risk so long as everything was finally settled as a result.

At this Caroline capitulated. Not at first, for she continued to storm against Emily, and she sat down on the same day and wrote an abusive letter to William. But on the following day she wrote to Emily's husband, Lord Cowper, begging him to discuss the matter with her cousin, Hart, now the Duke of Devonshire, and saying how anxious she was for a settlement which would keep them out of court.

This was surprising. The old Caroline would have revelled in a court appearance, and the opportunity it would have afforded her to deliver an impassioned speech in her own defence. But by now she had lost confidence in herself, and the mounting pressures against her were more than she could stand. Her brother's well-intentioned interference had achieved nothing, and in court she would have had to face the formidable opposition of the united Lamb front. It was then agreed that two of Caroline's cousins, Lord Althorp and Hart, should act as arbitrators in order to try and reach a just settlement.

The danger, as Emily realized all too well, was that even at this late stage William might weaken and retract. His lethargy and in-decision made him vulnerable, and he still found himself unable to avoid his wife completely. Moreover he believed in the promises she was making to him—of how she would go abroad and never trouble him again.

Finally the Deed of Separation was agreed upon in the summer of 1825, with a compromise settlement of £2,500 for Caroline and her undertaking to leave Brocket by the 1 August. In her last weeks there, facing a lonely old age in a strange household, she abandoned herself to grief.

'Every tree, every flower, will awaken bitter reflections,' she wrote in a letter to Lady Morgan. 'I would give all I possessed on earth to be again what I once was. I would not be obedient and gentle, but I shall die of grief...My life has not been the best possible. The slave of impulse—I have rushed forward to my own destruction.'

This mood of anguish and self pity was echoed in a long poem which she wrote in the Park at the time when she was waiting to leave. It concluded with the lines:

> My joyous days with youth are fled,
> My friends are either changed or dead,
> My faults, my follies, leave alone,
> They live in the mouth of everyone,
> And still remain when all is gone.
> This is my twentieth marriage year,
> They celebrate with Hagard's cheer,
> They dance, they sing, they bless the day
> I weep the while—and well I may
> Husband nor child to greet me come,
> Without a friend, without a home,
> I sit beneath my favourite tree;
> Sing, then, my little birds to me,
> In music, love, and liberty.

The fact that she had celebrated the twentieth year of her marriage only a few weeks previously added to her sorrow. Not all of the servants at Brocket were her enemies; the butler, Hagard, in particular, had served her faithfully and he had been one of those who had organized the celebrations in the village to mark this twentieth anniversary.

There had been little resentment of Caroline's behaviour in the surrounding district. The Welwyn band had always been happy to play for her in the Park, and the village maidens had danced willingly for her on the occasion of her sacrificial rites when she had burnt her Byron relics. These villagers had looked upon her as being a little mad, but her generosity had been proverbial. Now they witnessed her departure with genuine sorrow.

233

William had taken a small house for her in London, and she retired to this for a short time after the separation before announcing her intention of visiting Paris. But by now she was back to her old form, writing melodramatic letters to her friends in which she visualized herself living a pathetic and lonely existence in some cheap and dingy street 'a little way off the City Road, Shoreditch, Camberwell, or upon the top of a shop.' And she drew a tragic picture of herself eking out her pitiful little income by giving lectures to little children or even by keeping a seminary.

In fact her income of £2,500 a year was sufficient to allow her to live in considerable comfort, if not quite in the style to which she had been accustomed, and she spent much of her time going over expensive properties in Regent's Park and Chelsea.

By the 14 August she was in Paris, to the immense relief of the Lamb family, who were quite prepared to see her return uninvited to Brocket or Melbourne House. She had a very bad crossing to Calais which called forth from Emily the unsympathetic comment that it was to be hoped that it was *so* bad that it would discourage her from coming back to England for quite some time. In Paris she was befriended by—of all people—her cousin, Hary-O, who took pity upon her plight.

From Paris she wrote Emily a terrible letter, full of threats, warning her of the retribution she must expect for all her cruelties and concluding, 'The only alleviation you can now make to the agonizing sufferings you have heaped upon your victim is to write—do so then.'

Caroline returned after only two months in Paris. From an inn at Dover, where she landed, there came a stream of letters to her relatives in which she described the dreadful conditions under which she was living at the Ship Tavern, in Water Lane, 'in a dreary little apartment', in which her privacy was assailed by the sound of loud and heartless laughter from an adjoining smoking-room.

On arrival in London, she behaved more outrageously than ever and stayed for a time in Wimbledon, where she drove wildly about in the streets in a pony chaise with a jeering mob behind her. On such occasions she was usually half drunk.

She was existing, as she assured Lady Morgan, on the brink of destitution, with only one maid to look after her and without the simple amenities of civilized life such as servants, pages, a carriage, horses or even fine rooms. She remained as unscrupulous as ever in the wild charges she made. By now she had added a new crime to the long list which her husband had perpetrated against her—alleging that he had conspired with her doctors to have her branded as insane and adding that he was 'enchanted at the prospect of giving me nothing'.

Some of these highly-coloured accounts of her misery reached William, and once again he found himself unable to desert Caroline in what she so loudly proclaimed to be her hour of need. She had even gone so far as to pen a tragic poem to him, imploring his mercy and his permission to rest upon her bed 'with broken heart and weary head'.

The poem concluded with an exhortation that he should break away from the ties of his family, the final lines running as follows:

> You've yielded to a wicked crew,
> Who ruin me, who laugh at you;
> Sweep out the gore, and while you can
> Think for yourself, and be a man!

Whether or not William was able to convince himself that there was any gore requiring to be swept out is not apparent, but the sentiments expressed touched his ever-generous heart. Caroline, as he well knew, was playing another of her tragic roles, but he could not find it in himself to treat her harshly. Moreover Caroline's brother, William, showing more tact than hitherto, succeeded in making a moving plea on his sister's behalf.

William hesitated and was lost. He allowed Caroline to return to Brocket.

No one dared tell the aged Lord Melbourne of what had happened. Not even Emily could pluck up courage to do so. They all blamed William for being absurdly weak. But although he wrote often to Caroline, and sometimes rode down to Brocket to see her, he refused to spend a night under its roof, and certainly not one with her.

In her quieter moods, she and her father-in-law were now able to strike up a certain bond of sympathy. She was forty and had worn herself out by too much physical and mental exertion. He was now nearly twice her age and was also quite exhausted, and more than a little befuddled as well, his mind permanently clouded by alcohol, as indeed was Caroline's.

In the February of 1826 Caroline was involved in yet another melodramatic situation. There now appeared on the scene a figure who had so far been surprisingly absent from the Byron scene—the sinister figure of the professional blackmailer.

Signing himself J. Wilmington Fleming, and excusing his actions on the grounds of his financial difficulties, he wrote to Hobhouse to say that he had in his possession the confessions of 'a Lady of Rank' who had enjoyed an intimate association with the late Lord Byron. When Hobhouse ignored his letters, he revealed the identity of the Lady in question. It was Caroline.

As he received no encouragement from Hobhouse, Mr Fleming turned his attentions to Augusta, and writing still in the most apologetic manner and declaring that only extreme poverty was forcing his hand, he gave further details of the information which was contained in these Confessions. They included numerous items which would prove 'painful to a relative's feelings and interesting to the Public'.

Curiously enough the threat seemed aimed more at Annabella than at Augusta herself. Augusta was very simple, and the significance of all this seemed to escape her. She wrote to Hobhouse in quite an off-hand manner, mentioning that she had received an extraordinary letter, offering her the refusal of 'a *publication* of Extracts from Ly C. Lamb's Journal!!!!!' and adding, 'I cannot think what he is about.'

She informed Mr Fleming, through an intermediary, that she would have nothing whatever to do with any such things. Then, wishing to be helpful, she wrote a long letter to Annabella, warning her that she, too, might be approached. In this letter she said:

'of the truth of the Statement concerning the contents of the Journal I *have not the least* doubt—from all I *know* from those who have read it—& I believe it is shewn *à qui voudra lire*! That woman is a perfect *Demon* & one of the few I never *can* be charitable to. 'I cannot believe her *mad*—but EXCESSIVELY BAD...& it was a happy moment for me to meet her last night!!! when coming away with ye Dowr D[uchess] of Leeds from Ly Salisbury's. We were waiting for the Carriage in the *Cloak Room*—she suddenly jumped before us like Beelzebub MAD or drunk! accosted the D to her horror & to my dismay!...Imagine after that, her accosting me & absolutely thrusting her hand almost into my face! I believe I *just* touched it & made her the most profound curtsey! then she made off somewhere—thro' a trap door I believe—for the whole apparition was to me like something from the lower Regions! & I half expected like the man in Der Freichutz to find the *Fiend's Mark* on my hand—not my brow!'

236

It was now that Annabella began to reveal the animosity which she had been nurturing towards Augusta ever since the separation. Caroline she had always disliked, but Caroline was scarcely the sort of person to whom a salvationist could devote her attention. She was too hysterical and too stubborn. But Augusta was weak and almost cringing, and it was Augusta whom Annabella was now blaming for having caused the break-up of the marriage. Annabella believed that Augusta must be purged of her sins, but only after she had done suitable penance.

Now Annabella, with the outward purpose of helping Augusta, wrote to her suggesting that she should buy Mr Fleming's papers; and she also wrote to Mrs George Lamb—Caro-George—telling her that she must get in touch with William. She did so, but William was not interested.

There was no doubt that Caroline *had* written a journal; that she had threatened the Lamb family with its publication during the time when her separation from William was being discussed; and that she had—most indiscreetly—shown it to all and sundry. Presumably Mr Fleming had seen it and had made a copy of some part of it. It had been a long-winded affair, based on diaries which she had kept since 1806, and according to Caroline had run to no less than sixteen volumes in its original form.

Annabella was ready to hint that Caroline and Mr Fleming were acting in partnership in order to extort money. This was almost certainly untrue, but in Annabella's suspicious mind all the women involved in the Byron saga were wicked, unscrupulous and grossly immoral.

Now one of the most extraordinary aspects of the whole saga was brought to light, for it became increasingly apparent that Augusta was unaware of the main charge that was being levelled against Byron—that he had indulged in an incestuous relationship with his half-sister.

Augusta had always believed that the nameless sin which Byron was alleged to have committed was that of homosexuality. He had made love to boys at Harrow, and later with Greek boys during his grand tour of the Mediterranean. Even at this stage, when the blackmailer was writing of the indecent acts which Byron had committed, and which Caroline had recorded, Augusta still believed that they referred only to homosexuality.

Annabella was therefore in a position to condemn Augusta by suggesting that she had kept to herself a secret which she was too frightened to divulge. In fact she could not divulge it because she did not know what it was.

Annabella had already placed Augusta in her debt by lending her money at a time when she was desperately in need of it. By this act Annabella chose to demonstrate her nobility whilst at the same time punishing Augusta for something she knew nothing about.

Augusta, had she ever read the Byron *Memoirs*, would have been in a position to reply to Annabella. And Annabella, had *she* ever read them, would probably have been in no position to make the charges which she did.

Annabella, at this time, was still a little frightened of Caroline; for Caroline, if provoked, could prove a dangerous enemy. But Caroline, at this time, was weak and rather cowed. In a letter to her crony, Mrs Villiers, Annabella referred casually to her belief that Caroline was 'very miserable, I believe, about these effects of her imprudence'.

Neither Caroline nor Augusta was therefore in a mood to continue the fight. They were prepared to let Annabella dominate the scene with her veiled allusions and her exaggerated pose of defender of the faith and saviour of the wicked.

As for the mysterious Mr Fleming, he disappeared suddenly from the scene, and his communications ceased abruptly. He may, in fact, have been as penurious as he had always implied, and had been consigned to a debtor's prison. He was never heard of again.

But the mystery did not end there. In the years to come there were to be those who believed that one of the reasons why Augusta lived on in such poverty for the remainder of her life was that she had fallen into the hands of blackmailers.

When it finally dawned upon her just what was the sin that she and Byron had been accused of, she may have suddenly realized how deeply she was involved. If in fact she had ever allowed her half-brother to go beyond kissing and caressing, she would now have realized to her consternation that she was in a vulnerable position. Thereafter she might well have been ruined in her attempts to keep the blackmailers at bay.

There is no direct evidence of this, but the ways of the blackmailer are devious, and their victims are only too eager that all evidence should be destroyed.

One thing is certain, Both Caroline and Annabella had reason for feeling bitter towards Augusta, because they knew that Augusta was the only woman whom Byron had ever really loved. Had it not been for the question of an incestuous relationship it was clear to both Caroline and Annabella that Augusta, and Augusta alone, was the only woman in his life whom he could have married with any hope of permanent happiness.

There had always been two Carolines—one who was gentle and adorable, and one who was hysterical, vixenish and unlovable—but now, in the growing twilight of her life, a third Caroline came into being who bore little resemblance to the other two. This Caroline was a creature who had lost her vitality because she had lost the will to live. She was then the victim of time and despair. She was a faded butterfly sheltering in a corner of a garden and waiting for the first chill winds of winter to destroy the last impulses of life.

She and Lord Melbourne shared the tranquillity of Brocket together, a sad and ill-assorted pair, feeble in body and uncertain in mind. By now he was an old man who had lost all interest in the outside world, and who lived on—as old men do—with no other purpose but to sit and wait for the next meal, the next drink, and the moment for going to bed.

Caroline was now lingering on in life with only her memories to keep her company. And these memories were all of Byron. 'That dear, that angel, that misguided and misguiding Byron, whom I adore, although he left that dreadful legacy on me, my memory.' And gradually the bitterness ebbed away, and forgiveness took its place. The fatal passion had kindled both love and hatred in her heart. Now that it was dead, there was a place instead in her heart for compassion towards him, and even of understanding.

As she grew weaker, her affection for her husband grew stronger. In a letter to Lady Morgan she wrote, 'I never can love anything better than what I thus tell you. William Lamb first, my mother second, Byron third, my boy fourth, my brother William fifth.'

The order is surprising. Not because she placed Byron third, but because she placed her husband even above her adored mother.

It is one of the sad ironies of love that women so often quarrel with those on whom they most depend. Often it is because they *do* depend upon them so greatly that they blame the loved one for everything that goes wrong in their lives. In its curious way, this is a sign of the tie that binds them.

Caroline felt a certain guilt about the past and the manner in which she had made William's life a misery to him; but this sense of guilt was never very strong. Like a spoilt and wilful child, she was

239

ready now to run back to one whom she had always looked upon as a father rather than a lover. Byron had represented the romantic lover in her life—glamorous, exciting, passionate and cruel. He had treated her outrageously and she had never really imagined that he would treat her in any other way. But William was her haven—the father-figure to whom she could turn when all passion was spent and her strength to fight had ebbed away. He was the one from whom she had expected only kindness and understanding.

And what was William himself to make of this pathetic ending to her story? She was ill. He knew that. But was she very ill? How could he tell? She had cried 'wolf' so often in the past and had played so many harrowing death-bed scenes.

In him, ambition was now renewed and he became inspired with a sense of a destiny that had yet to be fulfilled. As her life force ebbed away, his seemed to take on a new lease, and the old lethargy disappeared. In the summer of 1827, which was to be the last summer of Caroline's life, she was forty-one and looked already an old woman. William was seven years her senior and yet he looked in the prime of life. His mind was clear and his brain active.

Caroline's hair was growing grey and it made her look old. William's hair was grey, but it only made him look distinguished. Grey hair was a contradiction of everything for which Caroline had stood for in her life—a denial of youth, exuberance and unquenchable spirit.

Unlike Caroline, William had not lost his zest for life, and although there were times when he suffered—as she did—from melancholy, there were still moments when he could laugh as uproariously as he had ever done. He could talk with animation on a wide variety of subjects; and he had by now borrowed some of Caroline's former delight in shocking people. He had no use for those who were 'stuffy' in their outlook or whose view of life was circumscribed. But by now he had developed tact, and a sensitivity towards the feelings of others.

He had suffered much in the past but this had not left him bitter. Rather had it strengthened his resilience and his ability to withstand adversity. He viewed life—and his career—with a humorous resignation. Fate had beaten him down once. He was not going to let it do so again.

His love for Caroline had lessened, but nothing could destroy his compassion. He knew only too well that he could never stand idly by and watch her suffer; or forsake her in her hour of need. Caroline

also knew this, and she tried to express her gratitude to him in a
poem which she wrote about him:

> Loved one, no tear is in my eye,
> Though pangs my bosom thrill,
> For I have learned when others sigh
> To suffer and be still.
> Passion and Pride and Flattery strove,
> They made a wreck of me,
> But O, I never ceased to love,
> I never loved but thee.
>
> My heart is with our early dreams,
> And still thy influence knows,
> Still seeks thy shadow on the stream
> Of memory as it flows;
> Still hangs o'er all the records bright
> Of moments brighter still,
> Ere love withdrew his starry light,
> Ere thou hadst suffered ill.
>
> 'Tis vain, 'tis vain; no human will
> Can bid that time return,
> There's not a light on earth can fill
> Again love's darkened urn.
> 'Tis vain, upon my heart, my brow,
> Broods grief no words can tell,
> But grief itself were idle now—
> Loved one, fare thee well.

George Canning became Prime Minister in February 1827, and in
the May of that year he offered William the post of Chief Secretary
for Ireland. Canning had always thought highly of William, but
William, in the past, had held back from joining Canning, for he had
little stomach for becoming a part of any Tory-Whig coalition.
Even now, in the spring of 1827, he was reluctant to commit himself, but the opportunity was a tempting one and so he accepted.

The curtain was coming down on Caroline's career, but it was
only just rising on his own. Now, in the autumn of 1827, the curse of
the Byrons seemed to be visited on Caroline as it had been visited
upon Lady Melbourne. She, who had always been so small, so elf-

241

like and so slim, developed dropsy and her body began to swell. There were many who were ready to declare that loose living and excessive drinking had brought about this malady and that she had damaged her liver and kidneys in the same way as Byron had damaged his. There were few who took the more charitable view that two miscarriages might well have had the same effect. Society was unwilling to look upon her condition with any sympathy.

She did not complain, for she had never been a coward. She lay weak and in pain, but her sense of humour did not desert her.

There had been a time when she had held a prominent position on the committee of Almack's Club. After the publication of *Glenarvon* she had been black-balled and forced to resign. Now she wrote to Lady Morgan saying that she expected to die but was encouraged by the thought that 'I shall no doubt go with an Almack ticket to heaven.'

Dr Goddard became increasingly alarmed by her symptoms. In a letter to William dated 2 October, 1827, he said, 'Lady Caroline has just desired me to let you know how she is—some time ago I had wished to do so, but her Ladyship prevented me, as she would by no means unnecessarily frighten or distress you.

It has been with feelings of the deepest regret that I have lately observed symptoms of water collecting about her—at present the cause is too clearly manifest, and from the quantity of fluid contain'd and evidently felt in the abdomen, and from other visceral obstruction and disease I have apprehensions of the greatest danger... Her conduct has been very amicable, indeed, her behaviour of late has altered very much in every respect for the better. She appears convinced she cannot ultimately recover but with feelings of perfect resignation says she does not mind to die.'

Dr Goddard also believed that she was dying, and was unable to hide this from his patient. Caroline chided him gently for his mournful expression and tried to bring a smile to his face.

'How glum you look,' she told him. 'You mustn't let my husband know how ill I am. I would not have him worried. He has so much to do and to think of over there in Ireland of more importance than my ailments and me. I will not have him told.'

And later she dictated a letter for the doctor to send to William, when she was too weak to write herself. In this she said, 'I really feel better; the medicine agrees with me and I have everything I possibly want...God bless you, my dearest William. I will write to you myself very soon; do not forget to write a line to me. Everything at Brocket is doing quite well.'

But to her sister-in-law, Maria Duncannon, she wrote, 'I consider my illness a great blessing. I feel returned to my God and my duty and my dearest husband...I broke that horrible spell which prevented me saying my prayers...I say all this, my dearest Maria, lest you should think I flew to religion because I was in danger—it is no such thing, my heart softened...I am quite resigned to die.'

Dr Goddard did what he could to alleviate her suffering and prescribed 'blue pills, squills, and sweet spirits of nitre, with an infusion of cascarilla bark' and the pain was reduced. Dr Goddard had done all that it was in his power and knowledge to do. He knew that Caroline was desperately ill, but he had only a vague conception of the cause of her illness. In fact she was probably suffering from cirrhosis of the liver, heart failure or cancer. There would be little enough that a modern doctor in such circumstances could do. He was quite helpless, except that he could ease her suffering to a certain extent.

William knew that she was very ill, but he did not know the full gravity of the situation. But when it became necessary in December to move Caroline from her beloved Brocket to Melbourne House, in order that the leading physicians might be readily available, he realized that the position had worsened. Yet she still wrote or conveyed messages to him, assuring him that there was no need for him to worry.

She wrote to Lady Morgan telling her, 'I am on my death-bed: say I might have died by a diamond, I die now by a brickbat: but remember the only noble fellow I ever met with is William Lamb.'

Soon after this Lady Morgan visited William in Ireland and found him deeply depressed. He had received a letter from Dr Goddard saying that Caroline no longer seemed to be suffering any pain; but he had added, 'Illness is a terrible thing.'

In his letters to Caroline, William tried to match her tone of forced gaiety. It distressed him that he could not leave his post in Ireland and he wrote to her, 'My heart is almost broken that I cannot come over directly...How unfortunate and melancholy that you should be so ill now and that it should be at a time when I, who have had so many years of idleness, am so fixed and held down by circumstances.'

By Christmas Caroline was suffering from long periods of semi-consciousness and could only speak with difficulty. In one of her rare moments of lucidity she whispered 'Send for William, he is the

243

only person who has never failed me.'

They sent for him and he hurried back to London to find her sinking slowly into oblivion. He sat by her bedside, but what passed between them remained secret. It may have been little enough. Perhaps no more than a clasping of hands and a few whispered words, spoken only with difficulty.

Had she been writing her death scene in one of her novels, Caroline would have died dramatically, surrounded by mournful relatives and with her husband kneeling in tears by her bedside. But death, as Byron had already learnt, could prove to be no more than an anticlimax.

William spent hours by her bedside, but when her last moment came, on 26 January, 1828, he was not in the room. By her side and holding the thin, white hand was 'Caro-George' who had been her playmate in the far-off, happy days at Devonshire House.

Caroline had lain quite silent and motionless, her breathing scarcely audible in the silence of the room. It had seemed to the watcher that she might already have set out on her last journey. Then there came a tiny sound that was no more than a whispered sigh from the unparted lips. Caroline, who had always been so restless in life, was now at rest for ever.

The doctors who soon crowded round her bedside made their last report upon the invalid's condition. She had died, they said, 'from complete exhaustion'. And on this point, at least, they were right.

Tranquillity had been so foreign to her nature that William, when they called him into the room, could only gaze down upon the lifeless figure in the bed and ponder on the problems of a future existence. True to his code, he hid his emotions from the world.

To the outside world, it seemed that he had suffered little from her passing. He had his political career to occupy his mind. He deeply immersed himself in his duties.

'He was hurt at the time,' reported Emily later, 'but he is now just as usual and his mind is filled with politics.'

He had always been her favourite, and it had distressed her to watch the manner in which Caroline had made him suffer. No one had ever been quite certain of Emily's parentage, but she was possessed of the Lambs' practicality in outlook. She had never understood why William loved Caroline. It seemed now to her that Caroline's death was all to his advantage. She comforted herself with the belief that he had only been hurt at the time—and then not greatly.

William grieved, but he did not show it. He accepted his family's

244

condolences with stoicism, knowing them to be insincere. But in the privacy of his room he mourned Caroline's passing. Would he ever meet her again in the next world? And, if he did, would she then be purged of all her troubles? Would she find in the after-life the tranquillity that she had never known on earth?

His father died six months later, and he became the 2nd Viscount Melbourne. He was now the owner of Melbourne House and Brocket Hall. Caroline had always loved Brocket, but Melbourne House had never brought her happiness. Now he found its size and palatial aspect were no longer in keeping with his mood; and he could not bear to enter the room where Caroline had died. He sold the house and bought a more modest one in South Street.

There were memories of Byron still clinging to Melbourne House. There were none at Brocket.

Nine years after Caroline's death, King William IV died in June, 1837, and was succeeded by his niece, Victoria. William was now at the peak of his political career, and had been Prime Minister since 1835.

The young Queen, who was eighteen and fatherless, turned to him instinctively for guidance. In him she found a father-figure, sympathetic and wise.

It seemed then to William that he had found a second Caroline. Here was the same mixture of child-like innocence and strength of will. The same transparent honesty, and the same tempestuous nature. The same imperious manner and the same strong resentment at being crossed.

But there was one great difference between Caroline and Victoria. Caroline's life had been without purpose. She had been endowed with a good brain, an artistic nature, a fine determination and the ability to fight. But her way of life never furnished her with a calling. She was ignorant of the world, and her existence was circumscribed by the social barriers that protected the privileged rich. In her childhood she had been shut in by the high walls of Devonshire House and had been encouraged to think only of herself. Lacking an outlet for her talents, she had grown up rebellious and frustrated. It had been a wasted life.

Caroline met William when she was young and impressionable, but she had derived little benefit from his strength and guidance. But the young Queen Victoria gained much from them. In the first months of her reign she came to rely completely on her beloved

Lord M., who initiated her into the duties of a sovereign.

William was fifty-eight when Victoria ascended the throne. A dangerous age—and often a tragic age—for an impressionable man whose path is crossed by youth and beauty.

William loved the young Queen. She aroused in him the same sense of fatherhood, the same longing to protect and guide, that Caroline had aroused in him. Fatherhood had, to all intents and purposes, been denied to him. He had been given a son, but only a witless, moronic creature on whom he had lavished his affection but from whom he had received little enough in return. He had died in 1836.

Now, for a few short months, he became a young romantic again. To some the sight was ridiculous—an old man making a fool of himself over a girl. A few smiled indulgently. Everyone realized that it was a romance which could have no future.

The first, fine blossoming of this romance made him feel a young man again. For a time he looked almost young, with his splendid figure and his old, irresistible charm. But soon he began to age. His appetite had always been healthy, now he began to suffer from indigestion. In the past he had always slept soundly and well. Now he turned restlessly in his bed and was worried by his dreams. His judgement began to falter and his temper became short.

In the spring of 1839 he was forced to resign his premiership, and although he was soon back in office the break seemed to accentuate his decline. He was beginning to feel old; climbing the stairs left him breathless and shaky. He became absent-minded and developed an old man's habit of dozing off when he should have been wide awake.

In 1840 the young Queen married her beloved Albert and thereafter there was only one man in her life. Lord M. was growing old, but she was growing up. She no longer needed a father or a protector. The bird had left the nest.

He spent more and more of his time at Brocket, dreaming of the past. The peace of the countryside soothed him now as it had soothed Caroline in her decline. London only tired him. There was change in the air, and the nineteenth century was moving too fast for him. He no longer had any desire to keep up with it.

He died on 24 November, 1848. He was sixty-nine and the days of his youth seemed far away. He died as Caroline had died—without fuss and scarcely conscious of his ending, with only a last, sad sigh to bid the world farewell.

He had loved three women in his life. His mother. his wife and his Queen. But of the three he had loved his wife the most. And yet she had given him so little of what he had longed for in marriage; just a few scattered moments of affection in a life of tumult and revolt. But he had never been able to forget her.

Often, in his latter days, he would sit at his study window at Brocket, looking out over the Park and thinking about her as a father might think of his child.

And always, in these moments of reverie, his eyes would fill with tears.

His poor little Caro! How he wished that he could have saved her from her fatal passion.

Principal Dates

1752 Birth of Elizabeth Milbanke (later Lady Melbourne).

1757 June 7: Birth of Georgiana Spencer (later Duchess of Devonshire).

1761 June 16: Birth of Henrietta Frances Spencer (later Lady Bessborough).

1774 June 6: Georgiana marries William, 5th Duke of Devonshire.

1779 March 15: Birth of William Lamb (later Lord Melbourne).

1780 November 27: Henrietta marries Frederick, 3rd Earl of Bessborough.

1784 January 26: Birth of Hon. Augusta Mary Byron (later Mrs Leigh).

1784 August 16: Birth of Caroline St Jules (Caro-George, later Mrs George Lamb).

1785 August 29: Birth of Harriet Cavendish (Hary-O—later Lady Granville Leveson-Gower).

1785 November 13: Birth of Caroline Ponsonby (Caro—later Lady Caroline Lamb).

1788 January 22: Birth of George Gordon Byron (later 6th Lord Byron).

1790 May 21: Birth of William Spencer Cavendish (Hart—later 6th Duke of Devonshire).

1791 August 2: Death of Captain John Byron (Mad Jack, the poet's father).

1792 May 17: Birth of Anne Isabella Milbanke (Annabella—later Lady Byron).

1798 May 19: Byron succeeds to the barony.

1798 Caroline falls in love with William Lamb at the age of 12.

1801 March 21: Georgiana Cavendish marries Lord Morpeth.

1804 William Lamb is called to the bar.

1805 January 24: Death of Peniston Lamb. William becomes heir to the title and gives up the bar for politics.

1805 June 3: Caroline marries William Lamb.

1806 January 31: Caroline gives birth to a still-born child.

1806 March 30: Death of Duchess of Devonshire.

1806 December 19: William makes his maiden speech in the House.

1807 August 29: Birth of Augustus Lamb, Caroline's only surviving child.

1809 May 17: Caroline St Jules marries George Lamb.

1809 October 19: Duke of Devonshire marries Lady Elizabeth Foster ('dearest Bess').

1809 December 24: Hary-O marries Lord Granville Leveson-Gower.

1810 Caroline's affair with Sir Godfrey Webster.

1811 August 1: Death of Mrs Byron, the poet's mother.

1812 February 29: publication of Cantos I and II of *Childe Harold.*

1812 March 25: Byron meets Caroline and Annabella at a waltzing-party at Melbourne House.

1812 March 27: Caroline writes her first love-letter to Byron.

1812 May-June: Byron takes refuge from Caroline at Newstead.

1812 June 13: Byron returns to London.

1812 June-July: Byron becomes friendly with Lady Oxford.

1812 August 9: Caroline sends Byron gift of her pubic hairs.

1812 September 7: Caroline consents to go with her parents to Ireland.

1812 October: Byron stays with Lady Oxford at Eywood.

1812 November 9: Byron writes a final letter to Caroline, signing it, 'I am no longer yr. lover.'

1812 November 10: Caroline returns to England from Ireland, determined to seek an interview with Byron.

1812 December: Bonfire scene staged by Caroline at Brocket.

1813 January: Caroline forges Byron's signature to obtain his portrait from Murray.

1813 July 5/6: Caroline in 'dagger scene' at Lady Heathcote's party.

1813 August: Byron's affair with Augusta Leigh reaches a climax.

1814 April 15: Birth of Medora Leigh. Rumours that Byron is the father.

1815 January 2: Byron marries Annabella Milbanke.

1815 Mid-January: Lady Melbourne takes Caroline to see Byron and his wife.

1815 July: Caroline in Paris, where she meets the Duke of Wellington.

1815	December 10: Annabella gives birth to her only child, Augusta Ada.
1816	January 15: Annabella leaves London with Ada.
1816	February 2: Byron is informed by Annabella's father that she wishes for a separation.
1816	April 25: Byron leaves England for ever.
1816	May 9: *Glenarvon* is published anonymously and meets with instant success.
1816	November 11: Byron settles in Venice.
1819	April: Byron meets Countess Guiccioli, who becomes his mistress.
1820	Caroline writes her second novel, *Graham Hamilton*, but holds back publication.
1821	November 14: Death of Caroline's mother, Henrietta.
1822	*Graham Hamilton* is published anonymously by Colburn.
1823	Publication of Caroline's third novel, *Ada Reis*.
1824	January 5: Byron arrives at Missolonghi, Greece.
1824	April 19: Death of Byron.
1824	May 17: The destruction of Byron's *Memoirs*.
1824	July 14: Caroline accidentally meets Byron's funeral procession near Brocket.
1824	July 16: Byron is buried at Hucknall Torkard.
1824	Christmas: Caroline's affair with the young Bulwer Lytton ends in acrimony.
1825	July: Caroline and William separate. She is made to leave Brocket. Altercation over terms.
1825	August 14: Caroline arrives in Paris.
1825	October: William relents and allows Caroline to return to Brocket.
1827	April: William made Chief Secretary for Ireland in Canning Ministry.
1827	December: Caroline is moved to London owing to the serious deterioration in her health.
1828	January 15: William is summoned urgently from Ireland.
1828	January 26: Death of Caroline at Melbourne House in the presence of Caro-George. Aged 42. She is buried at Hatfield.
1830	William becomes Home Secretary in Grey Ministry.
1834	July: William becomes Prime Minister.
1836	November 27: Death of Caroline's only child, Augustus, unmarried, at the age of 29.
1840	February 10: Queen Victoria marries Prince Albert.

1848 November 24: Death of William at Brocket, aged 69. He is buried near Caroline in Hatfield churchyard.

1865 *Glenarvon* is re-published in one volume under the title of *The Fatal Passion.*

Bibliography

It has always been my policy, when presenting the reader with suggestions for further study, to list books that are readily available in libraries rather than those which are only available to the scholar. Nor do I attempt to give a complete list of the books which I have consulted myself, because many of them furnish only small items of information, or merely confirm material that has been given in other sources.

There have been nearly as many books written about Byron as there have been about Napoleon, but curiously enough only two have been written in the last fifty years about Caroline Lamb. In 1932 Gollancz published Elizabeth Jenkins *Lady Caroline Lamb*; and in 1964 Heinemann published a novel by Doris Leslie called *This for Caroline*, which was based on fact and is in essence a biography of her.

However there is plenty of information about her in all the books about Byron, and in numerous others as well. For me the best portrait of her is that contained in Lord David Cecil's life of William Lamb, her husband, which was published in two volumes under the titles of *The Young Melbourne* and *Lord M,* and subsequently in one volume, under the title of *Melbourne.* These two books must be read by the reader who is anxious to make a further study of this rather tragic marriage, for the character of husband and wife is examined in depth. Personally I have only found myself in disagreement with Lord David Cecil on the subject of Lady Melbourne, Caroline's mother-in-law, who has always seemed to me to have been a rather less lovable character than has generally been supposed.

Obviously the reader who wishes to carry his or her studies of Caroline to the fullest extent should try to obtain a copy of Caroline's novel, *Glenarvon,* but this may not be easy.

Of the many books on Byron, I would consider that the following should be consulted:

Byron: A biography, by Leslie A. Marchand, published by the poet's publisher, John Murray, in three volumes in 1957, and the same author's *Byron: A Portrait,* published in 1971. Murray have also published *Lord Byron: A Self-Portrait,* comprising letters and diaries 1798-1824, edited by Peter Quennell, in two volumes, *The Complete Letters and Journals of Lord Byron,* edited by Leslie A. Marchand, and *The Late Lord Byron,* by Doris Langley Moore. Also *Byronic Thoughts,* edited by Peter Quennell, and *Byron's Poetry,* by Leslie A. Marchand.

Peter Quennell has also written *Byron: The Years of Fame,* and *Byron in Italy.* A further standard work on the life of the poet is *Byron,* by André Maurois, published by Jonathan Cape.

To this list I would add *Lord Byron's Marriage,* by G. Wilson Knight, published by Macmillan in 1957, and *Lord Byron's Wife,* by Malcolm Elwin, published by Macdonald in 1962. Also *My Dearest Augusta,* by Peter Gunn, published by The Bodley Head in 1968. This book, when read in conjunction with *Lord Byron's Wife,* takes us in some detail through the intricate paths of the Byron marriage and separation, and the rumours and allegations which resulted from them.

As a subsidiary work, which gives some valuable insight into the Byronic outlook, I would advise the reader to consult E. Tangye Lean's book, *The Napoleonists,* published by The Oxford University Press in 1970, because I consider the rise and fall of Napoleon played an important, if a subconscious, part in the life of Byron.

Biographies and histories concerning the Bessborough family, the Ponsonby family and the relevant Dukes of Devonshire should also be consulted. I suggest *Lady Bessborough and Her Family Circle,* by the Earl of Bessborough; *Georgiana,* being extracts from the correspondence of the Duchess of Devonshire, edited by the Earl of Bessborough; and *Dearest Bess,* being the life and times of Lady Elizabeth Foster, who became the second Duchess of Devonshire, by Dorothy Margaret Stuart. Also *The Letters of Lady Harriet Cavendish,* 1796–1809, edited by her grandson, Sir George Leveson-Gower, and published by John Murray in 1940. These give Hary-O's opinions of Caroline, as expressed in her correspondence. Also *Letters of Lady Palmerston,* edited by Tresham Lever and published by John Murray in 1957. Lady Palmerston was William's sister, Emily, and her frequent comments about Caroline and William are instructive. *The Ponsonby Family* by Sir John Ponsonby, published by The Medici Society, may also be consulted.

Caroline's brief affair in middle age with the young Bulwer Lytton is described by Michael Sadleir in *Bulwer: a Panorama* (1931).

Finally, the background to London Society in this period is given in full in J. B. Priestley's study of the Regency, *The Prince of Pleasure*, (Heinemann, 1969) which is copiously illustrated. Two other liberally illustrated books of the period are Dorothy George's *Hogarth to Cruickshank* (Allen Lane, 1967), and *Byron and his World* by Derek Parker (Thames & Hudson, 1968).

Index